Everything Passes, Everything Remains

Freewheelin' Through Spain, Song, and Memory

Chris Dolan

Saraband

Published by Saraband
Digital World Centre, 1 Lowry Plaza,
The Quays, Salford, M50 3UB
www.saraband.net

ISBN: 9781912235780
ebook: 9781912235797

1 2 3 4 5 6 7 8 9 10

Printed and bound in Great Britain by Clays Ltd, Elcograf S.p.A.

Contents

This entire book is a dedication –
to all the people in it, and connected to it.
Friends and family here and in Spain.

Only one member of my immediate family couldn't join
me at any time on the road, thanks to work pressures.
But for her support, for years,
I dedicate this book to my daughter…

For Emma.

Ever tried. Ever failed. No matter.
Try Again. Fail again. Fail better
Samuel Beckett

It started out as a bike ride. Three old friends, in every sense, cycling across Spain – a country that has obsessed and united us all our lives. It became a coast-to-coast tour of a distinctly iffy busking band. For two of the cyclists it was a celebration of retirement, moving on to the next stage of life. For one in particular, a voyage of remembrance and loss. We hadn't expected we'd be pedalling through the past as much as the present.

We decided to keep a record of our own and others' busks, interviews with people we met along the way, our reflections on the places we passed through, conversations and thoughts on memory – and the tricks it plays.

It's a risky business entrusting a book on memory to a man with a precarious grasp on what happened yesterday, never mind forty years ago, and who has a tendency to mythologise. But that's kind of the point. How we remember things, move forward, make personal and political decisions on a decidedly shaky basis. Believe me – this is not a reliable record.

The real starting point for me wasn't mounting our bikes in Vigo in 2019, but in Glasgow 1974.

When I was sixteen, I left home with my violin under my arm and a copy of Laurie Lee's *As I Walked Out One Midsummer Morning*, and headed with a school friend to Spain – a country I knew next to nothing about. Laurie Lee had left the Cotswolds forty years earlier, aged nineteen, to walk and busk across Spain, possibly knowing even less than I did. Lee's *Cider With Rosie* had been a favourite childhood book of mine and *As I Walked Out One Midsummer Morning*, the memoir of his exploits in Spain, became a life manual. My plan didn't work out – my brother had to save me. Lee was rescued for the far more dramatic reason of escaping the violence of the Spanish Civil War.

At the age of sixty-one, in the year of Our Lord 2019, I attempted to make good my teenage failure. This time, my cycling friends offered to come with me most of the way so long as we could add an extra dimension: pedal coast to coast, west to east, Vigo to Valencia.

Our journey was precisely 100 years after another celebrated expedition. Traumatised by the hell of the First World War a young soldier, Gerald Brenan, also from Gloucestershire, escaped to Spain in 1919, landing where I had first arrived, in La Coruña, north of Vigo. Brenan's book *South From Granada* is a classic of Spanish travel. Along the way I discovered or reacquainted myself with other writer-travellers, among them Nobel-winning Francoist Camilo José Cela who wrote up a number of his walks from the 1940s to '60s, Richard Ford in the nineteenth century, Irishwoman Kate O'Brien in the 1920s and '30s.

I didn't keep a diary in the 1970s, which bothered me for years until I admitted to myself that, even if I had, I would have lied. Lee supposedly did keep a diary, then supposedly lost it. There are many people, including some of his most ardent fans, who consider that much of his 'memoir' is fiction. Or at least, carefully embroidered renderings of what might actually have happened. This time round I tried to do the writerly thing and take notes along the way. Truth is, after a long day's cycling, lugging my unfit carcass, a fat old laptop, recording gear and bike maintenance tools I can't use, and with a fiddle strapped to my back, accurate chronicling was usually trumped by the need for food and sleep. And anyway, I'd just have lied again. Even when trying not to.

This result is a confluence of journeys. It's not *about* Laurie Lee, or me. It's a bit about cycling, a bit about walking, and a bit about buses. It's a kind of travelogue, over time, and through some lesser-known parts of Spain. Documenting people met along the way, things learned, or yet to be learned, or that I've given up trying to learn. Forty-five years after my first doomed stab at busking, I am now a (slightly) better violin player, (almost) fluent in Spanish, (nearly) solvent, and a (moderately) experienced writer with an ever-changing perspective on things. Themes emerged, Catalonia for one. What makes a nation, or a family for that matter, or a group of friends? In many ways it's as much about Scotland and the UK as Spain. The stories we tell ourselves, how the past plays merry hell with the present. And it's about songs and what they meant and mean. Along the way we played bits of Bluegrass, Basque and Catalan songs, Gluck's Eurydice, Aly Bain, compositions of our own. On one occasion, 'Chirpy Chirpy Cheep Cheep'…

Journeys are never what they seem, or what you expect. In 2019 my head was often in 2000, my friends' in 1978 or 2017, while reading about 1830, singing an old 1969 hit and discussing 1936. I've not gone out of my way to disentangle them. Memories and dreams accompany us every step of the way, every push of the pedal. Threaded throughout are bits of poems, song lyrics, short reflections by myself and others. Random memories that forced their way in for no reason I can fathom. There are pen portraits of people – some you'll know of, others I hope you'll enjoy meeting, some completely made up.

Cycling and tramping old roads and new slows you down, gives you time to think, reminds you of places you've been and who was with you, where you're bound and why. For walkers, the best surfaces are flat and firm but with a bit of give under the heel. For road cyclists, we want the hardest, smoothest tarmac. Whatever keeps you moving forward. And you don't need to turn around to see what's behind you – it's ahead of you too.

We recorded a song to sing along the road from Vigo to Valencia. I've always liked the prettier, older, tune of 'Auld Lang Syne' so I based my verses on that, and used – the nerve of it! – Robert Burns's chorus, adding a simple Spanish translation:

Los Viejos Tiempos

Remember me? I wandered here
your fields and streets and rocks,
seeking, hoping, long before
the ticking of any clock.

Recuérdame, I feasted here,
in and out these bars.
Dancin' round and falling down
beneath the scolding stars.

Mind me now, I dreamed here,
dreams that overwhelm me
Rebellion, love, hope and prayer,
Hasta la victoria siempre

¿Me conoces, no? – I slept below
your green-bathed balcony
Till you called for time and sent me home
on feet of beaten clay.

Por los viejos tiempos
Por la belleza de ayer
Brindamos por la simpatía
Los días de ayer

4

Everything Passes, Everything Remains

And here once more I return to you
to a land I've long held dear
Just another pilgrim on the Way
but no-one minds me here.

For auld lang syne, my jo
For auld lang syne
We'll tak' a cup o' kindness yet
For auld lang syne.

Dáme la mano, compañero,
here's a hand of mine
Together we'll sing the good old songs
of dreams and tears and wine.

PART ONE

Time Trials

GLASGOW 1974

This short description may have its interest, being a sort of record of a dream...photographed in youth upon the writer's brain...
Robert Cunninghame Graham, 'The Lazo'

Lee left behind the ancient idyll of his beloved Cotswolds, the world of *Cider With Rosie*, innocence, preindustrial pastel valleys where the same characters seemed to have lived, undying, for centuries. The Glasgow I left was black and bony, sooty tenements like rotten teeth, high-rises only a decade or two old but already soiled and skeletal. The pinnacle years of gang violence, life expectancy was as short as tempers. It was as scary to stay as to leave.

Lee was nineteen, a hearty country lad, a proficient violinist full of confidence and anticipation. I was a product of my city – clumpy, wan, and with precious little sense of self. On this last sortie I'm in my sixties, probably healthier than I was first time around, and can go a bike. Glasgow today still has its problems, thanks to an inadequate political class and savage capitalism, but washed and combed it is, on the surface at least, happier with itself.

Laurie left because he had an adventurous spirit, and he and the world were young. I had to get out. I had no reason for staying, and I felt older than I do now. My parents had pulled themselves up a class or two, from blue-collar Maryhill (Dad) and Gaelic-speaking, shoeless, peat-bog Donegal (Mum). My six surviving siblings had all done well, passed the necessary exams and were highly thought of by teachers and employers. I was the runt of the litter, and acted accordingly. I'd failed almost everything at school. So when my friend Brendan Hughes suggested a trip to Spain – leaving before our disastrous Higher results came out – we scuttled away.

Brendan had a brother in Spain. Brian Hughes's is another journey I'll map out later, one that fuses Scotland and Spain, and Ireland. I knew next to nothing about Spain. In the Glasgow schools' orchestra I played violin for the 'Habanera' aria from Bizet's *Carmen*. With a hazy idea of geography – enough to mix up continents – dark, tempestuous Victoria Montoya of *The High Chaparral* was the flipside of twinkly-nosed Samantha on *Bewitched*; boys my age wanted to be her mercurial, carousing brother Manolito. To this day, my Spain is infused with Tex-Mex borderlands. My sister Liz went on holiday with friends to Spain in 1970 and brought back one record, a single: 'Un Rayo De Sol' (A Ray of Sunshine) by Los Diablos. Listening to it now, it's typical '60s pop pap. When I was thirteen, I played it over and over, it was exotic, the sound of summer, of holidays I might one day have myself. Spain, somewhere between habanera and rumba, between knife-wielding *gitanas* and beach bars, seemed to me hot, sexy, dangerous, unpredictable. Half a century later, it's one of the few things I was right about back then.

Which way round it was, I can't be sure: I had read *Cider With Rosie*, was full of admiration and jealousy for Lee's talent and world, or did Brendan mention Spain and I then sought out the follow up, *As I Walked Out One Midsummer Morning*? Or had I already read it and that's why the idea of Spain was so appealing? Brendan thinks it was neither.

Let me introduce Brendan and his family from the get go. The first pen portrait of people who will be important in these journeys.

Coco

The primordial stew of mid-twentieth-century Scots-Irish Glasgow. First Holy Communion, Victorian school buildings, the belt, Celtic and Rangers and duffel coats. Keepie-uppie. Beyond our horizon, events around the time we were born would loom large later: Sputnik and the space race, Rosa Parks and Fidel Castro. Closer to home, big families and small houses, 'Rock Around The Clock', wedding scrambles.

Brendan Hughes was the reason I first went to Spain. The crack-dealer who slipped me the gateway drug. I can't remember actually meeting him. We'd have been in first year at St. Mungo's Academy. Whatever it had been before and might be again, when Brendan and I were there the Mungo was a madhouse. A comprehensive in an embattled part of Glasgow everybody was deserting. Religious brothers who couldn't control classes; vicious fifth years, swift to violence, who most certainly could.

Brendan was nicknamed Coco. He forbade anyone from using it as soon as we escaped that, mental, institution. When I teamed up with him, I got named, with a surprising facility for alliteration in the Mungo, Dodo. Coco and Dodo. I'd have preferred being another clown rather than an extinct, flightless, famously ugly bird. Coco was a compliment. Brendan made people laugh. He still does. Despite everything. A wit as dry as gunpowder in an assault rifle.

The nicknamers were thinking, really, of Pierrot. Coco – Nicolai Poliakoff – was on the TV from time to time when we were growing up. But the Pierrots, white-faced and comically melancholic, have been around in one form or another for 300 years. Brendan, the boy, had a long, elegant face, high forehead, gloomy and funny. His complexion was powder-pale, his default expression inscrutable, cool as a granite statue.

Fifty years later, Brendan entering a room is like being joined by an Incontrovertible Fact. He'll tell you, in measured monosyllables, that you are, by the way, talking pish. He's also Mr Inconvenient Fact, which will throw up lots of discrepancies in my narrative of discovering Spain. Brendan tells me that, the day we left, we travelled by bus to London, train to Dover, boat to Calais, and train again to Paris. I can barely remember any of that. But everything explodes into wild whirling Van Gogh colours with *steak frites* in a bargain bistro at the back of the Gare du Nord. Red and white checked oilcloth matching the blood brightly oozing from the steak, the *pichet* of deep ruby wine. The smell of Gitanes, the babble of French belying our six years studying the language. It had never interested either Brendan or me. Now we wanted to understand every word, every smoked, marinated syllable.

It was Kevin, another of Brendan's brothers, who took us to that restaurant. The Hugheses were mesmerising. Kevin soon settled in Italy, Rosaleen in the Isle of Bute, Eilish in the States. Eight siblings in all, each with their own strain of life-force. In *Cider With Rosie* Laurie Lee describes his many brothers and half-sisters as being notes in a melody. The Dolans were as numerous as the Hugheses, but while the chord we struck together was the opening of an Ave Maria, the Hugheses were a thrilling Stravinskian cacophony.

As soon as we could put together enough pennies from working as dustbin men, assistant psychiatric nurses, changing about a thousand light bulbs in a factory in Renton, Brendan and I were off. Overland to Galicia. Laughing, learning, looking for and never finding jobs, chasing and seldom catching girls, drinking, playing *futbolín*, pinball, Pacman. Nights with young people on beaches, playing Victor Jara songs on guitars, drinking *aguardiente* from *porrones* and lighting the alcohol so it looked, by the edge of the dark syrupy sea, as if you were drinking raw fire...

Sexagenarian Brendan bears his personal tragedies with discreet dignity, his pain clear-cut and sunk deep. There is no hint of self-pity, no halo for the painful losses. My friend has always stood firm. Cantilevered, his strong sportsman's legs the pillars of a bridge that will lead you... somewhere.

To be fair on my school days, they gave me friends who have lasted a lifetime. And they gave me the fiddle. Tom McAweaney, literally a lifelong friend, our families living across the road from each other, is a gifted musician. I looked up to him – he played fiddle, so I wanted to too. We played the folk clubs together in our teens and many of the songs I'll be playing again in Spain I learned from Tom.

The day I left for Spain with Brendan as a teenager was effectively the day I left home. There were a few terms at Glasgow University when I returned, between flats, but they were curtailed by going back to Spain the minute I could.

I have a memory of the evening I left. We were having tea (dinner to non-Glaswegians). Brendan and I must have been catching the night bus. At home at that time were my brother Paul and sister Maggie. When I finished my meal I got up and said I'd better be off. My memory is that my dad stood up to say farewell. He *stood up*. To the modern reader, or any Spanish person, this must make my old man seem cold and distant, certainly formal. But for a west-coast Scottish male at the time it was tantamount to putting his arms around me, crying and pleading for me to stay. Laurie's mum, remember, just waved at him from the garden in 1934.

All journeys bring new encounters, but they also must leave people and places behind. Each day, every step forward takes us a step further away. And memory distorts the past...

Zenith

The street looks different though I imagine nothing has actually changed. They say memory's a palimpsest. You don't remember real places, actual events, you just remember the last memory of them. I've been subtly changing my image of the old house every time I've thought about it. The stone redder, the road broader. The door is heavier and older-fashioned than I remembered.

The silence inside is new to me. A hush, like freshly settled dust. A taste in my mouth, of raw stillness. There's the phone, and there's the hallstand. A single old coat where there used to be a ruckus of anoraks and scarves and duffels and hats and brollies. Photographs on the wall. The kitchen's unrecognisable. It definitely used to be bigger and brighter. Certainly noisier.

And there's the wireless. 'Zenith'. I say it before I see it. Etched in gold jagged lettering on mahogany. I knew the word long before I knew what it meant, or thought to ask. It didn't matter. The word was enough. *Zenith.*

The radio was ancient, and big, even for then. A magic cask. The dial is the only thing I've remembered accurately in the whole house. Helsinki. London. Moscow. A wheel behind glass, turning like the world on a secret axis. Paris. Berlin. Madrid. Benghazi.

I turn it on, and it lights up; grumbles, as if rudely wakened. Then it makes the same old noises it always made. Whirrings and stutters and yelps. A kind of gargle, like emphysema in its lungs. Spin the dial and you sprint across the earth; an opera of barks and babble. I stall for a second on a woman's voice, like water running over pebbles. Istanbul.

I used to stand between it and the window, feeling the radio waves blow those sounds and voices and distances through me. I amplified them. I *was* the whole world. Little me. Full to bursting with hurried messages, world leaders intoning, orchestras and pop singers, all possibilities.

Women with voices like water on pebbles; soft hands covered in henna.

And here I am again now. I close my eyes, try to pick
up the past. Maggie, Mark, Theresa. Paul. Fine-tune Mum
soothing, hard hands hugging. Her distant voice, like me,
not quite on the station.

The journey we were about to set out on changed our lives. The
landscape we were leaving behind, in some senses forever, was
a kind of mental border territory. Families like ours were somewhere between Scotland and Ireland and if, like Brendan's parents
and mine, the older generation had done well in the new land,
between working- and middle-class. Our poetry was the Catholic
hymnal and our sisters' skipping rhymes. '*Deep night has come
down on us... We look to thy shining, sweet star of the sea... Up
in Aberdeen / There lived a fairy queen / Her name was Alice /
She lived in a palace...*' We sang 'Ally Bally' never having heard
of Coulter's candy, and only a faint idea what a *bawbee* might be.

Scottish literature was the dull hell of Scott's *Ivanhoe* at school.
We knew the odd line of Burns but the Suppers were for Proper
Scots. We half-celebrated St Patrick's Day, but really that was for
Proper Irishmen. At Hogmanay we watched Andy Stewart on the
telly and sang along with 'Campbelltown Loch' and 'The Skye Boat
Song'. What really spoke to us and bonded us with neighbours
from different backgrounds were Elvis and the Beatles. (When my
parents arrived at the house many of us would be born in, the
woman next door was Jewish and told my mother 'It's a case of the
Cohens and the Kellys here'.) For my generation, Billy Connolly's
'*The Crucifixion*' was exhilarating, something *ours* to hide from
parents. Only later did we recognize Connolly as a literary and
cultural trailblazer and influence.

LA CORUÑA

Everywhere being nowhere,
who can prove
one place more than another?

Seamus Heaney, 'The Birthplace'

Dado que "todas partes" significa
"ninguna parte" ¿quién puede probar
que un lugar vale más que cualquier otro?

(Translated by Brian Hughes)

Lee started his trek in Vigo. In 1974, Brian Hughes and Ana lived a little further north in Galicia, in La Coruña – *A Coruña*, in Galician. I was in my twenties before I discovered Gerald Brenan's *South From Granada*. Brenan has little to say about Corunna, as he calls it in English, with its overtones of Sir John Moore, British sea power and empire: 'discouraging', he called the town, dismissing the whole of Galicia in a paragraph.

The Galicia of 1935 and 1974 have more in common than they have with the place now. My teenage wonderment at the heat, light, the dark-skinned girls (and, disappointingly, equally bronzed and worryingly ripped male rivals), the bars, beaches, mysteriously tempting smells, was tempered by a dismay – even coming from Glasgow – at the poverty. There were mutilated beggars on every street corner and on the steps of all the numerous churches. Brenan and Lee report worse deprivation, but forty years of the Falangist regime had done nothing to make life better for the poor.

I've been back in Spain almost every year since: holidaying in the South and in Catalonia; at conferences in Madrid and other cities; for ten years I ran writing workshops in Pamplona; I've walked the Camino Santiago with my brother Paul, then cycled it and other bike routes with Liam and Eddie. And it is ever more evident to me that, after the death of Franco, the transition to democracy and joining the European Union, Spain underwent a fundamental transformation. The beggars have all but disappeared, people look taller and healthier, cars are bigger and prices higher. The toilets I used were like the ones Lee would have – holes in the floor, with baskets spilling over with cheap, used bog roll, swarming with flies. All that's gone. Even the most modest *hostal* or *pensión* is fitted out with two-speed flushes, bidet, and hand-dryers. In 1974, the Francoists and old civil disunities seemed, on the surface, to have faded, Spain settling into a centrist, avidly pro-European modernity.

We were luckier, in the mid '70s, than we realised. The young folk we met were of a new generation. They knew the old dictator was dying. They were preparing to construct *their* world. Pedro Almodóvar was already dreaming up his scandalous films. He made his first in 1978 called – and this tells you all you need to know about his intentions – *Folle, Folle, Fólleme... Tim* (Fuck Me... Tim). By 1980 he and Bigas Luna and others were filling Spanish – and international – screens with witty, jubilant stories of cross-dressers, night-cruisers, battered women taking exhilarating revenge, powerful gay characters, sad mums and kids on the run. Outrageous, hilarious and, at its base, warm and humane, art all over the country began to reveal a Spain that had always been there and kept secret. Yet, although the images and stories felt, in the '70s and early '80s, like a rupture, to a great extent they were updating a golden thread in Spanish art: the picaresque tales of Cervantes, Quevedo, the rogues and rascals of Lazarillo de Tormes, Goya's thrilling, and chilling, prints.

The churches were fuller in the '70s than they are now, with young people in the pews, a number of them voluntarily.

Catholicism was still a visible, controlling force across the land, the anger at either the Church's deadly collaboration with centuries of dictators, not just Franco, on the one side, dark tales of cruel murders of nuns and priests on the other. It was the era of Liberation Theology. Stories of Camilo Torres, the revolutionary priest, killed fighting for the Colombian National Liberation Army, Ernesto Cardenal siding with the Sandinistas in Nicaragua, were discussed in bars and sung about in rousing Latin American songs on the beach. For people of my age, growing up in the '60s, seeing civil rights marches and anti-war demonstrations nightly on the TV, hearing Dylan and Baez and Lennon on the radio, reading Harper Lee and Joseph Heller, Spain felt like a kind of battlefield of the soul, a place where opposing ideas might be reconciled in new ways. Unfinished business from the Civil War. Here, you could find people who claimed, electrifyingly, to be anarchist *and* Catholic, socialist *and* permissive.

Young Laurie, forty years earlier, had been clueless about the forces that were gathering on several sides. Not until his final weeks in Spain did he realise that communists, anarchists and Trotskyists were readying themselves to defend their Republic to the death, that Franco was powering up the Spanish Army of Africa. But he felt in the air that same excitement – a potential new world in the making. Vestiges of those old hopes and fears were re-emerging in the mid 1970s, Franco's reign coming to an end.

At Brian and Ana's there were always people and always talk. Debates, outright spats, nearly always about politics. Brendan and I were living through a revolution and, although in that venal teen way we had more immediate and self-gratifying concerns on our minds, we were aware of and excited by it. A couple of years later in Cádiz and with my Vigo friend Carlos, I found myself fibbing at doors to Guardia Civil officers, pasting up Trotskyist and

Communist and Galician nationalist posters in the dead of night, stuffing illegal pamphlets and magazines down toilet pans before the Guardia came knocking at the door. Slogans, songs, clandestine meetings, brushes with Fascist mobs. It was all so immediate and *dangerous*.

What hasn't changed since the Franco era, through Transition and Europeanisation, is the noise. Either side of the siesta every town, regardless of size, in every region of Spain is like having hyperactive pop radio played at full volume through earphones padlocked to your head. Endless talk, horn parps, bursts of blaring, incompatible music and muzak, announcements, guffaws... Add to that, mopeds with their silencers ripped off, discordant church bells clashing, street arguments, doors slamming. No Spaniard, it seems, is capable of putting a glass or cup down on a table or bar. They slam and wham them down. Nothing can be asked for softly or even at normal conversation level. Beers and coffees and *raciones* and bills have to be bawled out or shrieked for. On our first ever sunbathe on a Spanish beach – doubtless after our first ever night out on *Ribeiro* wine – Brendan said sleepily, 'Spaniards are born with bells instead of balls.'

And then it stops, and the opposite takes its place. The heat intensifies, even in Galicia, the streets empty, everything shuts, the siesta's spell takes hold and the silence becomes as intense as the noise. Spaniards' gas is never at a peep. It's turned off full at the mains then suddenly ignited again, burning on into the wee small hours.

The reason *why* Spaniards are so noisy, or we deem them to be, remains a mystery, to me at least. At a meal we cyclists will have in Valladolid on our way to Valencia, our hosts worry – noisily – that the image of the shouting, argumentative Spaniard is a damaging stereotype. It may have more to do with acoustics than culture. Spain being generally hotter than the UK has less soundproofing:

indoors there are fewer carpets, cushions, insulation. A glass being placed on a zinc bar top will be louder than on a wooden surface. Outdoors there is less rain, mist, grass, and other natural sound-deadening elements. Warmer weather brings people out onto the streets and communal meeting places, so that Spanish people live more publicly than we northerners. Spaniards themselves believe that the further south you go the noisier it gets. In fact, while we were crossing Spain this year, a report came out by the World Health Organisation ranking Spanish cities by decibel levels on the streets. Vigo came out tops, by far. Murcia, in the south-east, the quietest. In complete contradiction to the popularly held view. So heat may not be a factor at all.

Whatever the reasons, as a teen I loved the noise, the vivacity of Spanish life. These days I'm a little more appreciative of the afternoon silence.

Those first weeks Brendan and I spent in La Coruña were simply a holiday. We formed plans about how we were going to stay on, never go home and to hell with Higher results. Who needs qualifications if you're going to be a famous musician, or full time Lothario, or beach bum or, best plan of all, win the *Lotería* (though it might have helped if we'd had the cash to buy a ticket). Or, as it turned out, for a while, busking for pesetas and free drinks, and teaching English to bored children for a pittance. We spent days either on the beach, lounging, getting invited into the odd game of beach football, or else in bars, in viciously contested games of table football with Brian and friends or whoever we met. How we financed it I have no idea. Neither of us could have had much money. The pay for changing those thousands of light bulbs in the Polaroid factory in Renton couldn't have lasted long. Our parents certainly wouldn't have funded such a hare-brained escapade. We must have lived off poor Brian and Ana. The future academics and translators were, back then, just married, in their early twenties and trying to eke a living giving English classes themselves. But I remember Brian and Ana taking us out to restaurants, treating us to *parrilladas* of seafood: mussels, clams, outlandish *percebes*, prawns, *pulpo*, all arranged round a perfectly cooked lobster or, my preference, crab. For 1970s Scots boys we might as well have been eating Klingon or Vulcan food. I asked Brian what all these strange things were. He stroked his intellectual beard and pointed to each ingredient, pronouncing earnestly: 'In English? That there is coctopus, some keechties, the small ones flimsyfrucks, and in the middle, not sure but in Gallego it's *un huálaper*.' To this day, ordering seafood in Spain, I'm tempted to ask if they have any smudgerbutts or willywhacks.

At home we all cooked together, under Ana's direction. They presumably bought all the food. And the wine, and every other kind of drink for their numerous parties. I doubt we gave them a penny in return. The sheer cheek and entitlement of youth. Luckily, wine then cost – and I remember this precisely – two pesetas for a small ceramic quaich of young, weak, Ribeiro wine, and a handful of unshelled peanuts. We also found *futbolín* tables that were broken requiring the same coin to be used over and over again.

The owner of the bar didn't care. He was sitting in the same seat behind the bar every time we came in. His stool was a wobbly three-legged affair, positioned so he could pour us our cheap wines – about every ten minutes – and scoop up a saucer of peanuts, without getting up. Fat, and exhausted looking, at the time I thought he was ancient. He was probably in his forties.

'You boys never go to another bar?' he asked from time to time, irritated.

From time to time, while we were playing one of his broken machines, he'd belch. Occasionally a woman would come out the rope-and-bead curtain behind the bar. She would have been the same age but in clean, flimsy, clothes. She'd come round to pick up our china cups and empty peanut dishes.

'Who's winning today, lads? Can I get you something else?'

To my teenage mind she was flirty, in that loose top and skirt, light for working in heat. Victoria Montoya trapped in a down-at-heel saloon on the wrong side of the border. Then she'd vanish back through the curtain. Older and less impressionable, I now see she was cooking all day, probably in a small, hot kitchen.

But the cheapest place to be was the beach.

Riazor beach in La Coruña. It was spectacular then and has been upgraded since. The city now boasts the longest paved sea-front promenade in the country. At night, back then, the beach was a youths' paradise. Probably still is. Cool, in every sense. The lights of the city behind us and the islands ahead, shy lovers' eyes, sparkling at one another. The guitars and *aguardiente* came out, campfires lit. Singers sang, smoochers smooched, a ball was kicked about, names drawn in the sand, names forever entwined in waves washing out into the Atlantic.

Victor Jara, Lluis Llach, Violeta Parra, María Dolores Pradera, I first heard all these singers and songwriters on Riazor. Mexican *rancheras*, chic '60s *bossa nova*, my first hearings of flamenco, later to become an obsession. Georges Moustaki, too – Ana played his LPs in the flat Brel and Gainsboroug. The whole of Europe and the Hispanic world washed up on that beach: flotsam from Veracruz and Havana, Rio de Janeiro and Macondo; jetsam from Ortigueira, Sanlúcar, Lisboa. Paco Ibáñez's musical settings opened a treasure trove of Spanish language poets – Goytisolo, Rubén Darío, Alberti. Forty-five years later Joan Manuel Serrat's take on the poet Antonio Machado's 'Cantares' became our cycling anthem.

On first hearing the Spanish language, Laurie Lee talks of the hard, clanking sounds. This surprises me. The rapid-fire bullet consonants are more Castilian Spanish than *Gallego*. The language of Celtic Galicia, somewhere between Portuguese and Spanish, has always struck me as soft and lilting. What Hebridean Scots is to English.

We didn't first meet Teresa on Riazor. We met her in the, tiny, lift up to our nearby flat. She was like a character from one of our newly learned songs... *'like a samba that swings so cool and sways so gently'.* Brendan and I both made eyes at her, all of us inches apart. Coco won out over Dodo. Tere became a great friend to both of us and, soon, Brendan's girlfriend. She introduced us to so many people, took us to places all around La Coruña.

Most of the young people, if they could speak English at all, did so with an Irish accent. The school where Brian was teaching was Irish-owned and most of the teachers were from Cork. Take a look at a map – it's a direct unbroken line across the Celtic Sea from La Coruña to Cork. A few years later, at the folk festival in Ortigueira I met an old fisherman who spoke two languages – Gallego and Irish Gaelic. Not a word of either Spanish or English. Fishing those waters, they were the languages he needed.

Teresa's best friend was Flora Gallego. She and I pretended to be boyfriend-and-girlfriend. Despite all the radical talk and songs of freedom, this was still chaste, Catholic Spain – holding hands for a moment was as radical and daring as relationships got. Gentle and pretty, Flora lived up to her name, the Flower of Galicia.

Brendy and me, two eejits that left Scotland, no direction bound, found our *camino.* When we meet now we seldom discuss the old days. We talk about books and places and music, politics, friends and football. I'll leave us there for the moment, on Riazor: laughter and horseplay, two kids breaking open our full-to-bursting personal *piñatas,* stuffed with new discoveries and shiny promises.

* * *

Time Trials

Cantarte hei, Galicia,
teus dulces cantares.

Rosalía de Castro, *Cantares Gallegos*

Let me sing to you, Galicia,
your beautiful song.

When exactly I left Brendan in La Coruña – or he left me to go north to his in-laws in El Ferrol – and I took my violin to begin the vagabond trail in the wake of Laurie Lee, neither of us are sure. I simply remember heading off. First to some of the villages I had already visited with Brian, or Tere, or others. I had never in my life busked before. I was terrified. I also wasn't very good, which didn't help. On the other hand, busking wasn't a thing back then. Now, in Spain as in the UK or anywhere, there are buskers at every corner, the entrance to every tube station. Back then I was a one-off. People stood in astonishment rather than appreciation.

The loneliness of the busker. No one has asked you to play. You're getting in the way in a public space, a beggar essentially. Aware of your limitations, trying to catch strangers' attention but not their eye. Hoping for payment but unsure you deserve any. Part of me wanted to be ignored, another craved their approval – and needed their loose change. I had never busked in Scotland, had never met anyone who had. I stood as close to the wall as possible, kept my eye on my fiddle. I felt like a shadow, a smudge on the pavement.

Then passers-by began to throw pesetas into my opened violin case (eventually I learned to put in the first few – silver – ones myself, *pour encourager les autres*) out of sympathy and concern rather than for having been whisked momentarily to a haven of glorious music. I would usually make just enough to afford the cheapest *menú del día* in the village, and a night in the most basic *pensión*.

I didn't have the adventures, neither the highs nor the lows that Lee had in 1935. Inns in his day sound nineteenth-century in comparison. Bedding down with animals in straw, or in shared barns with entire families. His descriptions of single-room cabins and outhouses, or cheap dormitories in cities, run by drunks and crones and children – it all reads like Dickens. Or Stevenson. David Balfour, lost in the Highlands, taking refuge in black houses and crofts and among the heather. Stevenson wrote *Kidnapped* in 1886, and set it in 1751, after the turmoil of the Jacobite Rising. So Lee's accounts sound, in fact, eighteenth-century. Perhaps because he likes to tell a good story and his 'facts' are elsewhere dubious, it's hard not to suspect that he exaggerates his living conditions. But not by much. Spain was poor enough in '74, much more so in '35. Cut off from Europe by the Pyrenees, exhausted from a century of civil wars (the one in 1936 was far from the first), and another century of thrawn Church and landowners' conservatism, Lee's Spain had hardly changed in over a century.

The *pensiones* I stayed in – and would over the next few years on return journeys – were lugubrious, heavy old furniture, blinds down. There was usually a landlady, usually in her seventies – which back then was shockingly old to me. Almost without exception she'd narrow her eyes, look suspicious, demand payment, or part of it, up front. In every bedroom, hall, and bathroom there were crucifixes, dripping with blood and howling in pain. Stepping inside my room reminded me of going to confession as a child. Closed space, an air of pious anxiety, left alone with sins and penance.

But, just as usually, the old landlady would soon turn out to be kindly, offering you soup *a la casera*, seldom included in the final bill. If you stayed more than a night she'd even smile, ask you about yourself. You'd open your blinds, let in the light and the noise of the street, meet family and, what appeared initially as some murky house that held terrible secrets, became a family home, into which you were often, temporarily, accepted.

A few times, bar owners who had heard me in the street invited me to play inside, at lunchtime, or in the evening. Reimbursement was a few beers or glasses of wine and a thick, hot *caldo gallego* – a stew of a few bits of whatever meat was available but mainly cabbage and beans, garlic, onion.

Life was easier now that my Spanish was improving. I could ask for food, beer, accommodation, join in on very basic conversations, explain a little of the background to my songs and tunes. But in Vigo someone from elsewhere in Spain informed me I was talking *Gallego*. Or rather, the mix of Galician, Spanish and streettalk Brendan and I had been unwittingly learning in bars and on Riazor beach. To be absolutely accurate, I was speaking a mix of Gallego, Spanish, street jive, and west coast Scots. (A later version of which a student of mine in Pamplona dubbed *escoñol*.)

Maybe that's why I was destined to be The Man Who, unwittingly, Invented Fusion Music. Or at least one half of the duo that invented it. I was in Pontevedra playing my violin on one corner of the main square and some very noisy bongo player was attracting audiences at the other. I can't remember his name. A young black Brazilian guy. Twice my height, he moved slowly but played fast. After an hour or two he ambled – which implies far too much urgency – up to my pitch. Through his Brazilian-Portuguese-Spanish and my Gallego-Scots we managed to negotiate.

'*Oi, Branquinho. Vamos a play juntos, yeah?*'

Hoy, wee white man. Let's play together.

I've since gotten to know the music of Milton Nascimento and now, in my head, that bongo player is called Milton. Milton's thinking was right. We more than doubled our individual audiences. No wonder. The sound we made drew people from streets away. I'm playing the Irish Washerwoman and Milton is pulsing out a spliff-saturated slow samba. I switch to 'My Love Is Like A Red Red Rose', bowing with all the soul and misty romance I could muster, and Milton whacks hell out of his drums in some complex war cry.

Cacophony was only the half of it. What a *sight* we must have been. Milton sitting, but still nearly as tall as me standing. He's black and dressed in psychedelic tie-dye. I'm strawberries-and-cream, dressed in hand-me-downs from my brothers. I'm swaying awkwardly, his long arms are whirling and flailing like a shaman's.

We made a fortune.

We went back the next day, but takings were down. The world wasn't ready yet for fusion music. Our racket, heard once, seemed to be considered enough. I never saw Milton again. He disappeared from the streets leaving a whiff of ganja and a tincture of tinnitus in the air.

There was interest then – I notice it less now – in my Scottishness. These days, proper musicians top the bill in folk festival and concerts all over Galicia. Carlos Núñez, the Gallego piper, is at Celtic Connections most years. In the '70s too, the likes of the Chieftains were well known. (I have an old poster somewhere of the Ortigueira Folk Festival – 1979? – the Whistlebinkies topping the bill, and the name Chris Dolan at the very bottom – and here I'm not exaggerating – about thirty acts down. As I remember, it's hand-written on. As an afterthought. Quite possibly by me.)

But then, I was still a relatively rare sight. Porridge hair and raspberry skin, playing 'Annie Laurie', 'Danny Boy', 'Dashing White Sergeant'. At the end of, and for a while after, the Franco regime there was a renewed, more open, interest in Galicia's ancient Celtic connections. That helped me make some money. In one bar, in a barrio of Pontevedra, I was asked if I knew any Scots Gaelic songs. The bar had a guitar and I'd been alternating between singing and fiddle tunes. I knew roughly how to make the sounds of 'Fear a' Bháta' ('The Boatman'). So I did that. It went down well. I grew in confidence, making noises (truly racist, now that I think about it – and me the son of an Irish Gaelic speaker) that people who had never heard Gaelic in their lives happily accepted. I must have looked the part, the true lumpy son of Scots farmers. I used Scottish surnames as well as what I thought might sound like mouth music in my 'Gaelic' songs… 'Oh, Murdo McCraw, och naw och naw, aye Seamus wee Leitch'. I got invited back.

I think I made it to the third night – free wine, food, enough takings in the hat for a decent bed, my first, possibly last, truly spellbound audience – until the only other Scot in the entire province of Pontevedra walked in. I hadn't considered the possibility.

I remember the guffaw. I remember the sound of my heart plummeting. I stopped mid-ballad, 'Oh Catrii-ona hoo-roo MacNeice ach Sorley Loch Doon…' I don't remember his exact words, but they weren't complimentary. A mix of surprise, a degree of, I like to think, respect for the sheer *cara dura* – brass neck – but more explicitly an accusation of fraudulence. We spoke afterwards and my compatriot told me to carry on, he wouldn't tell a soul. But the game was up.

I like telling that story, been recounting it for years. But in fact, I think it was the beginning of the end of my Grand Plan. Things didn't go so well from then on and, soon, I left off, disappointingly not very far from where Laurie had set off. And more than 1,000 kilometres from Almuñécar, where I had intended on going.

SANTIAGO 2000

My first Spanish cycle wouldn't be until 2011, but I had walked it – well, 170 miles of it – eleven years earlier.

Throughout my adult life the Camino has cast its spell. The Way of the Stars. For the most traditional pilgrim, it is a journey towards a false tomb. Almost certainly James the Greater, son of Zebedee (after Peter the most important of the Apostles) is not buried in the crypt of Santiago Cathedral at all. Even alive, it's uncertain he was anywhere near Spain. More likely, the bones that lie at journey's end are those of the heretic Prisciliano. Yet the faithful will end their journey in Santiago de Compostela gripping – as we did – the pillar of the cathedral, and embracing the statue of St James. The mythic discovery of the Apostle's remains – in great Christian tradition by lowly shepherds under a field of stars, *campo stellar* – kicked off the wars of Reconquest, and the rout of the Islamic empire. The world-peace-loving modern pilgrim goes to pray at the altar of bloodthirsty power-mongering. Does it matter? The spirituality, sanctity, is still there, almost physical, like footsteps on snow, boots on grass.

In fact the Camino de Santiago predates St James by some time. The *Via Láctea* - literally, the Milky Way – was first an ancient Druidic road, a path for the wisest of men to tread to the then End of the World, the limits of experience. It links into Celtic mythology, to the legendary battle between the Milesians, a people from the distant land across the sea, Galicia, and the Tuatha Dé Dannan – gods. In a final peace treaty, the two sides decide to divide the island of Ireland equally – the Galicians (Gaels) living above ground, the gods below. Which is, if you like to believe it, the situation to this day. It was the warrior Breogán who first glimpsed the coast of Ireland from his tower in A Coruña. *Nazón de Breogán* is the national anthem of Galicia.

I like the Druid road idea immensely. Having set out with a group of, mostly, confirmed Catholics in the hope of rediscovering something of my own – once dearly-held – faith, the knowledge that for centuries not only Christians but ancient peoples too had trodden this road in search of enlightenment lent me some of the zeal of my companions.

The Scottish contingent of 2000AD – about twelve of us, mostly friends of my brother – became legendary along the line. Pilgrims would meet up with us, having heard stories of the bunch of joyous, partying Scots. Drinks were bought and hotel rooms paid for total strangers. At the same time, they took their sport and their pilgrimage seriously. We called out *Ultreia!* (the Camino's secret language: Keep going, Pilgrim!) to fellow pilgrims as we approached the legendary O Cebreiro mountain, 5,000 feet up. (The knowledge, and experience, helped me not a jot eleven years later when I pedaled up it).

My brother Paul and I heard, somewhere along the road, about the Miracle of O Cebreiro. The story goes that, many years ago in the midst of a storm, a farmer wanted to hear mass in the church at the top of the mountain. The local priest, understandably, wasn't keen on the idea. When we went up it we had to wade through knee-high snow – beautiful, muted, but cold and hard work. After complaining, the priest finally submitted, climbed the mountain and, exhausted, said Mass for his sole parishioner in a foul temper. Until, at Communion, the bread and wine really *did* turn into the living body and blood of the Saviour (in quite what manner, the story is not explicit). A statue of the Virgin Mary came to life and knelt before the miraculous transubstantiation. The priest repented his lack of faith and commitment. Wagner, we were told, heard the story and the opera Parsifal is the result. There are some who, to this day, believe that the story is proof that the chalice the priest used must have been the Holy Grail itself.

You're supposed, traditionally, to walk The Way alone, meeting and sharing with other pilgrims, strangers, as you advance. So after a few days with my brother's group, I decided to go on ahead and meet them again at the penultimate stop, the Mount of Rejoicing (well named). I fell into step with Suzete – a Brazilian woman from São Paulo. Tiny, her feet smaller than my then eight year-old daughter's, and carrying next to nothing she had trekked 700 kilometres from the south of France. She completed O Cebreiro in a pair of light shoes and the Brazilian equivalent of a duffel coat. It was Suzete who helped me understand that what matters is the walking itself. I was all about getting there. Waking and hitting the road early, head down, walk.

'If you're in such a hurry to get to Santiago', Suzete said, 'take a train'.

It's not about arriving. Nor is it even about thinking, or praying. It's tricky to ponder philosophically when your body is aching and you're trying to calculate where the next meal might be found, and that is what is liberating. The sheer simplicity of moving forward slowly, of having a single objective in mind, dealing with the practical problems along the way, meeting whoever it is you are destined to meet, it all conjures fantasies of some simpler, cleaner way of life. The body may be burdened, but the mind is not. A lesson that helped me on subsequent cycles.

You meet all sorts – which is the point. Diego, a Málaga policeman, seemingly pleasant and interesting, had some kind of Kabbalistic gesture that every passing National or Civil Guard immediately recognised. José María, a Basque pilgrim, loudly trumpeted the old Francoist rally cry of '¡Arriba España!' to everyone he passed.

Rudi was a handsome young Dutch lad who knew it, with a smile that could wash your soul clean. A court had decided that it would be better for the young delinquent to send him on a spiritual journey rather than to jail. So Rudi spent three months laughing, and talking, brightening everyone's day – and thieving his way from Amsterdam to Santiago. By the time he got to the pilgrim's Mass he was kitted out head to toe in new, top-of-the-range boots, jacket and backpack.

The last crossing into Santiago, just after a path that is naturally strewn with symbolic leaves and fronds like palms, is over a little river – the last cleansing place of the pilgrim in which, in the old days, wearied pilgrims would immerse themselves fully, Ganges-style. The township that has sprung up around this watering hole is Lavacolla – literally, Cockwash. The most crucial body parts to scrub were the ones that might have picked up unpleasant diseases along the way. The very first guidebook, not only to Santiago but arguably anywhere, is the twelfth-century Codex Calixtinus. Five books, the originals stored in Santiago cathedral, which include the stories about St James himself, a book of chivalry that Don Quixote would have loved following the exploits of Charlemagne and Roland. And, best known, the travel guide probably written by French monk Aymeric Picaud who brought the books together. Picaud is frank about the prostitution industry that grew up around the pilgrimage. As my brother put it, 'now that's what I call falling by the wayside'. And that other indulgence: rich people paying servants to do the pilgrimage for them (but keeping the blessings and hallowed boons to themselves). The Camino has been the subject of lots of eccentric books – by Paulo Coelho and Shirley MacLaine among others – and the *Liber Sancti Iacobi* can be pretty outlandish too. Picaud warns you to beware of the Basques because they are 'evil, dark in complexion, of aberrant appearance, wicked, treacherous, disloyal and false…thieves and murderers …who eat, drink and dress like pigs'. However, it's not their fault. They're the bastard offspring of an even more bestial and degraded people – Scots.

Our *credenciales* (the pilgrim's record of his journey) duly stamped, we were *compostelado* – presented with a Latin scroll rubber-stamping our acceptance into the community of pilgrims. After Communion at the Pilgrim's mass, the massive pipe organ strikes up and thunders through the 1000-year-old temple. Then they bring out the celebrated thurible – the ancient *botafemeiro*. Lighting a couple of pounds of incense, four monks hoist the enormous silver cauldron beyond the rafters, up into the gods, where it swings madly and perilously above the cowering heads of the faithful, belching out huge clouds of spiritual narcotic. The priest implores us to send up our prayers to heaven, buoyed by the music and holy smoke. Sheer smells and bells – pure theatre. Priests, nuns and monks in extravagant get-ups, the pulsing organ, siren singing – only the Spanish can pull off this kind of religious showbiz with such pizzazz. But if it worked for medieval peasants, it worked for me – a ritual of such colour and passion, only the most pious of cynics would fail to be moved.

Any pilgrim could be unlucky, like the story of the penitent who, at the fulfillment of her pilgrimage, lined up for the Eucharist and had her moneybag knifed open by the communicant behind her. But if you've kept your mind open to the comfort of strangers, to the ancient Druid wisdom of the Road, then be reminded that for every proto-fascist, or unfortunate prostitute, there's a Rudi who'll charm you (before stealing your shoes), a foreigner with vital advice, and a fellow pilgrim who'll offer you sustenance when you most need it. 'One begins the Camino', someone along the way had told us, 'as a traveller, but ends it a pilgrim'.

PART TWO

Gearing Up

SCOTLAND & SPAIN, 2011–2018

To record, even to record emotions, is to store up a fund of sadness...

Robert Cunninghame Graham, *Faith*

Next time I travelled the Camino de Santiago it was with cyclists Liam Kane and Eddie Morrison.

For much of this story we'll be in their company, so let me introduce them:

Eddie and Liam

We're the same age, Eddie, Liam and I. But I was the year below them at university where we met – my late arrival caused, in part, by this to-ing and fro-ing to Galicia with Brendan.

Like family politics, the youngest is forever the baby – the slightly annoying haunless one. Eddie Morrison and Liam Kane will always be the Year Above, the more advanced students of life.

There was always a crowd round Eddie Morrison. He doesn't tell jokes, but wildly embellished 'true' stories. His hyperboles – blatant exaggerations – were in tune with the fabulism of the Magic Realism we were studying. He's angular, Eddie – spiky, spry, sharp. And he's fast, at the top of any hill long before Liam and me. His glasses aren't the cause of that intense gaze – they simply frame it. A genuine scholar, rapt by his chosen subjects – Spain and Spanish, literature, sport, Scotland – his enthusiasm is contagious. After university, he became a teacher. Then head of department, then assistant head teacher, then head teacher. I've seen him in action. He knew every child's name, in a large comprehensive, plus their parents' and siblings' names – crucial details about their lives. It's not a studied tactic, but honest curiosity in and concern for the lives of others.

And now, the same thistly frame, quick edgy movements, the bright eyes – but also a hue, sorrowful, as opposed to sad, that's deepened over the years. Like all of us, the longer we live the more holes there are in our armour. In 2018, only a few months before we set out to cycle across Spain, Eddie's wife died. We'll hear more of Lizzie; for now, she exited as she had entered, suddenly, with theatrical timing, grace and wit. Eddie teeters on the chasm she's left behind.

He continues to tell his stories, find precisely the right quote from poems, songs and speeches, delighting still in discoveries, but we all know there's a quiet engine running in the background keeping the shadows and losses to a whisper.

Liam, *el Gran Organizador*. It's Liam who researches and maps out our cycling tours. Calculates distance, height gained, need for breaks, weather, books the hotels in advance. He is in charge of the funds – like wee boys, Eddie and I hand over our pocket money through the year, and Liam buys us food and coffee and ice-creams on the road.

Liam has no desire to do any of these things. At his happiest when he goes off on trips by himself, without having to worry about the weans.

Eddie has basic bike mechanic skills. I don't. Liam fixes the bikes. Also, being teetotal, Liam never sleeps in or has a hangover or is too grumpy to pump up a tyre or organise a breakfast. To give him his full title – which he himself refused to use while lecturing at Glasgow University – he is Doctor

Liam Kane. Linguist and expert on Popular Education, specifically the works of Brazilian educationalist Paulo Freire. Politically active, committed and thoughtful.

Both Eddie and Liam's fathers – and Liam's mother – had higher educations. Unusual for their generation – my parents left school without qualifications, though my mother, at sixteen, managed to talk her way into nursing training in London, lying about her age. Eddie's dad was a bandleader in the army, which led him to study at the Athenaeum. Liam's dad was in the Parachute Regiment and saw active service. Living and working in the west of Scotland, regardless of profession, you can't stray far from working class fixations and politics. Our generation grew up on a diet of Muhammad Ali and the Lisbon Lions, Jim Reeves and Sinatra, faith in Education, Labour, and Clyde Coast holidays. When we first took up our guitars it was to replace old songs and hymns with new ones by Neil Young and James Taylor and Dylan: *'He not busy being born is busy dying...'* Liam is an accomplished guitarist and ukulele player.

The believer, the agnostic and the atheist. Liam is our atheist. Resolutely intellectual, he is a natural scientist, looking for evidence and the practical – but diving for an oyster for sustenance, he often emerges with a pearl. It shouldn't really work, the three of us cycling long distances together. And sometimes it doesn't, quite. We each see the world from different standpoints, process the evidence contrarily. Yet we blunder along amiably enough.

Eddie and Liam's first Camino cycle was a disaster. It poured almost constantly. The odd time it didn't the scorching afternoon sun caught them halfway up tough hills. They hadn't booked ahead for places to stay (the lack of *planning!*) and they spent most of their evenings traipsing round backstreets begging for a bed for the night. Eddie's asthma played up. They had an average of seven punctures a day. (Again, lack of foresight, if you ask me. Wrong kind of bikes, wrong wheels, wrong tyres.) They lost their way often, adding miles to their routes, and generally were as miserable as stray cats, hungry and sodden for a fortnight...

There is not a single word of that that Liam and Eddie would agree with. Except maybe the punctures. And the lack of planning. And the asthma... In fact, they reached Santiago on schedule, enjoyed their time. So much so that I asked them to do it again, this time with me in tow. Having learned from previous mistakes, for the next outing in 2011 we bought the proper bikes, started to train, and began a whole lifestyle of day-, weekend-, and fortnight-long cycles in Scotland and Spain. Ten years now and counting.

SANTIAGO II

How perilous is it to choose
not to love the life we're shown?

Seamus Heaney, 'The Badgers'

¿Hasta qué punto es peligroso negarnos
a amar la vida que se nos ofrece?

(Translated by Brian Hughes)

A beautiful spring morning in León, olive and almond groves translucent 'neath a gentle blue sky... when over the hill come, panting and singing out of tune, three fifty-somethings, shocking pink and Day-Glo puce stretched over paunches and bony legs. We were cycling, early morning through a tiny village, just as an old man came out his door, no doubt to fetch the morning bread. He heard us, then saw us, stopped dead in his tracks. We waved, kept singing, '*Con dinero y sin dinero / hago siempre lo que quiero...*' The poor man stood gawping after us. I glanced back, to see him about-turn and go back into his house, troubled.

On this first long outing the Believer took the credit for the non-stop sunshine (unexpected in northern Spain in April), whenever we got the route right, and the astonishing fact of not getting a single puncture over a collective 1,000 miles. The Atheist was quick to point out that the latter had far more to do with his decision to make us all buy Schwalbe Marathon tyres. We had splashed out on decent tourers. Two Ridgeback Panoramas and one Specialized – the same bikes hauled out of cupboards and garages to take us coast-to-coast eight years later. We got old boxes from bike shops and put our luggage in them too for the flight. We've been using the same system ever since. Other cyclists, we've noticed, either hire bikes at their destination, or buy proper plastic bike cases. Hiring a bike abroad adds expense, and creates delays: finding, being fitted for, taking the bike away and returning it. The hard bike cases only work if you are staying at one location. With old cardboard boxes you can, if you like, get off the plane and ride out of the airport, on the comfort of your own bicycle.

2011, the Arab Spring. The second of my two children left home. Empty nest. An era gone. But the three cyclists were all still in employment. We had a week's holiday in which to do six days' worth of the *Camino Francés,* the oldest and most travelled pilgrim route to Santiago de Compostela. Roughly the same route I had walked with my brother and that Liam and Eddie had done the year before. Our starting point was Burgos, El Cid's Castilian city, a 350-mile journey in six days, giving an average of 58 miles a day. Not much, but we were touring without backup, carrying all our gear with us in panniers and backpacks. The first two days' cycles are flat, so the 120 miles or so were easy going, a perfect start, limbering up for bigger challenges to come.

The first of those loomed on the third day. Cruz de Hierro: 1,500 metres high. Had all the cycling up Gardner Street on rainy Glasgow evenings paid off? Cruz de Hierro – so called because there is, indeed, an iron cross on the summit – is a high point of the Camino in more than one sense. The practice of placing a stone brought from home goes back to Celtic times, serving the same marking and mystical purposes as Scottish cairns. Catholics think of it as leaving a great sin behind them before continuing on to the city of St James; others see it as a symbol of some problem they came here to resolve. For cyclists, it's a little less weight in your saddlebag.

O Cebreiro, the mountain of the reluctant priest, of the miracle and Grail. There was no sign of divine guidance for Eddie and me. Ahead of Liam, we were surprised that the ascent was so tricky. We had both been up this hill before and neither of us remembered it being so awkward. The road disappeared then too, the narrow path it had become, so we had to carry our bikes over burns and patches of moorland. Eventually we found our way back on to a tarmac road at last and remounted... And heard a distant voice on the wind. Looking round, we saw Liam cycling up an entirely different hill. The right hill.

We had to cycle, half scramble, back down the one we had gone up and start again at the bottom of O Cebreiro. The hottest afternoon in decades at that time of year. Three and a half hours, in 30° C+ heat. So slow we couldn't take our hands off the handlebars to get a drink. We sweated up 600 metres and nearly 20 kilometres. And we had to put up with Liam's laughter and derision – until we passed him. Our own little Miracle of O Cebreiro, the Golden Grail: getting to the top.

Above my desk at home is a photograph of the three of us on the top of O Cebreiro. The Camino cycle is the first of my Spanish journeys to be properly pictorially recorded, Liam being a keen photographer. Proof that we made it to the top, six arms raised. I seldom notice it but when I do it takes me, like a song, like a scent, directly back to that moment, every day further in our past.

A four-hour cycle up, but twenty sublime minutes back down. The road is perfectly smooth, almost empty of cars. The bends sweep wide below you so you can see what's round them. It's as if it was engineered for the most perfect downhill. Liam's handlebar computer recorded over 47 miles per hour. From there, full throttle all the way to the city of St James. Santiago, an intoxicating blend of Seville and Galway, bagpipes and incense, soft rain and seafood.

ANDALUCÍA

From then on three friends decided to spend portions of our lives on bikes, in a country we feel a constant need to explore and re-explore. We undertook two more Spanish tours, before the coast-to-coast, interspersed with day or weekend cycles in Scotland. East Kilbride to Strathaven, through Galston into Burns country; Glen Lyon and Loch Tay, spooling Perthshire never vanquished until Birnam wood come against us; Thornhill Dumfriesshire, a Scotland as seen on covers of People's Friend; further south to Scott's Lochinvar; north through David and Allan's escape route in *Kidnapped*, up to Glen Affric, Assynt, Lochinver in Sutherland.

2013: the year Prime Minister Cameron proposed a referendum on Europe, and a date for the referendum on Scottish independence was settled for the following year. We cycled south through

Gearing Up

Andalusia, Seville to Granada, through Osuna, Cabra, Montefrío, Granada, like pedalling through a Lorca poem, ending up in Málaga. Having risked changeable weather in Galician journeys we had chosen Andalusia not only for the beauty and the history we would be moving through, but in hope of better weather. In fact, we had had better luck in northern, green, generally wetter Spain.

You get to places on a bike you would never manage on foot or behind a wheel. By car, you move through roads and places so quickly you don't meet anyone, never feel the geology of the land beneath your wheels, let the scenery into your soul. All of us had been to Granada before, Liam living there for a year in the late '70s. It didn't disappoint, but it did rain – as it had when Gerald Brenan first passed through it in 1919. For us, though, the beauty of the place shone through, the Alhambra and Generalife glowing damply red (the word Alhambra comes from the Arabic for red), streets busy with multi-coloured umbrellas.

* * *

Two years later we toured the Pueblos Blancos. Scotland had voted to stay in the UK; in Barcelona Ada Colau and in Madrid Manuela Carmena were voted in as mayors, both radicals, both backed by the new, young, party *Podemos* (Yes We Can) which had risen out of Spain's own anti-austerity movement. From Ronda you climb into the Sierra Grazalema into *España profunda,* deep Spain. The provinces of Jerez, Sevilla, Cádiz. Heat, horses, the penitents in *Semana Santa,* sherry, fiestas, the heat again, birds falling dead out of trees, bulls and bullfights. We're going to hear lots of discussion on that bloody topic on the road to Valencia.

That 2015 Andalusian cycle took us through so many beautiful towns – Arcos de la Frontera, Zahara, Conil, Zuheros. Vejer de la Frontera… sounds exciting, exotic. It has a different effect on me now. The Sirocco and Poniente winds were blowing strong the day we cycled from Vejer, causing squalls and sudden gusts. In an early attempt at slipstreaming and drafting, I rode tight on Liam's back wheel. Terrified, I didn't take my eyes off the 6 inches between us. So I didn't see the truck come out unexpectedly on the right. Liam braked.

I went tapsalteerie. Straight over my handlebars, arse over elbow. But we straightened out the bike as best we could and ped- alled on for a couple of miles. It was problems with the bike that caused me to stop, cycle back to Vejer. Only when I had bought a paper, ordered a coffee and relaxed did the adrenaline stop pumping. Four years later and I still can't straighten my arm fully. Broken elbow, cracked ribs. At least we'd learned our lesson and would be more careful of any off us falling off and breaking bones in the future...

Not long after we got back from the *Pueblos Blancos* cycle, my brother Paul dropped dead. Impact, the ground rising sud- denly at you, you hit it, then go right through it, down into the black, back to black. His son, Michael, found him in his garden. People said later at least he died tending his roses. Paul hated those damn roses.

EXTREMADURA

We all stayed safe on our last cycle before the coast-to-coast, and our first as sexagenarians, to Extremadura in 2018. Liam and Eddie had both just retired. For Eddie it was a journey of healing and remembrance.

Extremadura runs alongside the Portuguese border, north from Seville up towards Salamanca. Driving out of Seville, we saw a Spain none of us recognised. The colour of the earth deep- ens from chalk white to rich amontillado. The broad, flat plains plummet down from the Sierra Morena like a sudden drop in blood pressure. It's so sparsely populated you become very aware of the sky – pale smoky blue with puffy white clouds, as if drawn by a dreamy child.

The origin of the name Extremadura – 'very hard' – had worried us. But it simply refers to the outermost secure border of the classical province. We worried, too, about talk of brutally high *'Extremeño'* temperatures. But the day we took to the road the blue skies morphed into soft, almost Scottish, silver. Even on A-roads we seldom saw a car. We did, however, see lots of lakes, reservoirs, rivers. Landlocked Extremadura is known as the 'Costa Interior'. There are thousands of kilometres of freshwater pools and gorges, inland beaches. So, weirdly, as you cycle along you hear peewits, see trees full of egrets.

Stranger still, it produced a plethora of sailors. Heartland of the Conquistadors. Francisco Pizarro – who kidnapped and murdered Atahualpa, the last Inca Emperor – was born in picturesque Trujillo. Hernan Cortés, the terror of Mexico, was from the little town of Medellín. Vasco Núñez de Balboa founded the settlement of Darien. (Scotland has little to thank Vasco for.) Hard to imagine such violence, pedalling past pastures and orchards and meadows. Figs, peppers, plums, tomatoes, cereals, oranges and lemons, artichokes. And another of Extremadura's famous exports – bulls, bred for their strength, size and aggression, for the *corrida*.

One magical day we came across a road that all of us agreed was among the best we had ever cycled. That would be put severely to the test, several times, from Vigo to Valencia. Nary a car for well over an hour. Beautiful white horses running alongside us, behind hedgerows bursting with fruits and flowers. Smooth tarmac, you could hear our Scottish tyres sighing with relief and delight, as we swept along. We were surrounded by oak groves. Extremadura is the epicentre of *Jamón Ibérico*. It's here they raise the essential black Iberian pigs and feed them nothing but acorns. Or oak-nuts, as Don Quixote called them, declaring them the basis of all great cuisine.

Heading up towards Plasencia, mountains suddenly erupt out of the plains. The Sierra de Gredos, with its scary Category 1 hills. Peña Negra is the highest point in La Vera – The Vale of Extremadura, home to high hills and brooks and, we discovered, Europe's best paprika. One of the reasons we were here at all was because Lizzie had insisted. Eddie's wife, and our old friend, had died in the summer. Throughout the ride we remembered Lizzie stories – and laughed, and gret. Eddie calculated hills not in metres or yards but how often he could say 'Elizabeth McKim Hamill Morrison'. Peña Negra got him into the hundreds, and to the summit long before us. 1,200 metres high, over an hour's climb – but the views from the top are a rich reward. A perspective to help you come to terms with loss, and a kind of spiritual profit.

The whole ride had a zen feel, each day, every hill and road, each push of the pedal melding into one long, calming, experience. 'I think I've mastered mindfulness,' I said, 'I forget where I am, just keep going forward, uphill or down'.

Liam thought about this for a mile or two then worried that I might be confusing mindfulness with stupidity.

PART THREE

Freewheelin'

SCOTLAND 2019

In January 2019 I met up with the writer Donald S. Murray in Glasgow. I had just read Donald's *As The Women Lay Dreaming*, a poignant family story beautifully constructed around the *Iolaire* Disaster: on New Year's Day in 1919 more than 200 men, survivors of the First World War, drowned off Stornoway harbour. A hundred years later Donald and I compare notes on how books have enlarged our idea of Scotland and our place in it. His book made connections for me not only between the Highlands and Lowlands, but between past and present. And that must have been how I got onto the subject of my teenage Spanish adventure.

The Scotland I had left, in 1974, seemed to offer me little, I told Donald, in terms of books and music. It was later that Kelman, Lochhead, Leonard and Gray changed my literary landscape. Peter MacDougall plays brought characters I recognised to TV drama. McIlvanney kick-started Tartan Noir. Since then I have thrown in my tuppence-worth, including crime novels sitting on shelves alongside exceptional writers like Denise Mina and Louise Welsh. Donald and I talked about Graeme Macrae Burnet's *His Bloody Project*, a novel that creates another kind of hinge between Scotland's past and present. He plays Cervantes-style games with authorship and reality: 'I subscribe to the view that it's difficult to set down an objective truth about any event in the past, even the recent past', Macrae Burnet has his namesake narrator say. Donald and I discussed time and memory and stories over soup at the Church of Scotland's Wild Olive Café. I told him about my attempt to walk Laurie Lee's route when I was a teenager.

'What age were you?'

'I was about to turn seventeen.'

'What age are you now?'

'Sixty.'

'Do it next year. Try again. Sixteen – sixty-one.'

It was a mad notion. I have a job. A family. I have limited funds and continuing financial responsibilities – debts. Rerunning a special time of youth sounded a bit midlife crisis. I had the original teenage trip perfectly edited and conserved in my head – why ruin it? It would mean being apart from my wife Moira, away from my family and home, from work for... I had no idea how long. It was a year or more of nineteen-year-old Laurie's life.

That would be impossible. But the idea took hold of me and a plan began forming in my mind as I said goodbye to Donald. There was nothing to be gained by simply repeating either Lee's journey or my own. My life had changed; I have different strengths and weaknesses, hopes and thoughts, from either young Laurie or young me. I would travel, I reckoned, roughly the same route. But I was a cyclist now, I could do part of it by bike. I'd ask Liam and Eddie if they'd be interested in doing some part of it with me, for a week, or even a fortnight. A new, personal pilgrimage. For Paul. A chance to think about all this *past* we carry around with us and see everything through.

A couple of months later I'm cycling the Duke's Pass route in the Trossachs with Liam.

'I've been thinking about your Spanish trip.'

'Fancy it at all? Any bit in particular? Doesn't matter to me.'

'Actually, I was thinking of doing a long trip this summer myself. Cycle the length of Spain, from the Pyrenees to Málaga.'

Lee travelled north to south, too, but from a starting point 500 miles west of the Pyrenees.

'Ah. Ach well. Sounds great.' The Duke's Pass was getting serious. Liam can keep talking. I can barely breathe.

'Then I thought... maybe I could do it across the way. North west coast to Valencia.' Two of Liam's children are currently living in Valencia, so it made sense to aim for there. 'I could start at Vigo. Accompany you to, I dunno, Segovia? You'd have to head south then, to follow Lee.'

'That would be great! Think Eddie might go?'

'He needs to.'

We were both worried about our friend. Such loss in his life and the absence of Lizzie still roaring like a mutinous wind around him. Liam and I get over the top of the pass, are cruising back down towards Loch Katrine, and I'm thinking, why not? This was never about retracing old journeys. Here's a new and exciting element. The whole of our beloved Spain, west to east.

'There's nothing to stop me doing that with you. The three of us, coast-to-coast. Why not?'

New roads, as well as old ones. Whatever it was that made me turn back in 1974 – soon enough I'd get a stark reminder – there would be less chance of failure, with Liam's organisational skills, and my mates having my back. At least for part of the way. Across Spain, with Eddie and Liam, then down – in the shape of a crucifix – to complete the last section of the 1935 route. I asked my family if they could join me at some point including, to complete another kind of cycle, my nephew Michael, Paul's son.

So much to think about, discuss, learn. How Spain has changed, Scotland, Europe, how *we* change. And in the present climate. The rise of the right again. Spanish independence movements like the Scottish one, gaining pace not only in Catalonia but also in Galicia, the Basque Country, and other 'regions'. What happened to the teenager's optimism about the end of Fascism and the bright, European, future? The Civil War continues to haunt the present, with more graves being dug up in order to confront the horrors of a past that still has the power to shape Spain's future.

Part of my plan was to busk again. I hadn't done that since 1979, but for my first few years of going to Spain it was my principal source of finance. Thinking of standing alone now on a foreign street playing those old tunes filled me with trepidation. Busking in my sixties, would I look like some old failure, no longer the young buck on a journey of discovery?

The narratives we tell ourselves, that we construct our personas from. How would any of us feel, if we could meet our teenage selves, a ghost on the road? Would we be happy, or amazed, perhaps disappointed, with how our lives turned out? Nye Bevan, on being asked his opinion on a fellow politician's memoirs, allegedly retorted: 'I like my fiction neat'. We all formulate self-narratives and explanations of the world around us to make sense of our lives and relationships. We edit – perhaps to keep us sane – the film reels in our heads, omitting or re-ordering details, make more of pleasant memories, less of painful ones. My university took an interest in the project. This was a trip about ageing, a data-gathering research mission. How do we – as individuals, as members of small, and local, national and international communities – record, protect or dismiss details of the lives that made us *us*? A venture into life-long, life-deep learning.

'You wouldn't, eh, fancy bringing your uke?'

I'd bought Liam a ukulele a couple of years earlier as a birthday present. He had taken to it at once and now plays very well.

'You mean busking? Why not?'

Not only was Eddie in from the get-go but, hearing of our plans to busk, he bought himself a penny whistle. Music runs in Eddie's family, informally and professionally. He's always been a singer, but had never learned an instrument. In three short months he learned nearly every tune Liam and I could play.

Both were happy that this journey would be documented. At sixteen, my plan had been to walk and busk, just as Laurie Lee had done, from Vigo to Almuñécar then write my own book. Not, as Lee had done, as an older man remembering, but fresh from the trek. We would post a blog of our journey, which would provide me with another kind of diary, other than daily notes. Liam's a good photographer, Eddie a perceptive commentator. This time, properly recording our journey, and remembering previous ones.

We needed songs we could make our own. We played around with a couple of completely new compositions, but re-setting two older songs worked out best. The new verses to 'Auld Lang Syne' fitted so many of our ideas and concerns, and it was a tune people in Spain would know and could join in with. Liam plays Joan Manuel Serrat's re-setting of Spanish poet Machado's 'Cantares' so I translated some of the lines to fit us and our project. It became our anthem for the road. A re-resetting – an idea that felt appropriate in itself.

Everything passes and nothing dies,
For us, the thing's to keep on going.
We find the route by our ain devise
weaving our way, o'er land and ocean.

Which way, pal? Wherever your footprints lead.
Friend, your footsteps are the road,
the only road there is.
The path you pick is the way ahead,
and behind you the road you'll never tread again.
Which way, ye say?
Nothing but the wake o' the water, ebbing.

Heel for heel, toe for toe
We make our way by how we go
Step by step, word for word,
One by one we make our road!

(After Machado)

SLAD 2019

In 1935 the Nazi Nuremberg Laws took German citizenship from Jews. *The 39 Steps* – Hitchcock's take on Scottish novelist John Buchan's story – was released. Mussolini invaded Ethiopia. Laurie Lee left his home village of Slad midsummer that year.

At the same time John Leven left school in the Gorbals, aged fifteen. He apprenticed, as his father had done, as a tailor's presser. My father-in-law was a quiet man who never spoke of his childhood and youth. There's a Loch Leven and a River Leven but it's a relatively unusual family name. He came from the Gorbals – once the largest Jewish community outside London – and the little we know of his family background, there are indications that he may have come from Levys or Levines. A history lost, but a man, ten years dead, who is still very present for all those who knew and loved him.

Neither Laurie nor John had the faintest inkling that Francisco Franco, having crushed an Asturian uprising, had been appointed the Spanish army's Chief of Staff. Wars were brewing that they, and everyone they knew, would soon be caught up in. And Cole Porter sang: 'You're the purple light / of a summer night in Spain.'

My latest journey across Spain began at exactly the same place as Laurie Lee's. Walking down the same lane he did in 1934, waving goodbye to his mother.

Discussing, in early 2019, my up-and-coming Spanish bike ride with a colleague, Mark Anderson, I mentioned the Laurie Lee connection.

'I'm from the Cotswolds,' Mark told me. 'I know Slad, Lee's valley and village well. In fact my mother is a local history expert.'

I had already considered starting my journey from the fabled land of *Cider With Rosie*. Given Mark's background, his memories of the place and the books, I decided to visit Gloucestershire with him before heading on to Spain. And just as well he was there – finding Lee's house wasn't nearly as easy as I'd imagined.

Even Maureen, as Mark had promised a genuine expert in local history, hadn't thought it would present such a problem. The pub Lee drank in, when he returned as an older man – The Woolpack – is openly advertised. I sat in his seat and supped of his favourite pint, as every tourist does, whether they know his books or not. The cottage he *returned* to is easily located. It's where his wife and daughter, Kati and Jessy, still live. To complicate things more it's called Rose Cottage; the original, family, house is Rose*bank* Cottage.

Lee, in his final years, wrote an essay, 'The Fight To Save Slad'. The last thing he wanted was buses full of day-tourists, their pamphlets the first they'd ever read about him, tramping around his sacred valley, leaving litter, taking selfies, and buggering off without connecting to the spirit of the place, or even buying a packet of crisps in The Woolpack. Today's inhabitants of the valley hold true to Laurie's stipulations. Normally congenial and helpful, giving directions for hill walks and viewpoints, they clam up the minute you mention Rosebank cottage. Suddenly nobody's got a clue. We asked a man, about my age, washing his windows. He furrowed his brow, looked around wonderingly, and replied in the soft local burr: 'Can't be sure, but I think that's it down yonder.'

'No, that's *Rose* Cottage. He lived there later. It's the *Cider With Rosie* house we want.'

The man peered down at us from the top of his ladder. 'Ah. Right. I think that's it down yonder,' and pointed again at the same cottage.

Another local, who lives in the building that was once Lee's school, was equally puzzled. 'Not sure it exists anymore, the old house.' In a way, he wasn't lying. Laurie mythologised his childhood so much that what 'exists' outside his own experience and rose-tinted reminiscence is questionable.

Barmen and locals in The Woolpack, a local walking guide herding his booted flock, the odd passer-by, all reacted the same way: furrow the brow, look baffled, shrug, apologise and bid you good day.

It's good, though, to be made to earn your rewards. Mark and Maureen and I spent two days researching and walking. We began to worry that the secret could never be hacked or, worse, that Rosebank no longer existed. (I was beginning to suspect it never had.) We scrutinised maps, searched for old photographs online, re-read passages of Lee's work, digging for clues. Through all this Maureen supplied me with local background.

Slight, neat, carefully coiffured, Maureen Anderson is in her eighties. She herself is an incomer. But having taught in local schools and immersed herself in the life and culture of the Stroud Valleys she seems to have been more readily received. Her stern school-mistress demeanour – if you haven't done your homework God help you – demanded, rather than asked for, acceptance. The whole family, Mark included, has been at the heart of Stroud's Am-Dram scene, so that will have greased the social cogs more.

Maureen talks with authority and grace about her adopted home. Place names, like an episode of The Archers written by Tolkien – Amberley, Minchinhampton, Woodchester, Eastcombe, Jack's Green – sound like poetry on her lips. Her and her husband Bob's story could be out of a Graham Greene novel. Robert Anderson (yes, of Scottish descent) worked for the War Office, went off regularly to do "Something In The City" while Maureen brought up the family, initially in a crudely converted barn in a neighbouring valley.

She explains to me how the local mud is in fact Fuller's earth. Together with the wide-open common land and the fast streams pouring down the valley sides the area was perfect for sheep rearing and wool production. Thus, The Woolpack.

Our industry – helped along by a bottle or three of Rioja and Maureen's ample cooking – finally paid off. We had seen a single old photograph of a path leading down steeply from, presumably, a bigger road to Rosebank. From the book we knew there had been an extension at the back, where Granny Trill and Granny Wallon had lived and battled. There had been a large front garden, a bend in the nearby River Frome, and of course the lower lane where nineteen-year-old Laurie had walked out, eighty-five years ago.

Mark and I – by this time his mum had given up on us – took all our line-drawings, bits of maps, quotations, and made a final, determined attempt to locate the place. And we did – orienteers, both. We were helped, admittedly, by a rather large sign, just off the main road, quite clearly marked 'Rosebank'. We must have walked past it ten times. So perhaps not that much of a secret (though, to be fair, you'd have to know it's called that in the first place).

A special moment for me. Forty-five years since reading *Midsummer*, half a century since *Cider*. Sitting up in bed, an asthmatic child, devouring the world of little Laurie, Annie and her blustery brothers, schoolmates Spadge Hopkins, Cabbage-Stump Charlie and, naturally, Rosie Burdock herself. There at the back, plain to see, was where the grannies had lived and waged their war. The garden looks wild and woolly now, but it was then too, in Lee's account.

And, clear-cut, as straight and level as a runway, the path that carried him – and soon me – from the cottage gate, all the way, economy class, from Slad to Vigo.

It was a moment for Mark, too. Mark Anderson had left the area many years ago. He's been back regularly to see his family, but agrees that memory works in mysterious ways. 'The distance from my childhood grows every day. I remember events, but can't be sure when, or exactly where, they happened. Snippets of images, places I've seen, or think I've seen, stories. They all get compacted into a kind of ideal of innocence and youth.'

Much the same as happened to Laurie. And perhaps me, with my first trips to Spain.

'I find myself looking around', Mark went on, 'for faces I recognise. But I'm looking for ten-year-olds or twenty-year-olds. Of course, they're all in their fifties and sixties now.'

Not all Mark's memories are *completely* innocent. 'There were discos and clubs in my day which didn't exist in Lee's time. But I don't remember them so well. More the walking to them, and back, on dark nights. All round about here. Old friends, girl-friends. Getting pissed on a combination of spirits and liqueurs in a jam jar – crème de menthe, drambuie, vodka – stolen from our parents.'

'Not cider?'

'Cider too. But we didn't need to nick that. It was everywhere, and cheap.'

We pass what I would call a lochan. We don't know, and anyway Lee's account in *Cider With Rosie* most likely isn't reliable, but it could be the water in which Miss Flynn, sad and left lonely like a character from a Carlos Cano Andalusian ballad, drowned herself. The report that she'd been found floating naked had had a profound effect on young Laurie's mind.

'So much still exists from Lee's day,' Mark said. 'For instance the Co-op.' Annie, Laurie's magnificently chaotic mother, couldn't work the brakes on the family's old butcher's bike. So – according to the book – she used to freewheel downhill and scream as she neared the store. Shop-boys were drilled to run out and stop the bike before it crashed into the wall.

Believe it if you like. I like. (Though I've always wondered how the bike got back uphill again.)

'My mum taught the boy who acted the part of Lee in the *Cider With Rosie* film.' Made by the BBC in 1971. 'But in my mind, she taught Lee himself. Though I know perfectly well that Lee is more than thirty years older than her... Everything gets mixed up. It's not about logic.'

Our minds, I say, seem to work in two different ways when it comes to memories. There's the analytical bit that, when you take a step back, can work it all out. Sift the facts from the impressions.

'But it's not a particularly effective sieve!' Mark laughs. 'All I can say is that the mental version of this valley is all *mine*.'

Whether or not we've assembled it with bits of books, misunderstandings, embellished memories.

'Or complete fictions. Who cares? Hands off – it's mine!'

He leaves, to let me walk the path from Rosebank, the first tranche of my journey, alone.

* * *

Looking up from Laurie's old gate you can see the graveyard where he now lies. We had already wandered around up there, talked to the gentleman who now lives in Laurie's old schoolhouse, across the road from The Woolpack. There are changes, of course – the school now a house for instance – but Lee's world is still surprisingly intact.

But what the locals want you to see of their famous son's life – the church, the school, the house he retired to – doesn't interest me so much. Nor, much as *Cider* is important to me, is his childhood. At least not on this visit. The Laurie Lee I feel a real connection with isn't here at all. The writer in his fifties and sixties, mainly residing in London, writing about his boyhood and young adulthood – that's my man. Diaries or not, lost or not, Lee mostly *recalled* his experiences. He is looking back on his youth and adventures as an ageing man. It's not that he edits out the bad bits. The story of Miss Flynn and, worse, his recounting of a planned attack on a young girl by a gang of village boys including himself, is more than enough proof of that. It's his storyteller's instincts, neatly wrapping up incidents, merging episodes into flowing instalments of an epic tale. It's what we all do, whether we are aware of it or not. Lee doesn't want us to *know* what happened, but make us *feel* how he felt. Both at the time and then, older, looking back. The excitement of boyhood and youth. He brings the past into the present. Into your life, and mine. *Cider With Rosie*, and *As I Walked Out One Midsummer Morning* are not histories. They are, for me at least, the present, happening now. Bizarrely, the road I've had inside my head for half a century still feels more tangible than the one I can feel beneath my feet, the crunch of the dry Fuller's earth. So, turning and waving goodbye to Annie, waving now to me as much as to her son, I set off, eventually for Spain.

PROVINCIA DE GALICIA

Desde aquí vexo un camino que non sei onde vai,
polo mesmo que non sei, quixera estiv andar.

Rosalía de Castro, 'Dende aquí vexo un camiño'

From here I see a path. I don't know where it leads. Which is why I want to walk it.

Friends of Moira and I have a house in Ardfern, Argyll. From their garden you look over Loch Craignish and the coiling tail of the peninsula, towards the Paps of Jura and Corryvreckan. No matter when you look at it it's different. The islands are closer or vanishing in the gloaming, the water every colour from billowy bramble to oyster-pearl. It was in Ardfern, among our friends' books that I first discovered another writer-traveller from these isles, obsessed – by her own admission, 'in love' – with Spain. Irishwoman Kate O'Brien's *Farewell Spain* records a number of journeys she took in the 1920s and '30s largely in Galicia, Castile, the Basque Country and Catalonia. We cyclists share her devotion. Just when you think you've seen enough, you have to go back, look at it all again from a different angle.

Weeks of planning finally came to fruition on the last day of May 2019. Edinburgh airport, old hands now at shunting heavy bike-boxes – on the edge of being expensively over the allowed weight – to Dublin. Then Dublin to Vigo; one Celtic town to another. A month of physical challenge ahead of us, of speaking Spanish, remembering and mistaking, and marvelling. Dodgy knees and dicky tickers. Would we all make it to the end? 1,100 kilometres, over 700 miles. Without broken bones, broken spirits? Would we still be friends by Valencia?

The sun was out – not a given in Galicia. People from all over Spain scramble up here to *escape* the heat, hoping for a wisp of cool mist, a day or two of tingling rain. The streets were bright and promising, the air sea-clean. The last time I had been here was to make a Channel 4 documentary on young Europeans, in 1995. Already, by then, there was a sense of optimism among continental young people about Europe, less in the UK. We bundled our bikes into a taxi into Vigo centre – the last motorised transport planned until our return. Staring out the window I recognised the view over the bay. The *bateas* – mussel and oyster farms – out into the estuary, and close into the shore. They had grown, considerably, in number and size. The sense of sea, the city crammed between it and the hills behind. That cocktail of smells, ever-present across Spain: olive oil, garlic, a smidgeon of sewage, black tobacco, lavender and lemon cologne and, here in the north, tomorrow's rain. Or, as Eddie put it succinctly 'figs and freedom'.

We had allowed ourselves an extra day in Vigo to get ready. We met an old university friend, George, who guided us to our first meal of our own minor *Vuelta a España*. But we ca'd canny, limiting intake of both wine and food – we've got twenty-one bike rides ahead of us, each with their own tests of fitness and character.

The hotel we set out from had, by chance, a balcony directly outside our three bedroom windows (we're good friends, but we like our privacy). We had to clamber out our windows to get to it, risking injury from Day Zero. But a perfect platform for rebuilding our bikes and packing our panniers. It had a panoramic view over the city. The houses climbing up from the harbour of one of the biggest fishing ports in Europe, the architecture getting more and more modern the further back from the port into the hills. Laurie Lee talks of his first sight of Spain almost in fear and despair. A barnacle of a town, he called it, where only the beggars move, and slowly. I saw little of that in 1975, and today we experienced something different again.

Galicia remains one of Spain's poorest regions (Gallego nationalists would say, Country). But Vigo certainly *looks* and feels a good deal richer now than in either '75 or '35. But every time I have been, Vigo has felt welcoming. The language sweet, the people cheerful. My visit in '75 is actually longer ago now – forty-four years – than between that and Lee's first encounter, forty years previously. Back then, much as I liked the city, I was astounded by the poverty on the streets – beggars, disabled people (rumours that some had crippled themselves in acts of desperation), babies in homeless mothers' arms. It's purely anecdotal, and we were only in the city this time for two days, but it so happened that we saw only two obviously homeless people, while the bars and restaurants were doing brisk trade.

We fixed the odd cycle-reassembly hitch, and we were ready for our training ride. The city of Vigo was not, in itself, our starting point. We had advertised this expedition, to ourselves as well as to others, as coast-to-coast.

It was the first time I'd seen this magnet town of mine, saddle-high. A fiesta (holiday) so the streets were quiet, but the seaside would be busy. Vigo is as higgledy-piggledy as most old towns in Spain, a hotchpotch of terracotta and buttery stone, like cranachan. New builds squeezed tight up against antique churches and markets. A traditional departure point for emigration, and now immigration, to and from the Americas, there are outcrops of colonial styles. All of Spain's history and hopes packed into a bay restricted by mountains and sea.

Down to the shoreline, a fresh breeze with a hint of Ireland in it, nobody swimming yet, not this early in spring, but walking, jogging, meeting in cafés. We pick a spot. This is our first public performance, so we want to make it as discreet as possible. We get out the recording gear, the instruments, the cameras. Set up the tripod, tune the uke and fiddle, decide a little set of songs. To make the point, we took off our shoes and put on our helmets – cycling and busking from sea to shining sea.

For no other reason other than we weren't terrible at playing them we decide on 'Danny Boy', a couple of jigs and, because I had referenced it in my take on Machado/Serrat's 'Cantares' ('*heel for heel, toe for toe...*') 'Mairi's Wedding'. Three sexagenarians, paddle-deep in Lycra mantyhose, helmets unfastened at jaunty angles, singing, seemingly to ourselves, playing ukulele, Irish whistle and violin to the rhythm of baby waves.

Nobody took any notice. Very deliberately so. Maybe they see the like all the time. We worried that our busking plans might not be quite the attraction we'd hoped. But there were signs. A woman, trying to camouflage the fact, was filming us. A lady, walking her dog, gave a little dance-skip and smiled at us. A guy on a hill waved down. We just needed a bit more practice.

We had one more job to do before leaving Vigo. Eddie and

Liam had decided it would be fun to mock-up an old photograph of me busking there, years ago. I found what looked like the same spot. In the original image there are six people standing listening. While Liam set up cameras, Eddie encouraged passers-by to come over, and then placed them to reconstruct, roughly, the old image. One even tried to give me money...

The 1970s Busker

He stands stiff, his posture unsuited to getting the best out of his violin. Flared jeans and pink shirt, dark hair although, the photograph having faded to a pinkish sepia, the real colours may have been stolen by time. His clothes are straining for a folk-rock look, Dave Swarbrick or Rick Danko, but the collared shirt isn't quite right, betraying other origins, another lifestyle he can't quite shed.

He has an audience, but he is resolutely not looking at them. His head is lowered. Perhaps he's looking at his fingering. There is something inside his violin case – it's too wide a shot to see if he has made any money – so he might be reading music. Perhaps the furrow on his brow is concentration, trying to play the tune correctly. Or he's just unsure of himself, tense being the centre of attention. A better violinist would say that he holds his instrument wrongly. The fingering hand not arched enough, restricting movement on the neck. The bow strikes the strings from too low an angle.

The people around the busker are young, darker-skinned, clearly locals. Four young men, one of them smoking, another could be either male or female. All of them are dressed for a warm day. Their clothing doesn't look very different than it would today – casual, open-necked shirts, jeans, two with jerseys tied around their waists. Fashion-wise, it could be almost any time in Spain in the last half-century. But this is the early days of a new era, the *transición* – the old regime behind them, these youngsters' world is going to be very different from their parents'. They're about the same age as the busker, in their sixties now. At this moment, they look serious – whatever the busker is playing it's not a happy-go-lucky number. It's reasonable to suggest that the air or the melody has slowed the day, the moment. The group seems tight, the audience supportive, if not stirred. They stand close enough to the busker for them to be acquaintances, but not friends. Unless the melody has drawn strangers in, closer than they had intended. One of them studies the busker's face, trying to figure him out. That worried look the busker has may be him trying to work himself out.

The background gives little away. The shop windows are barer than they might be today, less *stuff* on display. There is a female head bust. The wig on the bust looks, if anything, '60s, from a time before the photograph was taken. The shop, maybe a hairdresser's, is open. There is a weekend feel to the scene. Provincial, conservative. Far from bohemia, if that's where the busker thought he was.

* * *

Dawn, the day of the first cycle. We wake to a Tweet from the mighty Mark Beaumont, a rather more adventurous cyclist, wishing us well on our journey. An inspiration for years, his message is just the encouragement we need. I take a last look out over the city from that balcony, the sun half-opening a hungover eye. I had a faint inkling that Robert Cunnninghame Graham had a connection with Galicia's biggest town. His great-nephew confirmed it when we met up with him a few rides down the line in Segovia. Robin Cunninghame Graham reckoned his ancestor's home might well have afforded this same view over the bay below, sometime around the 1890s. Lee's description in 1935 – 'a steep terraced climb' out of the city – makes it sound like not much had changed since then. He looked down from a rock, rather than a hotel, then turned, and headed into Spain.

Eighty-five years later we head in the same direction for our first cycle of the tour. Stumbling and staggering onto our bikes, so heavy now that they're fully laden, it was hard to mount and dismount. The first few hundred yards that same steep climb, at rush hour. We made it, and made our own way east into our Spain – and straight onto a motorway…

Liam had done his homework before leaving. Cyclists are not permitted on *autopistas* (motorways), but they are on *autovías* (dual carriageways). The latter predate the former. Usually they're a godsend to cyclists. The Catalan government began a coun-try-wide revolution in roads when they decided to upgrade the, still relatively new *autovía*, motorway, system, for the Olympic Games in 1992. Over the next decade thousands of miles of bigger, toll-financed *autopistas* were laid. Essentially it means that across most of Spain there is a choice of three roads: the motorways, dual carriageways, and the older A-roads. So, generally, cyclists have two sets of well-surfaced roads to choose from. The problem is that, sometimes, the *vías* without warning turn into *pistas*.

As if the climb out of Vigo wasn't hard enough, none of the three of us had had much chance, for various reasons, to train for this major outing. We were carrying far more than we ever had before. A longer journey, twenty-one cycles in all, over twen-ty-seven days. We had all our gear, plus recording equipment, and we had our instruments. On the only practice cycle in Scotland, a fortnight earlier, we had tried all kinds of formulas for trans-porting the fiddle. It wouldn't fit into a pannier, stuck out too far behind, or across, strapped to the back rack. There was nothing to do but strap it across my back. Which would soon cause problems.

Laurie Lee tells us he carried his violin, wrapped up in a blanket. Surprising. Violins are fragile, an awkward shape. The slightest pressure on the bridge and it'll collapse. The tuning pegs are sticky things, one little knock and they unravel your strings. Heat and cold play havoc with the strings themselves – as I was soon to discover. Then there's the bow, which you have to loosen when not playing to stop it from distorting, the delicate horsehair, the rosin... He *carried* it, for up to two years, in a blanket, from Slad to London, and all the way through Spain on his adventures? It was difficult enough keeping the thing in two pieces in a hard-shelled case for a few months.

Within an hour of setting out, things were already going wrong. Sweating up a Category 2 hill, over 10 kilometres long, wasn't helped by the increasing traffic as we merged, innocently, onto the motorway. Ten-ton trucks thundered past, an inch from our shoulders. Horns blared angrily. The heat thickened. We stopped and shouted to each other over the bellow of the traffic.

'Is there any way off this thing?'

We peered at the map. None that we can see.

'Two choices. Either go back,' Liam said, 'but I can't see any other way out of the city.'

'Or keep going and hope.'

'That we don't die?'

'Well, that we don't *all* die.'

A steep concrete wall on one side, six lanes of max-speed-limit the other. Three burdened old guys, 5 miles per hour, Liam's ukulele sticking out his saddle bag, me with my violin case strapped to my back. Drivers hooted in more ways than one.

And then we heard the siren. The dreaded Guardia Civil.

I had flashbacks to all those illegal pamphlets I'd flushed down toilets, the posters I'd pasted up in the middle of the night, back in the '70s. The Guardia Civil were hated and feared. Franco's shock-troops. Armed to the teeth. They broke up demonstrations, arrested friends. It was something of a relief to see, as they flagged us down and pulled in in front of us, that their car was marked Guardia Civil *Tráfico.* So maybe just a few kicks and punches, throw us in a cell for the night. I really didn't want, not on Day One of my second attempt to cross Spain, to cause *another* minor international incident and major family embarrassment.

'*Caballeros, perdón.*' We walked up smiling, hands extended, shaking our heads at our own foolishness. They dismounted and stood waiting, sullen, arms crossed, mirror sunglasses like bad-ass cops in American movies.

'*Están ustedes en una autopista.*' Translating the body language as well as the language: you maniacs are cycling slowly on a motorway.

They hadn't expected we'd be foreigners. More surprised when we all spoke good Spanish. Surprised even further, I imagine, when we took our helmets off and they saw we were old maniacs. They relaxed, a little. We might not, after all, be dangerous anarchists on armed bikes... This Ukulele Kills Fascists.

Where were we from?

'Escocia.'

'*Escocia?!*'

Where are we going?

'Valencia.'

'*Valencia?!*'

What was I carrying?

'Un *violín*?!'

Hard-headed police distrust was turning, through disbelief, to unconcealed smirking. We explained what had happened, that there was no sign announcing the end of the dual carriageway, which does permit cyclists.

Manolo and Juancho. Jesus, I'm now on first name terms with the *picoletas*. They seemed to accept the nature of the problem, softened their stance, took off their shades. But what's to be done? How do we resolve this situation? The trucks and buses and motorbikes are still battering by us. I'm roasting, knackered. The – friendly – filth had just about enough room in their vehicle to fit in three bikes and three Scotsmen. But oh the failure – a coast-to-coast cycle and we're in motorised transport within an hour?

The Guardia guys came up with the answer. The next exit was about 6 kilometres down the road.

'Okay gentlemen. Back on your bikes.'

They're going to *let* us continue with this death-ride? Bastard *Guardias*.

'We'll escort you.'

And they did. They got back in their car, and blue-lit us to the next exit.

If my friends from the old days could have seen us. Police protection by the Guardia Civil.

Truckers and commuters stopped beeping us. We tucked in behind the flashing lights and followed. Whether Manolo and Juancho had more faith in our cycling skills than we had, or they were having a wee cop joke, I don't know, but they tore along that road at about 50 miles per hour. Liam, when he wants to be, the strongest cyclist of the three, was ahead of me, his legs spinning in top gear for all he was worth. I'm nearly hyperventilating. Eddie's pushing me from behind shouting over the traffic noise for me to keep up. Maybe our friends back home would be impressed – cop car being chased down the highway by three mad Glaswegian cyclists.

To be fair to our policemen I'm pretty sure they passed a possible exit or two, ones that wouldn't have suited us, that would have taken us well off our road. Eventually, we're led off the highway.

They stop, by now half a mile ahead of us, in a village.

'Okay, guys, take the third exit at the roundabout ahead. The road will take you all the way to Ourense.'

'Quiet road,' says Mano.

'Pretty, too,' says Juancho.

We take selfies with them. All radical street cred gone. We shake hands. They slap our backs. *'Buen viaje, chicos!'*

We probably shouldn't read too much into such incidences. I suppose it was perfectly possible that, back in the dark days of the Regime and its immediate aftermath you could have found two friendly traffic officers every bit as courteous and understanding. But I wouldn't have risked it. You kept out of their way. At all times. And today? I'm not sure I'd want to have to deal with the non-traffic version, who are gunned up enough as it is.

We had left Vigo early in the morning, the day after the 2019 Spanish national elections and the final results were coming in slowly as we made our way to Ourense. We got updates on our phones, and in shops and bars when we stopped for water and coffee. Fears that Vox, the far-right party, would increase their support, possibly enough to be a dealmaker for any coalition, were allayed. Still, 10 per cent of the population of a country which has suffered the wounds and indignities of dictatorship relatively recently had seen fit to put their cross next to a party who, like all the new right-wing populist parties globally, make no attempt to hide their misogyny, racism and homophobia, scorning empathy and probity.

Exactly how the old forces that used to protect the Franco regime are reacting to change is going to be interesting to watch. There's a town I'll get to know after this cycle is over, where people worry that their allocation of two policeman might be reduced to one which would be a nail in the town's coffin. As it stands, the two officers walk or ride their motorbikes slowly round town.

They chat to everyone. They shop in the market. They're relaxed – though still armed. Perhaps most importantly, they speak Valenciano, the local language. Until not long ago all Guardia came from somewhere else. The police in La Coruña would be from Cádiz, in Cádiz from Barcelona, and so on. Making sure there was no fraternising. No getting to know, and understand, the people they are there to serve. Liam had learned just how distracted Eddie and I can get on the road. So he had prepared daily cards for us, and provided a master key card, convinced that we'd take a wrong turn and end up in Andorra. Here's the key card:

KEY

L = turn left
R = turn right
O = Roundabout
T = T junction
→ = head towards ...
O, X2/3 = take the second/third exit at the roundabout.
[22] = at 22 kilometres
Road numbers are highlighted in blue
Place names are capitalised and highlighted in green
Climbs are highlighted in grey
4.7: 12.4, 5.2%, C2 = a climb starts at 4.7km into the journey and goes on until 12.4km, it has an average incline of 5.2% and it is classified as a Category 2 climb.

You can see how Dr Kane rates our intelligence. L means Left, R means... It's almost as if he expects that Eddie and me, involved in some important conversation about an Adam McNaughtan song, or discussing why Third Lanark *is* third rather than second, might miss an important turn-off.

The daily cards, in all seriousness, were essential, and accurate. Here's the first of twenty-one:

Day 1, 2nd May: Vigo to Vilasoboroso (37km, 905m)

[0] → Gran Vía, Plaza de España
[0.6] L, → A55/N120/A55 Estr Porrino-Vigo
[3.2] L, Estr Velha Madrid; [3.4] R, Rua Paz Pardo (turns right)
[4.2] L towards Autovia; [4.4] L, Rua Recaré
[4.9] L, Rua da Vinha Grande
[6.2] O, X, Estr das Plantas, EP-2005
[9.6] L, EP-2605; [9.7] R, Caminho do Monte
[11.2] CABANELAS, T, L, weave; [12.7] ROUBLIN, R, weave.
[14] L, PO 331; [19.3] → N120; [17.5] O PURRINHO
[28] PONTEAREAS
[34.9] Pass EP4402 (L), take 2nd R, Hotel Cantaruxa on L
[35.1] 2.4: 10, 5.2%, C2 16.6: 21.9, 2.4%, C4 27.3: 35.1, 2.7%, C3

The code is clear. It has to be for Eddie and me. From our Vigo hotel you take the high road to the main square, then left onto the Porrino road, its number clearly on the card. The numbers along the bottom line are the ones we checked first, every day. They're the hills we had to tackle. So that first ascent out of Vigo and onto the motorway was a Category 2.

The origin, I am reliably told by Eddie, of deciding the categories of hill climbs comes from what gear a French car had to be in, for how long, in the 1930s. It takes into account not only gradient, but length. A Category 1, originally, meant that a car had to be in first gear for, well, a long time. Category 5 is therefore the easiest. *Hors de catégorie* are the ones that really worry you, and we had one of them coming up in a fortnight's time. On Day 1, the ascent out of Vigo, began 2.5 kilometres from our city-centre starting point and lasted for 7.5 kilometres. Which doesn't mean, as we discovered, that the hill stops. It merely isn't as steep thereafter. In fact, that road kept climbing for over 20 kilometres.

Roads, and trying to map them out. At every breakfast we poured over the day's route, working out when and where to stop for food, worrying about the climbs or, worse, the motorways, or sections where the road forward wasn't clear. But also, for where the beauty spots might be, areas of historical interest, places associated with writers and songs. Where we might busk and where best to meet people.

The keen cyclists might well raise an eyebrow at the paltry number of miles we covered that first day. Remember, all that gear to carry, including inner tubes, sets of bike tools, kit for every kind of weather (which we did, indeed, encounter), clothes, not only for cycling, and to last us a month. We had to leave time for interviewing people, editing, saving or posting the results. We're not as young as we used to be, or as energetic. So on that first day, without any pre-training, we had to cope with a Category 2, then a 4, then a 3 – and that last one nearly did me in.

It was mesmerising, moving through the Galician countryside. Every journey here has been significant for me. Brendan and I, kids, going to fiestas and *vaquillas*; I had busked in Ourense, so I must have travelled, on foot or hitching, along this very road, sometime before the age of twenty. Both Camino routes, walking in 2000 and cycling with these two in 2018, lie a little north of this road. The same mountains, but from the other side.

The road to Vilasabroso played like a movie in front of us, the first birds of spring tuning up. Hills and mounds, shamrock and olive greens, the *hórreos* – little stone granaries on stilts in farms and crofts – silvery houses, the smell of rain. There's a sense of Celtic diaspora, a preference for hills and damp, soft air. The Milesians of mythology, still searching for their homeland. A soundtrack played in my head – Luis Emilio Batallán: *'No niño novo do vento*

/ *hai unha pomba dourada*' (In spring's sweet breeze, nests a golden dove). Songs that, in the bad old days, got past the censors posing as innocent love songs but were listened to and sung in public as declarations of passion for Galicia and freedom. The '*Himno Gallego*' (Galician anthem): '*a nosa voz pregoa / a redenzón da boa / nazón de Breogán!*' (we proclaim the redemption of Breogán's nation). Valleys and villages flickering past to the buzz of *gaitas*, higher-pitched and busier than the big Scots bagpipes, more akin to the uilleann or the Northumbrian pipes; the sweet local accordions and taut *pandaretas* (tambourines). Echoes of Scots and Irish music, but inflected by more southern breezes, quarter tones and grace-notes, whiffs of a different history and a warmer clime.

We got to Vilasabroso quicker than we had anticipated, despite that last slow hill. A perfect place for a first stop-off. Cantaruxa is a *casa rural* off the main road. Frogs burped comically in a rock pool, so an ideal spot for our first band practice. Just as we hadn't trained for the cycling, we'd had one single rehearsal in my house a fortnight before leaving. Liam and I have a small set of songs, in Scots, Spanish, Basque and Catalan, but we were keen to play some of the music Lee mentions in *Midsummer*, plus a couple of jigs and reels. Things we reckoned might go down well in the streets. And, surely, we couldn't sound worse than those belching frogs.

We'd noticed there was another couple staying at the *casa*. But they had gone out for lunch, so we took our instruments outside to practise in the cooling afternoon sun. After half an hour of easily beating the frogs at their own game, the other guests appeared. And they didn't complain but sat down and asked us to play on. Sabine and Egbert. Our first voluntary audience. Here was something I could share with Laurie Lee – his first musical associates, who encouraged and advised him, were passing Germans too. Later, we got talking to Hr. and Fr. Classen; neither of them was hard of hearing. We played the songs we had tried out on Vigo beach. They smiled, nodded their heads and tapped their feet in time, hummed along to tunes they half recognised. Then they suggested we go into the lounge to record our efforts.

Sabine found a bottle of wine and some biscuits. Egbert set up his phone for recording. This German couple became our first musical consultants.

'I think you should sing more with that one.'

'Maybe try it with all the voices together?'

'Play that faster. As fast as you like.'

'Not so sure about that one.'

Egbert, tall, bearded, perhaps early fifties, girder forearms and a default frown. A mix of knowledge, inquisitiveness, practicality and physique that makes an engineer an engineer. Sabine his corporeal opposite: small, quick to smile, deft little movements, her radar picking up every faint passing mood and reaction.

They chose which songs to record, which became, essentially, our set list for the rest of the tour. Pieces to grab the attention, a few slower airs, some sing-a-longs. They suggested arrangements, an order of play. 'Danny Boy', then 'Dashing White Sergeant', 'Raglan Road', Gluck's 'Che faro senza Euridice', 'Whiskey In The Jar', 'Ashokan Farewell', 'Red Red Rose', 'Irish Washerwoman'. And the three songs we had worked on specially. Our hispanified version of 'Auld Lang Syne'. 'Cantarés' – Liam sings it beautifully and Eddie recites it with verve and drama (and it keeps him off the penny whistle.) But the single off any future Grammy-winning album will be 'Mairi's Wedding'. Sabine and Egbert knew the tune, it has gusto. And it's easy, all three of us can play it – almost together – with a degree of confidence.

After the recording session we got talking about more interesting matters. Sabine and Egbert were on holiday.

'Touring Visigothic churches.'

Egbert has a particular professional interest in late- and post- Roman architecture. We admitted, abashed, that after a combined century and a half of studying Spain, Spanish history and culture, none of us knew that the Iberian Peninsula has a rich supply of still-standing churches dating from the fifth to the eighth century, between the decline of the Romans and the rise of Muslim Spain.

An even more painful topic, and one that would crop up time and time again with people from different countries... 'What is going on with you guys and Europe?'

We tell them we are not those guys, and that we are just as mystified, and as worried, as they are. We get into the knotty subject of Scottish secession. So many people we met, non-Brits, are automatically, romantically, on board. (The subject of Catalonia will soon get thorny.) But it's important to explain fundamental issues.

'There is still a small, nationalist anti-English rump,' says one of us. 'But the recent rise in support for independence is, paradoxically, a vote *against* nationalism. Against this resurgence in British nationalism.'

'They used to say *España es diferente*. The cry of the right back home is, Britain is different. Britain will be great again. Alone.'

'It makes no sense,' say the perplexed Egbert and Sabine.

The following morning, they came out to bid us *bon voyage*.

'*Tschüss!*'

'Busk, my friends, and have no fear!'

We rode back out into the fresh Gallego morning. Nowhere near a motorway or the Guardia Civil. We behaved ourselves as elderly cycling gentlemen should. Confident now of our talent and our plan.

Until the bullets started flying.

* * *

A sweet day for cycling, hilly but manageable, our legs getting stronger, still Ourense-bound. I lapsed back into daydreams and memories, mixing themselves up. Mile after mile, on this camino or any other... Paul and I laughing, lagging behind the main group. Brendan and I exploring the new-born world. A fallow field behind a village reminds me of us showing off at the *vaquillas* at a fiesta. Pretend bullfighting with calves. Jumping over the barricade, running, scaredy-cat, from baby bulls. Cows, more likely. Showing off for the Teres and Floras, and failing, which was better, making them laugh. Before either of us knew anything about *toreros*, before the invention of animal rights, pre right and wrong. 'I was innocent then of my ignorance,' writes Laurie Lee in *Midsummer*. Galicia then was our playground; now, a hard, bonny land of poetry and conflict and song, and after so many visits and experiences, I still know only its shallowest surface.

We passed through village after village, climbing all the time into the Galician hills. We stopped over at a Val de Pereira, the centre of the Ribeiro wine-producing region – where they make all the hundreds of two-peseta *copas* Brendan and I had downed, indifferent to the labours that created them. This time round I supped with a little more respect. Don't imagine that, just because we were undertaking an athletic feat that Eddie and I stopped imbibing. Far from it. Liam worried that I was single-handedly exhausting Ribeiro supplies. And, as we progressed, the Duero, Rioja, La Mancha and Valencian stockpiles... Like a lot of men, I'm in a love-hate relationship with my own addictions. I cited in defence another coast-to-coast cycling book. Alan Brown's *Overlander*, bikepacking over rough terrain through the Scottish Highlands. Alan always ensured that, at the end of a hard day's pedalling, he had a decent red wine in his pannier. And a *glass*, no less, to sup in a refined manner. In a tent or bothy on a boggy hillside.

The next day, after a few hours' cycling we spotted a quiet road.

Freewheelin'

We miked up. Pete Murray, journalist, Manchester Metropolitan University lecturer, old friend and expert podcaster, had given us a lesson or two. We wanted to try recording as we cycled along. We each had our own recorder, and a lapel mic. One loud clap before speaking means you can line up the three recordings for later editing. We got all that right, but then we cycled off in three different directions. Regrouping, we cycled three abreast along the backroad. Listening to the recording now, I'm impressed by our lack of breathlessness. We hadn't planned anything to discuss, just bantered, about roads that lead nowhere, a hill that didn't need to be climbed. We sound happy. Relaxed in each other's company. When we heard the first shot.

On tape, the report is as piercing and unexpected as it was at the time. There's a moment of genuine shock and fear. There are signposts all over the Spanish countryside for *cotos privados de caza*, hunting estates. Had we wandered off-grid…? More shots. Closer. Whiff of gunpowder. Then a few jittery jokes. 'That's the last time you'll disagree with me…' It's a matter of seconds before we realise what's happening.

Fireworks. Of course. This is Spain.

Spaniards will set off fireworks at any hour of the day and at the slightest excuse. Regaining our composure, ridding ourselves of mics and wires, we knew what to do. Follow the source: there's a fiesta in town.

The festival of the patron saint of the tiny town, Santa Cruz de Arabaldo. We had actually met the band a little earlier along the road. I'd assumed they were *gaiteros*, a pipe band, going to play *muñeiras*, not very distant relations of reels. They turned out to be a brass band, in full flow as we arrived, salsas and rancheras, pasa-dobles. Horns parping, drums pulsing, they were the embodiment of a party. The good folk of Santa Cruz de Arabaldo leaned against a makeshift bar, sipping small glasses of beer, eating tapas. At this early stage, around forty people in all. They paid little attention to us at first, far too concerned with listening to the music, running after their toddlers, chattering amongst themselves. But they smiled and made us feel welcome.

Beatriz was touring the tables selling raffle tickets. But it was an excuse for the two sides, locals and sweaty interlopers, to parley. We all know a Beatriz. Women In The Community Who Get Things Done. Every village in Scotland has several. When I was writer-in-residence in Easterhouse, it was the women in their middle years, with more than a handful of problems of their own, who were the activists, the representatives, the sorters-out of problems well beyond their doorsteps. We bought a few tickets and Beatriz explained about the patron saint.

I recorded the band, and asked Eddie to explain what was going on, on tape:

'A wee celebration. It's so relaxed, so family orientated. And that band! Playing music from Cuba, Mexico, Spain, Colombia. It's one of the great joys of this country, intimately connected with 420 million Spanish speakers. It's a local festival but the world is here. This is why we come to Spain, you and me. Why we loved it in the first place. What this journey is all about.'

They were taking turns to serve behind the bar. A young woman, her two children at her ankles, saw us as an excuse to move the party up a gear. We never got her name, but let's call her Maruxa (like Jean in Scottish songs, Maruxa is the archetypal *Gallega*). When the band stopped for refreshments Maruxa organised an impromptu singsong. Here's something else Galician culture shares with Scots-Irish: a never-ending supply of drinking songs and anthems. It didn't take much encouragement for about twelve folk standing around to join in. I knew some of the songs: 'A Santiago Voy', 'Se Chove' (It's Raining), 'Pousa, Pousa'. There was one song I remember in particular from my first visits. I asked

Maruxa if they knew 'O Andar Miudiño'.

Imagine asking a bunch of Scots on a sunny day to give us a chorus of 'Wild Mountain Thyme', or '500 Miles'. The gathering, generally, had grown, and our personal choir swelled to twenty or more...

¡Que eu traio
unha borracheira-a
de viño,
que auga non bebo mira
mira Maruxiña, mira
mira como eu veño!

(I've got the wine. Never mind your water. Come on, my little Maruxa...!) Members of the band put down their saxes and trumpets and joined in. The song is about being tipsy, staying for one last drink. Burns could have written it. On tape, you would swear that it was after midnight and every one of them was blind drunk. At most, some of them had a bottle of beer.

And everyone knew the words. Bairns, teenagers, oldies. It's something we would witness all across Spain – far less generationally divided than Britain. It was also cheering to know that a song sung by everyone in the '70s was *still* being sung. By everyone. I don't know how old it actually is, but I guess that Gallegos have been convening at fiestas like this and singing their traditional songs for decades. More.

We saw our chance to try out our own wee band. Our first official busk. They were delighted, and tickled, that we were cycling with instruments. Beatriz introduced us, after a quick briefing:

'Ladies and gentlemen, your attention. The village of Santa Cruz del Arabaldo is very pleased to welcome, all the way from Scotland, on bikes from Vigo to Valencia... *Los famosos*

SexYgenarios!'

We had a name for the band. We gave them a few tunes, every bit as sozzled-sounding and exuberant as they had been – still mid-cycle with another 30 kilometres of hills to go that afternoon, we'd had nothing more than juice and coffee. For our encore, 'Auld Lang Syne'. They knew it, joined in lustily with Gallego, Spanish, mispronounced English, and made-up versions.

They demanded we come back for the *real* celebration tonight. A free meal – well, for the price of the raffle tickets we had already bought – at the village hall. Everyone would be there. Babes-in-arms, grannies, no doubt the local priest and Guardia. There would be wine, best of local food, singing and dancing…

But the road calls. We still had over 1,000 kilometres ahead of us. And a hotel room booked in Ourense.

* * *

pues rosas hay que manchan y emponzoñan,
y abrojos que a través de su aspereza
nos conducen al cielo.

Rosalía de Castro, 'I In My Bed Of Thistles'

For there are roses that stain and spoil,
and thorns, on the way to heaven.

At a recent Christmas gathering old friends were reminiscing about an incident from our collective past. We all laughed, adding our own details, such as we remembered them. One of them said to me: 'But you weren't there'. I know I was. But I've now abstracted myself from the incident. In some sense, perhaps I wasn't there. Or, I wasn't any longer.

Something happened on the road from Santa Cruz (as Manolito himself might have said, but for rousing cowboy reasons). Cycling along, the interior landscape changing faster than the topography. Memory and dreams whipping themselves into daymares. A much-loved country became almost subconsciously foreign, unfamiliar, the spring sun hot and dangerous, close friends distant. The weight of all that's remembered.

Dodo

How useless a creature that allows itself to be hunted to extinction even though its meat was famously greasy, crude and bitter. It is mocked by its very name – probably from the Dutch *dodaar*; meaning 'fat-arsed'. We only recall it now in the phrase 'dead as a dodo.' It makes an appearance in *Alice In Wonderland*, organising a race with no starting or finishing points and where the prizes are your own possessions handed back to you.

In real life the dodo was probably even more ridiculous than Lewis Carroll's caricature. A 1627 description: 'The body is round and fat...It is reputed more for wonder than for food... its meat offensive and of no nourishment. The visage darts forth melancholy, as sensible of Nature's injurie in framing so great a body to be guided with complementall wings, small and impotent...the bill is crooked downwards, the eyes small, round and rowling; the clothing downy feathers, the train three small plumes, short and inproportionable, its legs suiting its body, the appetite strong and greedy...'

Dodo inhabited a cruel world, murdered by laughing assassins who didn't even want to eat it.

Which is why it returns, ghostly, to hound us in revenge. Or some of us. Statistically, around a quarter of the people reading this already recognise Dodo, albeit in a different form and with your own name for it. (The old joke: if you have three sensible mates, you're the bamstick.)

Depression, be it persistent, bipolar, seasonally affective or manic, situational or mood disorder touches us all, directly or indirectly.

Fat and clumsy, Dodo still manages to skulk into your head when least expected. It waits for no particular set of conditions to set about its work. It's always there or there-abouts, hiding in the rushes of your subconscious, suddenly, uninvited, flumping out directly in front of your eyes so you can't see beyond it. And it sits there spitting and snarling and telling you how things *really* are. You're a daftie, a nutteloos, a coof. Cycling across Spain? You're a slouch, a self-serving birkie in your own rash wee tinsel-show... Whatever the situation, Dodo finds a way of revealing the underside, the pointlessness of it.

It eats your unspoken words for sustenance so that next time you're in company all you have left are grunts and silences, wary eyes. For those who don't have a dodo, or black dog, or shadows of their own, you seem deliberately sullen, spiteful. (You want to explain: some folks get the sneezes, some get the runs. I get this fucker.) You get anxious about everything: your tyres, some small thing that happened ten years ago you thought you had forgotten about, why all drivers seem to hate cyclists, the state of the world... You'd have to be crazy not to be mental.

There's no sure way I know of to get rid of Dodo. It comes and goes as it pleases, before lumbering back into the undergrowth. Or it can stay with you, for an hour, or a month. For some unfortunate people, it never backs off. God love them.

These bouts do make you self-obsessed. What can help, is reading. Poets. Novels. Songs (*'I think I've failed when I'm only starting*'; Dumb Instrument's 'Suffering From Scottishness'). Montaigne's essays – a man stepping outside himself to study, dispassionately, his moods and actions: 'There were many terrible things in my life and most of them never happened.' Cycling helps. It's tiring, it's out in the open air, and it's mechanical, repetitive – cyclical. Keeping my distance: having stable, sensible friends isn't always best when they're utterly bamboozled by your state of mind.

Sometimes, and only after the gloom lifts, I get a cloudy insight into possible triggers. This time, maybe I'm just tired. Not just from the cycling but from months of working double-time so I could get away from the day job. But often, I find them not in negative things that have happened, but in positive ones. Like busking with my friends, being accepted into a village *fiesta*. Stereotypically Scottish? Guilt and foreboding after pleasure. The highs prompt the lows. The 'ancient misery' of Alastair Reid's 'Scotland': *'We'll pay for it, we'll pay for it, we'll pay for it!'*

Back in the first night in Vigo, we'd met up with an old friend who had asked if this expedition of ours was somehow… epiphanous, was the word George had used. We'd laughed, but perhaps he had a point. The last few days had been, without me realising it, challenging in a way I hadn't prepared for. We'd all had a great time, in Vigo, on the road, at the fiesta in Santa Cruz. Once we had taken our bows, and our leave, we cycled happily on to lovely Ourense. It was the first time I had busked, properly, in over forty years. More, in Galicia. I sang songs I hadn't sung in a lifetime. Felt things I hadn't felt in as long. Sang the words of a song that was central to my youth. Cycling on, I'm hearing echoes, including those of people no longer around.

At the hotel in Ourense I looked at the photograph we had taken in Vigo.

The 2019 Busker

The busker is the oldest person in the shot. It seems five people have been drawn to his music and stand around him, listening. They're relaxed enough, though one of them is looking searchingly at the busker, trying to figure him out.

The busker himself looks like a proper street musician, the real deal. Smiling, he's enjoying his own playing. He's got a belly on him. So he might be quite successful at this game, or he has another life, one that is not dependent on the meagre takings of most buskers. He's giving movement to the music, his right leg in a kind of dance mode. But he's resolutely not looking at his audience. Perhaps concentrating on his playing. He's not supporting the violin between his chin and shoulder. A better musician would advise him to straighten up his stance, allow for more fluid movement in both bowing and fingering.

The onlookers are much younger, from mid-twenties to mid-thirties. They could be the children of the audience in the 1970s. How different is their world to that previous generation's? What will their world, their Spain, Vigo, be like when they get to the busker's age?

The shop behind the group looks art-deco and the all but empty window suggests a much earlier era. It isn't clear what the shop sells. Perhaps furniture? It's a bright day, a ray of sun highlighting the violin case – plainly empty, no coins or notes – at the busker's feet. But it's cold, the audience wearing coats and jackets. Another jacket – the busker's? – is lying in the closed shop's doorway, so this is a Sunday, or after opening hours.

The scene is not in any way unusual – buskers are as common in Vigo as anywhere else. But it's far from bohemia, if that's where the busker thought he was.

The photograph was fun to take. But it is also pictorial evidence of the passing of forty-five years, likely more than half my lifetime, gone. I felt the 'rending pain of re-enactment,' as T. S. Eliot describes it; all that I have been and done, and the time all gone.

Happily, Dodo seemed sated biting a single lump out of me, taking it to gnaw at in the back of my head. In Spain I see Dodo more as a gecko, waiting, absolutely still, unblinking, blending into the hinterland of my mind. But I know it can jump in a trice. Or flash its tongue, as long as itself, in a thousandth of a second.

After a shower and shave in Ourense – a town that glimmers of memories from forty-five years ago – I'm feeling a little numb. Until, exploring the *casco Viejo* – old town – we hit a celebration. At the cathedral a ceremony is just ending: the wedding, we learn, of two local notables. Lining the church steps is a full traditional *gaitero* group – a sound as flamboyant and rousing as a full Scots pipe band. The wedding guests were in their best bib and tucker. Fascinators and feathers, evening gowns in the late afternoon sun. Antonio Banderas lookalikes. The whole scene reeked of money. When, after a tense wait, the bride exited the church and took her place on top of the stairs, the streets erupted. The pipes powered up, several drummers putting their back into it, cheers and shouts: '*Mira, ¡ahora viene! ¡Ay qué guapa! ¡Ala, venga!*'. She is, as they say, radiant, and even to my inept eye, exquisitely dressed. When the groom appears – apparently Cuban, but weel-kent round these parts – he's as cool as cucumber in *sangría*. Cameras flash. More bangers, naturally. Confetti and rice, rose petals, even coins – reminiscent of scrambles at Scottish weddings of our childhood – are thrown every which way. The couple descend the steps like Ferdinand and Isabella themselves. They are clearly in love, and loving their Big Day. A waft of happiness breezes around the *plaza* below.

The scene brightened my mood, but I still felt a little… detached. This failure to respond, be more aware of my surroundings, almost brought the Dodo back out, howling and hungry. About 3 miles up a steep hill out of Ourense I had a feeling something was missing. I was cycling too freely. My back felt cool and unburdened…

I had decided not to take my own, reasonably good and fairly old, fiddle on the journey. I have form, when it comes to Spain and violins, as we'll see when we get to Cuenca. I'd bought, in Glasgow's Violin Shop, a cheap 'student violin', complete with hardy case, for 75 quid. So it wasn't the cash that made me panic when I realised I'd left it in the hotel in Ourense. I already loved that wee fiddle and, without it, I'd be dumped out of the Sexygenarians. More seriously, my entire project was based on busking, playing violin in the streets of Spain. I shouted apologies to the boys, about-turned and flew back down the hill.

It was still in my as yet uncleaned room. The gecko had coiled, tensed, but its opportunity had gone.

The rest of that day went past in a dwam. Keeping memories at bay rather than awakening them. A slow day of intermittent cloud, roads winding, ever upwards. A day of zen cycling, the mechanical rhythm of push-down-left, push-down-right, keeping eyes on the road rolling beneath your wheels, the purr of rubber on tarmac, the mind emptying.

Except, not quite. Memory can't be turned off and on at will, like a tap. Perhaps the dodo, or black dog, or gecko, or whatever those who suffer from it call it, frees up parts of us that we don't know are there or that we stifle. My memory of my first busking days in Spain is a period of excitement, meeting people like Milton the drummer, earning some cash, making good of a little adventure. But one day – I have no memory of it whatsoever – I must have gone to a booth and used all my takings to call home.

Freewheelin'

Travelling these days, virtually anywhere in the world we can keep in touch daily with family and friends by email, text, social media. I video call my wife and children regularly. Back then, especially if you were moving around, there was only the odd letter – an art neither my parents nor I had much of a knack for. But that day I didn't call my parents. Failure, and shame, had already taken hold. I phoned my brother. Paul, a lawyer, gave me a series of instructions. Three days later I was back in my old bedroom.

Why call so sudden a halt? As I remember it, I was doing well, following roughly in Lee's path, generally making enough to eat and find a place to stay. I know that, most of the time anyway, I was enjoying it. I always hated setting up and playing the first tune, but once people started dropping coins in my case, tapped their feet, wished me well, I got into full swing.

On this new cycle from Ourense I began to remember – or at least figure out – what might have happened, forty-five years ago. I had stopped playing, clearly. My only source of income. I can only think that I had lost confidence. The negativity and self-loathing and venom of the Dodo's bite had taken hold. I hadn't realised that the vicious little bastard had been with me for so long.

I don't hold it against my younger self. He was brave in his way, and imaginative, in at least trying (more than once) to pull off a big adventure. Quite possibly too, he did the right thing. Realised how low he might get and how dangerous that could be on your own in a foreign country, with no back up. Dodo acting as a kind of protector; a guide into corners of your own life. How to recognise and deal with our limitations. Another unforeseen benefit was that, until then, I had not been particularly close to my brother. That call, from some village in the province of either Pontevedra or Ourense, was the start of a lifelong friendship.

Now with Liam and Eddie, arriving in Xinxo de Lima – far less exotic than it sounds – I had planned to busk solo for the first time. I didn't. I wasn't ready to play in front of people alone yet. We didn't get round to it as a group, either. We couldn't find the right place and anyway we had lots of other stuff to sort before moving on. I was quietly relieved; still trying to stop me and myself fighting with each other. Eddie finally takes the sting out of it all by adapting a Margaret Hamilton poem in Scots for the occasion: 'Lament for a Lost Violin'... 'See ma pals? See ma violin? I pit it in ma room, And they cycled oot a toon. See they hills we didnae have tae climb?'... I laughed out loud for the first time in days. Such attacks are often followed by a kind of euphoria, potentially just as dangerous and socially awkward. Out of the blues, I'm jack-the-lad again. Like scoring a tab of MDMA, the system flooding with rapture and bonhomie. I count my many blessings and am as confused as anyone why I was so low before. Dodo never reappeared, centre stage, for the rest of the trip.

I'd have thought that, if it was going to make an appearance at all, it would have felt more at home in the next stop than in the relative refinement and bustle of Ourense.

Vendas be Barreira – in Spain, the longer and more elaborate the name the smaller the place. We climbed over 3,000 feet. To this point there had been no killer hills, but the constant ascending was tiring over time. The culmination of the day's hard work was hardly, at first glance, inspiring. Hotel Bayona – it had sounded so chic and French. It ain't.

It's a truck stop. There's the 'hotel' and a, closed, John Deere tractor garage and outlet. That's it. Barreira is so far from anywhere that none of the rules apply. Customers – travelling salesmen, local farm hands and, of course, truckers – smoke in the bar and in the dining room. A crazed-looking dog howled sporadically from a cage at the entrance that didn't look nearly securely enough locked. The rooms were tiny, basic, but warm and clean – except for the smell of the last guest's black tobacco.

Freewheelin'

It was Eddie who the dodo bit here, though he wouldn't identify with my representation of it. His is a different pain, one with much more, and more recent, justification. It's still less than a year since the loss of his wife; Liam and I recognise when the pain gets too much. Without a word between us we know when to back off, when to let him cycle on, or (extremely rarely) behind, with his own thoughts and grief. When to judge the moment of re-engagement. Crack the joke, ask him for one of his shaggy dog stories. In Venda de Barreira Eddie stayed in his room and, tellingly, even declined to come down and watch the football.

We're not so underfunded as Laurie Lee to have to sleep rough or in hovels. Nor are we rich enough to buy land or rent houses like Gerald Brenan or Robert Cunnninghame Graham. Being two retired and one part-time gentlemen of limited means we have worked out a system over the years for our cycle trips. Liam looks for deals wherever he can find them. There will always be one or two genuinely comfortable and upmarket stops. To balance that we stay in as many cheap places as we can. There's also the challenge of finding a place at just the right distance, taking into consideration the amount and gradient of hills.

Hotel Bayona served its purpose. They stored our bikes safely and had a piping hot meal on the table within an hour of arriving. Family run, the daughter was on duty and was our point of contact for the evening and the following morning. She introduced herself as Fanny – such an old-fashioned name, fallen into disuse thanks to its more recent double entendre, I didn't know it ever existed in Galicia. Fany? Fani? was around six feet tall, broad shouldered, what my aunts would have called 'saucy'. Or handsome. You wouldn't want to pick a fight with her, but there was good cheer in her eyes and healthy scepticism about us and our venture. She, her brother – possibly her twin, you definitely wouldn't upset *both* of them – and her parents could have been

Scots. Their bluntness, their take-it-or-leave-it nonchalance. Asking for Ribeiro wine drew a scornful look. The evening meal was chips. And more chips. Home-made chips, to be sure, lusciously saturated with olive oil and enough salt to cause three heart-attacks. There might have been a frozen hamburger in there too: all I can remember is the chips.

After tea, the bar filled up and the television went on, for the football. Semi-final of the Champions League, Liverpool v Barcelona. Liam and I were cagey at first, not wanting to support a British team against a Spanish one too vocally. We needn't have worried. And anyway, Liverpool didn't stand a chance. Three down already from the first leg against one of the greatest teams in history. No Mohamed Salah, no Firmino, Origi playing out of position, our hero Andy Robertson crocked before half time. Against Messi, Suarez, Busquets... The first Origi goal, in seven minutes, was strong enough cheese to tempt Eddie out of his bedroom refuge. Liverpool won 4–0. Dumped the great Barça out of the competition and supplied one of the most entertaining games of football we've ever seen.

The Bayona bar was in uproar. It turns out *everyone* – truckers, farmers, barflies, our hosts including Fany – *hates* Barcelona. We're in Galicia, a northern region of Spain, further from Madrid than Catalonia with, like the Catalans, its own once discouraged language. The crowd in the bar weren't actively supporting Liverpool, it was ABB – Anyone But Barcelona. We noticed for the first time the Real Madrid pennants and photographs behind the bar. We were nearing the Galician border and border towns often look to their more powerful neighbours than back into their heartlands (not unlike Tory-leaning, more Brexit/anti-independence voters in parts of the Scottish Borders). Anti-Catalan feeling is powerful all over the rest of Spain, including in Galicia. The caricature of the Catalan is rich, snobbish, entitled, and always causing problems for the rest of the country.

My father was at the European Cup final in Glasgow in 1960 between Real Madrid and Eintracht Frankfurt. Forever after, Dad said Real's Di Stefano was the greatest player he had ever seen. In Spain there have been rumours, always vague, that Di Stefano, an Argentinian, was signed to Barcelona but Real and the Spanish football association made sure he went to Real instead. Real was Franco's team and has long been associated with the right in general. Barcelona, on the other hand, represented (to many) anti-Franquismo, anarchism, the left, Catalan pride. For those people, Di Stefano, despite his extraordinary abilities, was bought off by fascists. I now wonder – because it would suit me better – if it was Puskas my Dad had said was the greatest player he'd ever seen.

In Vendas de Barreira we watched Liverpool players, and the irrepressible Jürgen Klopp, do the Walk of Life round Anfield, a thousand miles away, while the men of Hotel Bayona paraded around us. They shook our hands, embraced us.

'Leeverpol!'

'Viva *Real!*'

'*Oye, amigos, ¿cómo se dice?*...Fuck Barthelona!'

Breakfast the following morning was chips. A mountain of chips, but this time with three eggs apiece and – here I do not exaggerate – twelve rashers of bacon. Each. We could barely saddle up, let alone cycle. Whatever the politics of Vendas de Barreira, it was our last overnight stop in Galicia and I had the feeling of leaving Scotland all over again. Some of the same mixed emotions. Same hopes and hankerings.

* * *

Galicia gave us a final day of hills in farewell. Over the route we rose over 1,000 metres – higher than Ben Lomond – and it got colder as we pedalled up. Along the way we passed through valleys and Eddie and I found ourselves singing 'The Massacre of Glencoe'. Perhaps one of us had mentioned the similarity. Or, inwardly, we were making the same connections. *'They came in a blizzard...'*

Eddie is my cycling partner. More often than not, just ahead. Sometimes miles ahead. Sometimes pacing me from behind. Regularly pedalling side-by-side. Liam is usually behind. Either on the same road, or the correct one. He enjoys cycling slowly, stops more than we do, to take photographs or to check the map. Cycling with Eddie keeps my pace up, and on difficult patches takes my mind off the effort. Stories and songs, mutual encouragement. At the top of *Fumaces* (Misty Hill, in Gallego) we had to haul out every semi-warm article of clothing in our panniers. The view was open and wild, but it was too cold to linger and savour.

Coming back down, we levelled out into more gentle slopes – a sign that Galicia was ebbing under our wheels. The wind was behind us. Cyclists will know that if you are aware you have a following wind, it must be strong. Ordinarily we're only aware of wind when it's against us. Until now the violin strapped to my back hadn't been as problematic as I'd feared. Today it was a positive boon, acting as a kind of sail, drafting me along, turning my hefty old tourer into a swift square-rigged vessel pushing me over the road's surf and surges.

The lack of effort allowed us to take in the topography, and life, around us. Shepherds out on their pastures, the odd pilgrim on their way to Santiago – a long distance ahead of them, no whiff of incense yet. Cuckoos, bashful in the trees, tribes of brash and noisy goats. Starlings pretending to be other bigger, maybe better birds, for protection, concealment, the sheer joy of it. Skirting a wooded area, a deer ran alongside us. Leaping, bounding, racing us along the road. The very spirit of youth and vigour and joy, mocking our slow progress, creaky crank-arms and knee-joints.

It vanished delicately into the trees leaving a rustle of its freedom behind. Sorely MacLean's great Gaelic poem came to mind: '*Time the deer, is in the wood of Hallaig... the mystery of the hills*'. Youth, the land, wildness.

After a magnificent 6-kilometre descent into the town of Verín, the three of us, exhilarated, jabbered about the power of cycling to return you to childish bliss and wonder. Even if cycling fast downhill wasn't part of your childhood. I never had a bike as a kid. So it's possible to experience a false, if delightful, memory. My companions tell me I have selective cycling memory, numbering every uphill and discounting every descent. 'Even you can't forget that descent,' they said. The Verín descent is indeed unforgettable. So too was the 20-kilometre Category 2 climb back out of it.

Stopping for coffee at the regional border with Castile y León we come across a trio of Cork men who, embarrassingly, tell us that they're doing just about as many kilometres as us, in only ten days. Off-road (Spain's *Vía Verde* – often old railway lines turned into off-road cycle routes) on mountain bikes. And they're drinking *beer* while we have coffee and water. To be fair, they were twenty years younger than us, clearly practised and avid cyclists, and carrying next to nothing. Still.

So, it turned out that we Scots waved cheerio to Irishmen at the last stop in Celtic Galicia.

PROVINCIA DE LEÓN

When I get into the final stop of day eight, Lubián, I'm ahead of Liam and Eddie. I soon discover that's because Eddie had come off his bike. They had been going through one of the many unlit tunnels that cut through the hills. Generally, these are welcome, avoiding sharp ascents. This time, though, the gutter that ran along the edge of the road wasn't visible, even with bike lights. I had been lucky; I hadn't even noticed there was one. Eddie fell foul of it. He wrenched his knee, which subsequently played up from time to time all the way to Valencia.

The wind that day toyed with my violin-sail. Sometimes pushing me on, other times pulling me obstinately back. There were a lot of bridges over rivers, with barricades of only about four feet high. I found myself cycling in the middle of the road, even around blind bends, rather than risking being blown over into a ravine.

Waiting for my companions in Lubián, rain smirring, I had myself a beer. Another bar, another uproar. This time there were only three people there. I initially thought there was an acrimonious domestic building up. Grandmother, mother and daughter, at a guess, were speaking, or yelling, still in a form of Gallego even though we had crossed the border, so it took me some time to get the gist of it. Languages don't obey political boundaries, they ebb like tides up against the shores of other lands, other ways of speaking and thinking. Eventually I managed to pick out some Spanish words – *cariño, chica, guapa*: love, hen, gorgeous – in the raised voices. I think they were discussing the pleasant time they'd had last weekend in the big city of faraway Vigo.

There were TV sets in our rooms at Lubián and we took the night off to catch up with the news. Britain barely features these days in Spanish news. Up to, say, a couple of decades ago, what happened in the UK was deemed important in Spain. Perhaps it is a reflection of Great Britain's waning importance – in contradiction to the prevailing populist mythology in parts of the UK itself – but also of Spain's attachment to and alliance with the European Union. Even Vox, the ultra-right party, somewhere between Farage's Brexit and Britain First, mutes whatever anti-European feelings it might have, knowing that stating it would cost them a lot of votes. Spain for centuries felt on the margins of Europe, geographically, politically and culturally. EU membership helped break the grip of a deeply conservative Church and landowners who jealously protected their wealth and privilege. Now that it's in with the in-crowd, and plainly the richer for it, it has little intention of going back out into the cold. You have to get three quarters of the way through an extended late-night news show, or page twenty-seven in a daily newspaper, to hear the latest about Brexit, Theresa May resigning, who might take her place. Even then the tone varies from incredulity to outright derision.

Two subjects take up most of the print and broadcast news – the coalition that Pedro Sánchez, the Secretary-General of PSOE (Labour Party, more or less) will make to keep him in power. Come the election, the safe money is on Unidos Podemos. Pablo Iglesias, the Podemos leader, stands out, physically and in every other way. Pony-tailed, tie-less, jeans, backpack, he is the eternal geeky student. Pablo Echenique, Podemos's General Secretary, has Spinal Muscular Atrophy and equals Iglesias in eloquence and political fluency. However, there have been policy splits in their party which may cause them damage in the following week's general elections – and weaken their hand with Sánchez. The other subject is Catalonia. It plays in the rest of Spain the way Brexit plays outside Westminster. Everybody claims to be bored silly by it, but they'll talk about it for hours as soon as you mention it. The debate is heightened, as it is in the UK, by feverish and furious language, accusations on both sides of Fascism ('Catalanazis' v 'Falangistas').

* * *

Rionegro del Puente. Sonorous name – another truck stop. Another cheery family. Another football match. We walk half a mile in a very Scottish dreich gloaming, to see Spurs beat a young

Ajax side, then tramp back to our digs through puddles, only our hi-viz cycling gear reflecting.

Maybe a traveller never really leaves. Robert Louis Stevenson writes more clearly about Edinburgh and Scotland from France and Samoa. Lee conjured up *Cider With Rosie*'s Cotswolds from downtown London. The Andalusias of Lorca and Cernuda feel dense and true observed from New York and Glasgow. Watching and studying other nations and peoples, we hope, gives us some understanding of them, but we cannot but reflect, compare and contrast, with our own experiences and the land and landscapes we hail from. Tethered, like overly curious dogs on long leashes in which we get tangled.

In one village, on one side or the other of the Galicia/León border preparations for the next day's market reminded us of George Mackay Brown's 'Hamnavoe Market', where some Orcadian locals drink till they fall in a ditch. None of us, we discover, has ever been to Orkney, but we know that market. And we see it here, in various guises all over Spain. We're in a Leónese village, reciting Mackay Brown, and thinking about Lanarkshire.

Not all our conversation is so elevated. The following day, we would reach the city of Zamora. We'll be in Zamora, the Morra. We laughed, simple souls. It's another kind of return, travelling with old friends. Lads on the road, reclaiming youthful blithesomeness. Keeping something of home in language, old words revitalised.

Laurie Lee says little about the entire road from Vigo to Zamora, Galicia into León. Brenan says even less, travelling from Corunna to Granada in little more than a page. A literary Jean-Luc Godard, twenty-five years before the French director mastered the jump-cut, Laurie Lee snips out all the boring bits, and perhaps the inconvenient ones, to make a ripping good yarn of his life and travels. He does mention, and this would be true throughout his journey, that children in cities and villages, on country roads, would crowd around him, convoy him along his route for a kilometre or two. Cela makes the same note in his travel books, in the 1940s to 1960s. And it was true of my earlier wanderings in Spain in the '70s. Bairns stood close, staring, while I played in the streets, young teens would follow from one busking spot to another, not always with the best of intentions. None of this happens anymore. The most remote village in unfashionable parts of Spain are now yawningly used to foreigners. Even odd old foreigners with fiddles and whistles. And the country is so much richer now. The kids playing in the square around you, on their electric scooters and BMX bikes, loftily snubbing your musical efforts, have already holidayed in Edinburgh and Donegal and Mexico. They've probably been dragged around more of London's attractions than I've managed to visit.

By the time we reach Valencia we will be debating keenly which was the most beautiful city we passed through. There are several contenders to come, but Zamora is very much in the running.

The ride to it heralded flatter lands ahead. The Brownie points we had earned ascending every day since leaving Vigo began to show a few dividends. But the wind persisted. More bridges, over rivers, canals and railways, with those waist-high barriers, keeping me worrying that a gust would lift me, bike, heavy panniers, over the edge. My only hope was that my 'sail' violin might act as a kind of parachute and soften the 100-foot drop.

Pilgrims got thicker on the ground, ironically the further we got from Santiago. Some possibly on the Camino de Madrid, another major hike. We spotted Dutch, German and Italian pennants. Mainly on foot, a few cycling, one elderly gent on a recumbent bike, another family towing an infant in a trailer – when we passed it was Mum's turn. Some of them might have been timing it to arrive on 23 May, a fortnight hence, for the feast of the Apparition of St James – during, allegedly, the ninth-century battle of Clavijo, which almost certainly never took place, the Apostle helping the Christians knock seven bells out of the Muslims. It's one of the occasions they bring out the *botafumeiro*, and light enough incense to smoke out the devil himself.

One lady, equipped with the necessary staff and shell, flagged me down. She had tried to flag down Eddie, half a mile ahead of me, but he must have been counting Elizabeth McKim Hamill Morrisons, passing her unheeding. A case of not waving but needing directions. Her name was Margaret, Australian in her mid-seventies. This was the eleventh time she had done the Camino.

'Not all the way from Sydney?'

'That would have its obstacles. From Paris, the Pyrenees, Rome last year...'

Her husband's not a walker. He goes motorbiking while Margaret patiently walks hundreds of miles, alone.

'What got you into it?'

'A book.'

I'm thinking the *Codex Calixtinus*. Possibly that annoying Coelho one. Or the Bible. None of the above:

'Shirley MacLaine's.'

We've all read every book we can get our hands on about the Camino. I like Shirley MacLaine as an actor, and the little I know about her as a person, but that book is deranged. Crystals, her past lives, androgynous beings and the search for Atlantis... Put like that, it sounds fun, I must read it again. I have more respect for it now that I know it has changed the life of a bright, hardy, kindly soul like Margaret.

'My pilgrim's map says I should go off-road here.' We were on a B-road, and she pointed to a narrow path heading up over a wooded hill. 'But so far this road's been quite nice. Quiet, too.'

Liam has caught up by this point and we assure her that the

road continues like that. We've just cycled the last eight miles and hardly seen a car. Liam can also confidently inform her that the path she's referring to does indeed join this road, just outside of the last village. We take the compulsory selfies and exchange the two cries heard along The Way:

'¡*Ultreia!*'

'¡*Buen Camino!*'

An hour later I'm cycling, alone again, through a small town. As I stop for a mouthful of water at the village cross, two ladies pass on either side of the road. To the left of me, a local. In scuffed, practical shoes, apron on, grubby from work, her hair tied back out of the way. She'd be in her fifties perhaps. A little world weary, tramping back from the shop with a trolley shopping bag and a flagon of water. On the other side a pilgrim. Probably about the same age, but she looked twenty years younger. Head to foot in Gortex, merino wool, top-of-the-range rucksack, shiny walking sticks, and Ray-Bans. Fresh as a daisy, exuding self-confidence. Neither woman acknowledged the other. It was ever thus on the Camino. You just wonder why the pilgrim, as was accepted practice in days gone by, didn't just pay her home-help to walk it for her.

The approach into Zamora hugs the river Duero, its water to Rueda and Duero wines as spring water is to Scotch whisky. Running a few feet below us the river sparkles golden in the sun beside the buttercups and honeysuckle. You feel you could dip your cup in it, sip it with a tapa of *jamón serrano*. Round one slow bend in the river and, ahead, the spires o' the toon full view we could see. Shades of cream and pink, a cool pastel oasis after a long, if undemanding, ride. (*'Are we in Zamora ahora?'*)

After a quick freshen up at our hotel we're out on the streets. Turns out it is Graduation Day for *Bachillerato* – high school – students. They pour out of the town hall in their Sunday best, excitable, happy. Zamora seems to be a city small enough for everybody to know everybody else. Hugging and kissing, a few tears, chatter and shouts and waving. A banger or two, naturally. Inching our way through crowded streets towards one of the main squares, we pass a *fiesta particular* – a private family bash. We can't be sure but almost certainly a First Communion party. It was the season. We had passed scores of them on the way down from Vigo; had been refused entry to restaurants thanks to them – no room at the inn. It's the same back in Glasgow, for Scots-Irish families like ours. I had missed at least three First Communions, and regretted it. I'm not a church-going man, but I enjoy my great-nieces' and nephews' excitement, and the family gatherings, almost as noisy as the one up that Zamora street.

Zamora was one of the first cities to sign up for the Franco's rebellion against the Republic, as early as July 1936. Which doesn't mean that all Zamorans, or even the majority of them, were Falangists. Those in power were. And after several hundred years of rigid control by the landowning oligarchy, in cahoots with a deeply oppressive Church, it wasn't easy to mutiny, or take a contrary stance. The reprisals Franco took against anyone suspected of disloyalty were savage, from the start of the War, and through its aftermath. (Paul Preston's *The Spanish Holocaust* is a work of meticulous research, the blood dripping from every, tragic, page.) Thousands of brave men and women still fought in whatever way they could, often clandestinely, and to this day none of them are properly recognised, including in Zamora...

The square was quieter than the festive streets. Strictly pruned trees, the centrepiece a statue of, the inscription says, the Lusitanian hero Viriathus who kicked the Romans out of town in the second century (well before the Moors took it from them again – Zamora's name is, elegantly, Moorish.) We were taking photographs of both the square and Viriathus himself when an elderly lady, sitting on a bench with three friends, called us over.

She pointed up to the statue. 'Look at it from here. From this angle.' We did as we were told.

The hero's sword was sheathed by his side and, from the ladies' point of view, its hilt made him look as if in he was in, shall we say, a state of physical excitement. War gets some men like that.

The ladies screamed with laughter watching our reaction. '*¡Mira!* It's like his willy!' They've probably performed this trick for years with passing tourists.

'*Tengo noventa años.*' I'm ninety years old, the most talkative of them, the one who had called us over, told us proudly. 'Ninety-one in two weeks.' We get this a lot on our travels. If I get to ninety-one, I'll tell everyone too. With us, they're talking to people with very open ears. Memory, personal and historical, local and national. It's what this trip is all about. If you were born in the 1920s or '30s, you've seen a lot of history. And here in Spain, history most people don't like talking about. So when we find someone like this lady, who offers her story, perhaps sensing that we would take an interest, we make ourselves, and hopefully her, comfortable.

Visi was eight years old in 1936. On the 18th of July that year Franco launched his attack, green-lighting Falangist fighters, police, anyone who felt authorised, to round up people unsympathetic to the Nationalist cause in positions of power, no matter how minor, or how weak the evidence.

'My dad was the mayor of a wee town just over there,' Visi said, pointing south over the Duero into southern León. 'We had known – neighbours had warned us – that men would come for him. He tried to dodge them but of course they caught up with him. In the little shop my mother ran in the village.

'They hung about outside for a bit, then one soldier burst in, and raised his gun. Pointed it right at my dad. We all hid behind the door that led from the shop into the house. Did I tell you there were eight of us? Including my mum.'

Her full name is María de la Visitación Lastre. Immaculately turned out. Perjink, in a coat my mum would have said was 'good enough to wear inside-out'. Neatly combed and made-up, a faint scent of jasmine, like a girl from a María Dolores Pradera song. Visi laughed when she admitted she was so scared, aged eight, that she wet herself.

'The gunman backed off. But said they would come back for him. Dad went into hiding, living rough in the fields and woods for a month. But they eventually caught up with him.'

The small-town mayor, father of seven, was imprisoned and the family feared that he would never come out alive.

'But he was one of the lucky ones,' Visi said. 'They released him at the end of the war.'

It wasn't Visi's only story. She told us how the family had to move to the city. This city, where she still is.

'During the war there was no school, really. But I was always keen to learn. *Siempre se aprende, ¿no?*' You live and learn. She went back to study, a mature student, in a school set up by local women.

We spent some time with the ladies of Zamora, the youngest of them in her seventies. Chatting, laughing, remembering. There was not a hint of bitterness among them. Finally, we did the obligatory selfie and were a full five minutes shaking hands, hugging, being reminded of names and sharing ours again, waving as we walked away.

María de la Visitación Lastre: vibrant, funny, articulate, a living example of lifelong, and life *deep*, learning.

'*Recordados,*' she called after us. '*Visitación. Me Llamo ¡Visi, Visi, Visi!*' And chortled happily.

Half an hour later, still buzzing after our meeting with the girls (my aunts, in their seventies and eighties, still referred to themselves and their friends as the girls) we stumbled upon Zamora's

Freewheelin'

Poets Corner. The side of an old building overlooking the Duero, quietly singing to itself below, is festooned with the full text of about fifty poems. By writers old and new, celebrated and forgotten, voices as yet undiscovered. One or two of them have the look of concrete poetry and we discuss Eddie Morgan and Ian Hamilton Finlay. Liam and Eddie, over the opening line of a poem that deserved better, fell into a heated discussion over a minor point of the use of the subjunctive. (This is an everyday occurrence, students and lovers of language obsessing over details, wanting to correct the holes and fissures between words, exploring the gaps in meaning.)

A local couple – as it turned out ten years older than us, though they looked much younger – were reading the poetry wall too. I asked them to referee the mounting dispute between my colleagues. María cleared the grammatical problem up with admirable brevity. Her husband, Ángel, got round, with a little prompting, to his family story. This one set on the other side of the conflict from Visi's or her father's.

'*Hermano contra hermano*,' Ángel said desolately. Families and communities divided, by forces beyond their control and often their understanding. Ángel, born in the 1940s, is too young to have witnessed the events but, though his father didn't like to mention it, he heard the tale eventually.

'My father had tried to stay out of the fighting.' Ángel speaks gently, but not furtively. Like Visi, his townswoman, he is impeccably dressed. Everyone in Zamora is. Jacket in the *Americano* style, waistcoat, open-necked shirt, soft shoes and sternly pressed trousers. 'But with the rebel army in power it was impossible. Back then, the choices... When they forced him to sign up, he had a plan.

'He bought an old *furgoneta* and offered himself as a driver.' It worked. A man with a van.

'He drove army personnel all over Spain, across battlefields. He never held a gun, never got shot at. Then, one day, around the start of 1938, he was given the command to drive a colonel to Teruel, to join the fighting there.'

He did as instructed and dropped the colonel off. But, worried he might be asked to do more at the front, Ángel's dad turned the car round, didn't sleep, and drove all night. Straight back to Zamora.

Perhaps the people who offer their stories do so because they have a happy ending. Too painful for those whose family luck didn't hold out, who have atrocious memories.

'They never came after him. He kept expecting it, but he lived quietly and they forgot about him.'

That was a bigger stroke of luck than Ángel's father had realised at the time. The battle of Teruel went on to become one of the bloodiest and most brutal of the entire Spanish Civil War.

We went back and joined the others at the poetry wall. María pointed at a poem by José Ángel Barruecos. A love poem. She said it could have been written for the two of them – María and Ángel. But it also spoke to us: '...*el viaje, a pesar de las postales / de los monumentos y las tabernas / de las librerías y las catedrales /es en el fondo una ruta hacia / el interior de uno mismo...*' (journeys, after all the postcards, the monuments and taverns, libraries and cathedrals is, finally, a voyage into your self). We walked back through town and they insisted we had a drink with them.

For many years I travelled to Pamplona, in the Navarre region, working with theatre writers. As is the Spanish way, we finished most days by going for a drink and a bite. There were several bars and restaurants in the old part of town we frequented. Some of them we never entered. Once or twice, unaccompanied, I tried them out. They seemed to me every bit as good as our regular places. Next time, I asked a friend, 'Why don't we go into those bars?'

Normally talkative, he simply said, 'We just don't.'

Three quarters of a century after the war. Then again, at the time I was working there, less than quarter of a century since Franco's rule.

So you cannot stop yourself from wondering, taken to a new bar in new city, whether it's one of the bars my Pamplona friends would have side-stepped. The one that María and Ángel took us to was certainly more upmarket than the bars Liam, Eddie and I tend to frequent. We drank crisp, nettly white wine (not Liam, a teetotaller), sampled rich salty *jamón ibérico*, some local cheeses. The owner looked like Willy Nelson, the clientele gracious, the atmosphere hugely congenial.

The funeral of a leading PSOE politician, Alfredo Rubalcaba, had been on the news on radios and TVs all day. Rubalcaba had been around for much of our time visiting Spain, generally regarded as a centrist social democrat, veteran of the Felipe González era. María knew him personally and had considered going to his funeral that day in Madrid. They had been chemistry students together at the Complutense University of Madrid in the early 1970s. They had organised together, with others, a strike demanding more pay and better conditions for early academics. My daughter, Emma, would approve. Anyone working in a university in the UK might want to bring back the spirit of young Alfredo and María. María spoke of Rubalcaba, and of her memories of student life in Madrid, with emotion and pride.

Then we got to singing songs. Our hosts were genuinely impressed at our knowledge of Spanish and Latin American music. We discussed our favourite musicians. Moira and I are life-long devotees of María Dolores Pradera. Victor Jara, too. Eddie talked and sang Victor Manuel. Liam and María sang Mexican rancheras and mariachis. I took away the names of artists and songs I didn't know.

Walking back towards our hotel, María made us promise to stop the following morning and take in the view of Zamora – *'mi ciudad'* – from the bridge out of town. We made our farewells. The young-old couple joined hands, she fair and slight, keen eyed, effusive; he dark and unobtrusive, placid. They walked off close together into the fading hubbub of the Zamora night.

PROVINCIA DE VALLADOLID

The view from the bridge didn't disappoint. We dismounted, stood gawping. The scene was like a photoshopped Spanish Tourist Board fantasy of Spain – castle, cathedral, Moorish-influenced architecture. Under a crayon-blue sky. A stork sailed over our heads to its nest on a high tower. The morning sun poured fresh as an invigorating shower while the Duero stretched sleepily below.

Laurie Lee's Duero in 1935 was 'wrinkled mud'. The air of Zamora thick with flies, the citizens poor. Yet we had felt it rich, certainly richer than anywhere in Galicia. It had worked out alright for Laurie in the end. This is where he met his German bandmates, and they busked and played at a local dance, and had a drunken time of it.

The difference time can make? Or the luck you have in the people you meet, the places you see, the state you're in, physically and mentally? How often have any of us lauded a particular place only to hear that somebody else experienced the opposite? Looking over that bridge, on that particular spring morning, we couldn't have cared what anyone else thought. We were lucky to be alive and there, to see it.

It was hard to get back on our bikes and leave. We finally did, and the minute we passed the city boundary, I declared: 'Boys, we're that ahead of the curve, we were in Zamora yesterday.'

Tragically, I'd been saving the line since we first arrived. They smiled nicely and we cycled on.

And then new friends appeared. Our personal guides who would lead us, every day, on every road, high or low, all the way into Valencia. Our journey had coincided perfectly with the poppy flowering season. They lined either side of the road, botanical cat's eyes showing the way ahead, keeping us safe. A necklace of rubies and garnets, the occasional meek amber-petal. They awaited us at every bend, applauded us as we passed, sang their joyous song softly, swaying in a bolero performance. They stayed with us even at the end of the day, perfuming our nights with opium dreams of cherry blossom. I know that, in the future, when I think back on this trip, I will see first those humble, kindly poppies. *'Pleasures are like poppies spread…'* A line of Burns for a Spanish road.

The entire next fortnight would be a treat of nature. The stork we saw from the Duero bridge was the first of many. In every village we went through they sat on their thrones, smug on the highest spires and towers. They seemed birds of fables, out of fairy tales, fantastical. The world of Hans Christian Andersen breaking through into reality. We stopped to take photographs in a village, and as one improbably large but graceful, almost computer-generated, stork floated over our heads, I asked a woman, doing her morning shop, when they arrived and left.

'Here, they turn up around February.' Later, Robin Cunninghame Graham told me that in his Segovia village the males arrive first and sit shivering in their nests until the females turn up six weeks later. 'They go south again,' the woman said, 'around midsummer.

'Wow. Six months of these beauties.'

The woman shrugged. 'You wouldn't say that if they were destroying *your* roof. The damn things cost this town a fortune. That church over there? Derelict. They couldn't raise the money for the repairs.'

One man's wonder is another woman's everyday reality. 'And you ought to see their shit! *Jolín!*'

But I'm smitten. They turn the day into a scene from Gormenghast, or dreamed up by Ursula K. Le Guin. I thank the woman and, as she turns to get on with her day, she glimpses up at the storks, and smiles fondly.

Out on the open road, there are birds of prey of all shapes and sizes. I think I recognise a few pairs of red kites. As we progress and more birds appear around us, I ask in bars and shops, check the internet when I can (rarely) and try, at last, to learn what these creatures are that I'm seeing. That said, there is some joy in ignorance, a simple marvelling, an acceptance of a world more diverse and manifold than we can label and file away.

Our plan had been to stop at the town of Toro. But we dillied (*'and dallied, dallied and dillied… and don't know where to roam…'* as the old music hall song goes) distracted by fields of poppies, panoramas, a hundred photo opportunities, conversations with pilgrims and townsfolk. By the time we reached Toro we were seriously behind schedule. And the town was up a severe looking hill. We decided to give it a miss and, anyway, we had got what we'd wanted – the view of it from the road below. Coral pink, in the afternoon sun, teetering over the edge of raw red rock, sweating in the heat. That perspective inspired Laurie Lee, master of the epigram, to describe Toro as 'dried blood on a rusty sword.' The perfect description, given Spain's long, embattled history. We continued on, delaying lunch and rest till we were nearer our day's destination. We soon thought that that might have been a mistake, all signs of village or communal life absent, in any direction. Until at long last, we cycled into a place best described as a hamlet. San Roman de Hornija (wee place, long name). With one restaurant. It didn't look promising, but we needed to stop and eat *something*.

This inn, and it felt like a place Lee or Brenan might have stopped at, or José Camilo Cela, had one or two elderly people sitting outside in the shade. Though Spain lunches late we worried we were still too late for food. Inside, we were the only clients. A woman in her thirties was running the place by herself but she assured us she could feed us. There were few choices. *Lentejas* (lentils), always welcome to cyclists. Filling.

Later we'll eat in some very upmarket restaurants, and we enjoyed Spanish food all along the road. But I guarantee, if asked in a year's time what was the most memorable dish, all three of us will say that *lenteja* stew. Served with spicy raw green chillies, I have no idea what the other ingredients were, but it was archetypal Spanish *casera*, home-cooked, food. Perfectly satisfying, piping hot, faintly exotic.

Liam had picked up on the accent of the woman who had served and cooked the food.

'I'm *Colombiana*.'

She had come to Spain, she said, because she couldn't find work in Colombia. Full of praise for her new home, she was withering about her native land. She reminded me of my mother. Until her death at ninety-three she spoke with an Irish accent. But if anyone – an aberrant uncle, or one of our friends – dared to support Ireland against Scotland at football, rugby, whatever, Kay had her line ready. '*This* country,' she'd say, 'shod, fed and educated my children when *that* country couldn't.' She wasn't anti-Irish, she loved the Oul' Sod in her own way. She was just truthful about her own experience. Despite anti-Irish, and anti-Catholic, disposition in Glasgow. In Spain, Latin Americans have to contend with similar problems. Language heard in the UK – 'flooding', 'swarms' – has been applied by far-right groups to all immigrant communities. Ecuadorians and Colombians are amongst the largest of those groups and have borne the brunt of racist chants, attacks and politics. Our hostess in that little town either didn't care or hadn't been singled out.

Liam is an aficionado of Colombia, his daughter was living there at the time, and he later defended the country. But he kept his peace at the time. Working, perhaps owning, a small, apparently ill-frequented, restaurant in a remote part of rural northern Spain had worked out for this woman. Perhaps it was where her family had emigrated from, generations before. Maybe she'd found love. Or she simply loved making world-class lentil dishes for passing cyclists. She seemed happy enough, chatting to us and the odd farmer who popped in for a beer, humming, singing, dancing to herself behind the bar.

'Definitely Colombian,' Liam said.

Getting on our bikes a jeep pulled up. On its side was written *Teso de Tras de Macada*. I asked the driver, a weather-beaten man about our age, portly, his jeans and boots dusted with earth and white, dry clay, what *Teso de Tras de Macada* means.

'The wine I make,' he said, pleased that foreigners had taken an interest in him and his work. 'It's good. I sell it abroad. Maybe you'll see it wherever you're from,' not bothering to ask where that might be. We're about to pedal off when he says, '*Espera.*' He rummages around in his jeep, harrumphs, goes into the bar, and comes out with a bottle of wine. *Teso de Tras de Macada*.

'Let me know what you think of it.' Though we all know we'll never meet again.

'*Buen camino!*'

Wine, I quickly discover, is a heavy thing to add to an already heavy pannier. But reinvigorated by lentils and *cumbias* and reggaeton – and our uncalled-for gift – we continued towards Tordesillas. Seemingly on our own private road, offering itself to us, open, fresh and smiling. We rode three abreast, talking, laughing, singing.

One last stop before Valladolid – this was a day to savour, one none of us wanted to end. Simancas's castle is another set out of Gormenghast. All turrets and crenellations, cloud-capp'd towers, shiny as if it had just been drawn for a Disney film. A damsel quite possibly could appear at a high baronial window and let her hair down. Sipping coffee in the town square we witnessed a more down-to-earth apparition. Campaigning for the European and some local elections had been put on hold for a couple of days, out of respect for the passing of Alfredo Rubalcaba. It was back to battle stations today. A group of people, all ages, began to set up their stall. We tried to guess which party they were promoting but there was nothing to give that away. Well-dressed, middle-class and middle-aged, chatting among themselves as they worked together. Then the orange-coloured pennant came out. Ciudadanos, the party to the right of the Partido Popular (Conservative party) but left of Vox. Throughout the campaign Ciudadanos were the most evident party on the streets. They were everywhere – posters, stickers, cars blaring out their message, stalls in squares and high streets. It wasn't till Cuenca, four days before the election, that we saw a PSOE campaign. Apart from a series of posters, very little sign of Podemos.

* * *

Why do they speak Portuguese in Brazil?

Tordesillas was the only stop on the route that Liam had insisted on including. So he knew about Tordesillas. Eddie and I had never heard of it.

Tordesillas is in the province of Valladolid – the fourth to date we had cycled through – and part of the greater Autonomous Community of Castile and León. We would be moving through Castile in one form or another – old, new, Manchego – for days to come. In its various forms it takes up nearly half of Spain, incorporating the provinces of Valladolid, Burgos, León, Salamanca, Zamora, Palencia, Ávila, Soria, and Segovia. Kate O'Brien in *Farewell Spain* describes the ancient kingdom as 'empty, blond, austere'.

Tordesillas is small, but it's a favourite day out for city folk from all sides, so is well furnished with bars and restaurants. One of its attractions is its history, and the standing architecture that links us to the past. The churches, the monastery of Santa Clara, the museum housed in an old palace, the 'Treaty House', where the Catholic Kings themselves, Ferdinand and Isabella used to stay. These places have a direct influence on us all today, not just in Spain, but worldwide.

We went to see the chapel first. Drenched in gold leaf, the insignia of the Inquisition on display, softness in the cool alabaster walls and statues. That stone, quarried locally for hundreds of years, is graceful but also very soft. Time and wind and heat and rain have eaten into it making monsters of saints, zombies of heroes and kings.

'What jumps out at me,' Liam whispers in the echoey choir loft, 'is how scary the iconography is.' He doesn't just mean the semi-erased faces and severed limbs, like a gallery of fifteenth-century lepers. He means what the original sculptors intended – trodden-on snakes screaming, blood-drenched Christ figures, gargoyles seething.

'It reminds me of St. Patrick's Primary School.' Coatbridge in Tordesillas. 'Five years of age and the first thing you saw as you entered St. Pat's was some saint tramping on a snake, just like that one. But even worse, it had long sharp bloodied fangs, and it was a deal more pissed off than this one. It looked like it might take its revenge on *you*.' Carrying Scotland and old Catholicism on your back, like a snail. New places throw light on old ones. We carried on to the palace and the museum.

'Most people have never heard of this place but, actually, it was of enormous significance. Two years after Christopher Columbus supposedly 'discovered' the Americas in 1492 – although people who were already there felt they didn't need discovered – there was a meeting in this palace. The Spanish and the Portuguese were already arguing about who was going to 'own' these newly found lands. They were ready to go to war over it.'

But the courts of the Catholic Kings and of King João I of Portugal decided that jaw-jaw was better than war-war. Mainly because neither side was confident of winning. And then there were complex and long-standing Papal bulls and alliances to consider. But why Tordesillas?

'Well, we're pretty near the Portuguese border, and both royal houses had connections and properties here. To even things out, the agreement they finally came up with was rubber-stamped the following year in Setúbal, in Portugal. The Catholic Kings' daughter, Juana, had her court here.' *Juana la Loca*, Mad Joanna. And no wonder – the daughter of the Catholic Kings, they tortured her cruelly when, as a teen, she dared question their faith. Later, they imprisoned her and ignored her cries for help. Juana's story, at the threshold of Spain's richest and most powerful era, is tragic, and telling.

'At the negotiations,' Liam continued, 'they drew a line down from the north pole of the known world to the south and agreed that everything west of that line would belong to Spain and everything east, Portugal. The Spaniards had thought they had outmanoeuvred their rival neighbour, but they still hadn't explored most of South America yet.' Eight years later, in 1500, a Portuguese fleet under the command of Álvares Cabral anchored at a shoreline that turned out to be the massive landmass that sticks out, eastward... Brazil, as it was later named. '*That* is the reason why the vast majority of Central and South America speaks Spanish, but in Brazil they speak Portuguese.'

Of course, as Liam was keen to point out, the story is much more labyrinthine and open to interpretation than that brief introduction. Unfortunately, the main museum was closed for repairs. But there was a guide, Patricia, who knew some more about the history of the treaty.

'We are very proud of the treaty in Tordesillas. It prevented a war. Many, many lives were saved.'

The stories we tell ourselves, individuals, communities, nations. The *Tratado de Tordesillas* did indeed prevent a war. But what they were agreeing was the total colonisation of a vast part of the world that led eventually to millions being enslaved, and in some regions, outright genocide. To lands being stolen and exploited, all the riches and produce sent back to Spain and Portugal. Churches and holy places all over the Peninsula are still 'decorated' by gold and silver and gems torn from conquered lands.

An argument often cited for deeds done in the past is that the mindset was different. That we look back from the vantage point of more enlightened times and judge the past too harshly. But there were always voices speaking out against colonialism, exploitation and slavery. There were organised and popular protests against enslavement of people as early as the 1680s. Thucydides argued against the idea of imperialism in the early fifth century. In a Spanish context, the Dominican friar Antonio de Montesinos gave a sermon in 1511: 'By what right of justice do you hold these Indians in such a cruel and horrible servitude? On what authority have you waged such detestable wars against these people who dwelt quietly and peacefully on their own lands? Wars in which you have destroyed such an infinite number of them by homicides and slaughters never heard of before. Why do you keep them so oppressed and exhausted, without giving them enough to eat or curing them of the sicknesses they incur from the excessive labour you give them, and they die, or rather you kill them, in order to extract and acquire gold every day.'

Yet that Spanish past is even now being vaunted as an ideal, something to attempt to regain. Vox and other political parties invoke it. Just recently Pablo Casado, leader of the Partido Popular, has said it was, 'the most important landmark of humanity, in my opinion only comparable with Rome. It is probably the most brilliant era, not only of Spain, but of Man, together with the Roman Empire'.

O little town of Tordesillas, what an impact you made on the modern world! How colonialism played out, the consequent slave trade, the foundations of today's inequitable international trading system. The rise of the Spanish empire, then the British, then the American. And it's still being cited, the Treaty of 1494. In the early 1980s, the UK and Argentina argued over its interpretation to determine who 'owned' the Falkland Islands. And there is another direct consequence, one that links Spain's past with Scotland's. Over the last decade, since publication of my novel *Redlegs*, I have been involved with our own problems of historical memory. Liverpool, Bristol and other English cities have museums, plaques, bearing witness to how the wealth of the nation owes much to the most audacious, far-reaching and cruel slave industry in history. Scotland has been slow to come to terms with itself and its own past. Only now, through the work of Dr. Stephen Mullen, Sir Geoff Palmer, Professor Tom Divine and others, with those in the Caribbean, the southern States and across the old British colonial world, are we beginning to bear witness to the source of our wealth and seek ways forward, to at least try and find positive responses to that most inhuman trade.

A 525-year-old pact. Yet we've heard, and will hear more in the coming days, about how the Spanish Civil War is too long ago to bother about anymore. How Franco was our grandparents' time and should be left there. While other past events and agreements, as we are about to see at our next stop, are deemed to be important, even essential to the future.

The museum was closed but there was a little gallery run by a man who was every bit as informative. He told us about the 1481 and 1483 agreements. He brought out maps, old and new, replicas of those used at the time, he discussed contemporary longitudinal and latitudinal understandings, and consequences. Everything that led up to the Treaty, and lots that came after it, complicate and obfuscate its terms, the benefits and penalties. But this gentleman was again at pains to tell us how his little town prevented a world war.

And why shouldn't he have civic pride? We all want to present our best faces to the world. The jump-cut. Stitching the best bits together, trying to make sense of your history, and your own place in it.

After our educational afternoon and evening, I get back to the hotel to write up notes. From down the hall I hear this cacophony of ukulele and, well not quite singing. Eddie and Liam were singing their own version of an old Bluegrass song:

In fourteen hundred and ninety-two
Before you was borned-oh
Columbus and his motley crew
Knew that they was scorned-oh.
He knew the world was round, though
He knew what could be found-oh
He sailed the sea for you and me, Christopher Columbus!

* * *

Laurie Lee's Valladolid, 1935: '...a shut box, full of pious dust and preserved breath of its dead...' Cycling into the same city in 2019: a warm inviting town, busy with colours and daily business; a statue to the poet Zorrilla; cafés, families, buses, sensible, regular architecture.

On an evening of 'red stale dust' Lee found little life. We arrived in a city gearing up for a grand fiesta (what Spanish town isn't, ever?). Another festival for the city's patron saint, Pedro de Regalado. (We never found out who he was, or what he did. It was hardly the point.) We were staying in a hotel just off the main square – which would cause something of a problem at night. The hullabaloo started just as we hit the streets. A massive stage erected, an orchestra playing De Falla's *The Three-Cornered Hat*. Music brought to the people. And they listened, in their hundreds. Yes, they talked, and laughed, and chased after their children, licked ice-creams and *granizados*. But they took in the music, moved to it, and by it, held the little ones up to see the orchestra playing. The whole scene was an illustration of an ongoing conversation Eddie and I had been having – high art and low art, what defines them and how too often they are seen to be mutually incompatible. As if you can't enjoy both *paella de mariscos* and fish and chips, Bach and ABBA. The weighty does not take it all.

The orchestra was joined on stage by a troupe of female flamenco dancers. Amateurs, probably a club that meets one night a week to practise. Of all ages, and levels of expertise. Their joy in performing, the odd giggle of nerves, the occasional mistimed step, it all made it more enjoyable, and admirable. The crowd gave them an enormous cheer. We wandered off and had a look around the adjacent streets. The formal lines of the buildings, erect and foursquare, you could begin to imagine how, in more meagre days, the stone perhaps unwashed, Lee might have felt the city to be austere, stern – 'chisels and chains'.

Perhaps in Lee's day, or even now when the city is not in fiestas, something of Valladolid's past seeps through. It's where Tomás de Torquemada, first Inquisitor-General, was ordained and where the whole notion of *autos-da-fé*, the Inquisition's system of enforcing confessions and punishments to 'heretics', was born.

He had a terrible time of it in Vallodolid, Laurie. Witness to a wife-beating, his own health failing. It was here he tells of trying to get his permit to play violin in the street. A story that *Valisolitanos* are suspicious of. Even if not correct, or correctly remembered, in every detail it tells you something about officialdom not only in Spain, or back then, but now and everywhere. For our part, we decided to get an early night. And the square festivaled on into the early hours.

On Sunday morning Valladolid was, temporarily, shut – taking a breath for the next lot of festivities later that day. Valladolid has twice been capital of Spain. Columbus himself retired to the city and died here. If Granada is the southern version of *España profunda*, with its dream-like Moorish Alhambra, its flamenco, Valladolid has a claim to be its northern counterpart – land of El Cid, Fernando y Isabela, the Castilian *jota* and *pasadobles* with their strict steps and rhythms. Catholicism more orthodox, less wantonly pagan than in the south.

We eventually found a little café, with coffee, orange juice, toast, *bollos*. Yesterday's papers. We breakfasted with the unfortunate few who still have to work on high days and holidays – a nurse, a cleaner, fireman, a roadie or two about to restyle the stage set in the square. Sitting, dunking fresh *bollos* in strong coffee, reading *El País* and *La Vanguardia* newspapers, orange juice and fresh tomatoes… a glimpse of how our mornings might generally have been had any of us decided to live in Spain. A decision all of us have, at some time or other, come very close to. The Spanish versions of ourselves breakfasting, getting ready for the working day, like our companions in the bar.

Freewheelin'

Liam and his wife Anne had, for the last couple of months, welcomed a young friend of their son's into their home. Lucía's parents, to thank him, insisted on taking all three of us to lunch. We had never met these people, but we suspected that the restaurant they were taking us to would be pretty upmarket. Now, halfway through cycling across Spain, we barely had a clean T-shirt between us. We were concerned at the impression we'd make. Especially Eddie and I, who had done nothing to deserve a slap-up meal.

If María's and Ángel's bar had been smart, this place was smarter still. And a vegetarian's nightmare. Valladolid is famed for its gastronomy – what Spanish city isn't? The speciality dish, 'don't order it anywhere else, *caballeros*. Only in Valladolid do we know how to do *lechazo asado*.' Roast veal. Made from calves slaughtered at 1–2 days old having consumed nothing but their mother's milk. Entering the cellar establishment, bare stone and candelabras, on proud display was just such a calf. Intact, except for its skin, legs stretched out as if killed and shucked mid-jump. The three Scots glanced at one another, concerned about the ethics... But when in Valladolid...

Lucia's parents, Marta and Ángel, and their other daughter Marta junior, had brought along their old friends Arturo and Rocío to meet us. We needn't have worried about our appearance, or how we would get on with these strangers. Talk erupted the moment we sat down. Just as well Ángel had booked a private back room for us – the endless chatter, shouting over one another, the ensuing debates, toasts and the clinking of glasses. It was noisy, exuberant, argumentative, and quintessentially Spanish, eating, drinking and socialising late into the afternoon.

Marta junior had just qualified as a doctor and was about to take up her first job in a hospital in Segovia. My son is about a year ahead, junior house doctor in Manchester Royal Infirmary. So we compared courses, career plans, remuneration. Doctors in

Spain, I discovered, have a hard time of it in their early years, getting paid little. Daniel is better waged at MRI. However, here they move up the grades more swiftly and as they do the rewards get greater. We touch on the difficult subject of comparative health systems. Spain, like the UK, has a Universal Health Care system and, depending on which ranking you believe, is often placed above ours. But there is also a voluntary insurance factor. This was not the time to start on British fears of how Brexit, a swing to the hard-right, might affect the NHS.

Arturo tells me that Valladolid is the capital of Spain's growing rugby scene. We both played the game in our younger years and we exchange a few dodgy rugger tales and jokes. I tell him I used to be a hooker (cue rugger joke) and, from time to time my two props were my brothers Charlie and Paul, collectively known as the Dolan Sisters. Arturo roars and laughs at everything, including some of his best pal's political opinions. He is tall, lean, a veterinary surgeon, strong-armed. Second row if ever I saw one. (He wasn't; he was *tercera línea*. Flanker. Cue more rugger jokes...) I'm sat next to his wife, Rocío. Charming, animated, tall and blonde, we immediately took to her because she was genuinely impressed by our cycling feats. Marta senior is petite, dressed in muted honey and cinnamon shades. Quieter spoken than any of us. An accountant, when we all start on politics she's more measured, a conciliatory smile.

But this is Ángel's gig. The paterfamilias, respected lawyer of this parish. And he's footing the – considerable – bill. Intellectually bespectacled, northern complexion, healthily plump like a Clyde Valley plum, he is all energy and bonhomie. A man who prides himself on saying-it-like-it-is.

Picking me out as the one most responsible for our blog – they have all been following us faithfully – he gives me a few ticking-offs.

'You shouldn't talk about "Two Spains". This is dangerous.'

I don't remember using the phrase (originally, Machado's), but I can see how Ángel thinks I might have. In the beam of his keen eyes, I feel like I'm in the dock. Not a dangerous offender, in fact one not to waste too much time over. 'Let's not bring back the past. This country has changed.'

We all understand the argument. Spain is doing well, opening up the past could, potentially, be ruinous. Franco's the past. 'We need to discuss the issues of *today*. I was just a toddler when he died.'

We're aware of being their guests. More importantly, we like these people.

'But the past doesn't just go away,' we say. 'There are still problems, like the Valley of the Fallen.' That's where Franco is buried, and a shrine for the far right. The Socialist acting Prime Minister, Pedro Sánchez, has promised to exhume the dictator's remains and find a way of honouring all those who died in the Civil War, not just Francoists.[1]

The mention of Sánchez doesn't go down well. Nor any politician for that matter. As in the UK, there is a deep distrust and distaste for politicos of all stripes. By now the *lechazo* has arrived. Great platters of it. Our consciences have been well dampened by creamy white and syrupy red wines, and we gorged like cyclists who have had nothing but tortilla and *lentejas* for a fortnight. Chins dripping, taking seconds and thirds, we'd forgotten to worry about the impression we might make.

---

[1] On 24 October 2019, Franco's remains were moved from the Valley of the Fallen – to chants of ¡Viva Franco! – to a lair next to his wife's, at their old residence in El Pardo. A highly publicised and ceremonious echo of hundreds of Republican soldiers' corpses being exhumed from mass graves all over Spain.

They were as impressed by our language as we were by theirs (beautiful Valladolid Spanish) and we got onto the – as it turned out, prickly – question of whether Romance languages are inherently sexist. Just as English uses 'he' referring to the unspecified or general, even though that may contain more than 50 per cent women, Spanish uses the male form in verbs in much the same way. But, as with French and Italian and others, every noun has a gender too, so the language problem gets more complex. Part of the debate in Spanish-speaking countries is whether to always add the female to the male plural, to be inclusive. *Señores y señoras*; *pasajeros y pasajeras* on aeroplanes, etc.

'It's ridiculous,' says Rocío. 'I don't need them to spell it out in planes or theatres. *Señores y señoras!* It's such a mouthful, it's unnecessary.'

Marta agrees. 'We're all included in *señores*.' Their husbands, sensibly, stay out of it. But the women's argument isn't universally held. There are a lot of people in Spain, women and men, who think you should absolutely use the feminine form as well as the masculine. It seems very little effort to make to include half the human race. The idea that language in itself can be chauvinist keeps us going over another bottle of wine and platter of *lechazo*.

'That's the kind of feminism that gives feminism a bad name.'

I've noticed that, in written text, there is a movement towards transcribing gender nouns like this: *trabajadxr*, or *pasajer@s*. Not much later I saw my first example of the same approach in English: *womxn*.

I find the subject interesting, not only ethically, but linguistically. English, to counteract its sexism, has stopped using words like 'actress' or 'waitress'. But the logic of the battle in Spanish is to use '*actriz*', or '*directriz*', specifically feminine forms. David Sedaris, the American essayist and commentator is, hilariously, confused about gendered nouns in his book *Me Talk Pretty One*

Day. He notes for instance that, In French, 'vagina' is a masculine noun, but 'masculinity' is feminine.

My daughter is deeply interested in this subject and I remember some of her thinking. That language is both created by and in turn creates gendered knowledge. European languages are often constructed around the binary logic of masculinity and femininity which might seem random, but actually reinforces gendered lines of thinking. For example, masculine nouns are more often described by adjectives associated with masculinity *(sol fuerte* – strong sunlight) while feminine nouns are more frequently described with adjectives traditionally considered feminine *(luna suave* – delicate, gentle moon).

Then someone mentioned Catalonia.

Bang.

This is purely anecdotal, just my own experience, but I have yet to meet a non-Catalan in Spain who doesn't feel disturbed, offended, and heartily bored, by the question of Catalan independence. Across political lines. Our hosts here were equally as frustrated.

'Of course they should have a referendum,' says Ángel. *'¡Que se vayan si no quieren quedarse!'* – let them go if they don't want to stay. But there's hurt in every Spaniard's eyes every time I hear this. Like the woman who had complained about the storks in her village, the same sadness.

'The Spanish Constitution of 1978. Everyone agreed to it. Including the Catalans. Everyone had their say, and everyone signed. It works for us all. You can't just turn your back on it now.'

Why not? Why can't it be tweaked, updated? That constitution prohibits any part of Spain holding a referendum, or even considering self-determination. Franco died in 1975, and that is, apparently, ancient history, but 1978 is not only still relevant but binding.

Arturo takes the middle ground. Or rather, the debunking line.

He throws in quips and observations. He's having a great time. He rugby-tackles his opponent, low, and from their blindside. He gets Ángel into a headlock with obscure 'facts' (all queried and all dismissed). It's clear that this is how his relationship with his best pal has been for decades.

'What would you know about it?' Ángel retorts to one of his mate's put-downs.

Arturo rejoinders with a terrific line: '*¡La ignorancia es atrevida!*'

Later I discover it's a line from Thucydides, the fifth-century Greek historian who argued against colonialism: 'Ignorance is bold and knowledge reserved'. I use it for the rest of the cycle whenever I take a wrong turning, develop a problem with the bike, or state something that is factually disputed.

One of the joys of being with these people, apart from their generosity, their *joie-de-vivre*, their craic, is the Spanish they speak. Valladolid, and Zamora, are the Inverness of Spain. Their Spanish is considered the most correct, the clearest, most perfectly enunciated. There's no confusion as with Gallego or Asturianu, Catalán or Valencià, or the difficult accents of Andalusia. Their phrasing is lyrical, every utterance a lesson in the proper and imaginative use of Spanish.

By coffees, nothing is resolved. Not the constitution, not the Catalans, animal rights or rugby tactics. We pour out into the street, sunlight hurting our subterranean, sozzled eyes (except Liam's of course). The kissing and the hugging. We're no' awa' tae bide awa'. They're all coming to Scotland to visit their daughter, in a couple of months' time. Liam says, when they're out of earshot, 'Return game. We'll have the advantage on home turf.' And we'll disagree all over again. And laugh and shout and disturb the neighbours. I'm already choosing the whiskies.

* * *

Freewheelin'

Each of us has our special place in Spain. Our personal Spanish creation myth. My Spain begins with Galicia. Eddie's is Santander and Cantabria. Liam's is Valladolid. Over a quieter coffee that evening he tells us why.

'When I finished sixth year at school I bought a European railcard and took off with a friend. We toured France and Spain. And ended up, on the advice of another friend, in Valladolid. It was my first experience of non-tourist Spain and it changed my life.

'Two and a half years later I was driving overland in a Citroen Diane to spend my year abroad in Guadalajara. I took a detour via Valladolid, not least because I was enjoying the company of a girl from Coatbridge who had cadged a lift from me at the last minute. That was a good decision on my part – six years later Anne and I got married.' Valladolid is an important place for Liam in many ways.

We order more *cortados,* reflect on the fact that we were only twenty years old or less, *asistentes* in Spanish schools in the '70s. Without modern communications, away from home for a full year, thrown headlong into a different culture, a language we didn't speak well yet. We were all truly on our own.

'I remember being told that a percentage of students went home before the first month was up. Another percentage committed suicide, they felt so lonely and isolated. It was a test of social and learning skills.'

The first Spanish song Liam had ever heard was four years before he started learning the language. His music teacher taught the class a *'Tuna'* song. Nothing to do with the fish, *'tunas'* are traditional bands of students, playing guitars, mandolins, lutes and tambourines. They've been singing in the streets, under sweethearts' windows, at student parties, since the fourteenth century. We had seen a *tuna* when we were cycling through Jerez a couple of years ago, with their capes and caps. Nowadays they play old songs from Spain, Mexico and Cuba. *(¡Ay, ay, ay, ay, canta y no llores…!)* Like flamenco, some people associated them with Franco's regime, but now that he's no longer around to appropriate them, they can be enjoyed as colourful, fun and, generally, skilful musicians.

'Funny how things work out,' Liam says as we pay up and head back out into the Valladolid night. His and Anne's three children have all learned Spanish. And two of them will be there in Valencia to welcome us.

Back at the hotel, the orchestra in the main square had been replaced by the Spanish equivalent of an Irish showband, playing every kind of music from traditional to pop. They could give The Who a run for their decibels. There were thousands in the square now. The noise of a large Spanish audience can compete with any amplifier or speaker system. So it was a little harder to get to sleep that night. But eventually the strains of joy and fun soothe over the pumping of the bass and sleep came, assisted by the aftereffects of expensive Rueda and Rioja wines, plates of *lechazo,* and all that argy-bargy. We slept the sleep of Spain.

PROVINCIA DE SEGOVIA

On the road out of town the poppies were already in line, all set to greet us and show us the way. 'Where've you been, lads? Hey ho, let's go!' They nodded and bobbed, full of oomph.

Smooth roads, six knees and legs all still spinning smoothly enough too. Bernard MacLaverty in 'Midwinter Break' talks about 'ailment hour', when the leading characters, a couple getting on in years, agree to confine bouts of complaints and fears for their health to an hour a day. We all of us felt right as rain and as young as our friends the poppies. But cycling long distance in your sixties, even early sixties, betrays weaknesses, mysterious little aches and discomforts that you hope will just go away. Eddie's knee's been playing up since his fall in the tunnel. Liam has had a dodgy foot since before we left. My head has settled down, but my hamstring plays up after a few hours in the saddle. We're halfway through our endeavour and, if anything, we're feeling stronger. But you can't keep pretending you're twenty, and your body reminds you on a regular basis.

We can't resist playing for the poppies, our biggest fans. We busk outside a small town in a wheat field, bordered by the crowd-surfing *amapolas* – the sweet Spanish word for poppies. It's a quiet road but a few people still pass by. They don't give three old Scottish guys in the middle of a field playing jigs in cycle helmets a second glance. ('*Whack for my daddy-o, there's whiskey in the jar-o…*')

The day, the road, the tarmac, it's all lovely. But every time we cycle through a village we're aware of the problem afflicting rural Spain. So many villages and little towns feel too quiet. Only elderly people on the streets, if anyone at all, shops and restaurants shut. Play parks rusty and overgrown. A report in 2018 found that the country has nearly 4,000 villages with fewer than 500 residents. A third of them, fewer than 100. Village Spain is at risk of extinction. It was an issue in the General Election, and still is for the upcoming European and local elections. There have been marches in Madrid, demanding that something be done to help the countryside. The Spanish interior is emptying out. Look at a map of Spain, all the thriving cities, with the exception of Madrid, are on the coast, from Barcelona, through Valencia, to Almeria and Málaga; Vigo, Seville and Cádiz. In villages from Jaén to Guadalajara they need doctors, dentists, banks, post offices, shops, young people.

Urbanisation is a global problem, and each country has its own particular conditions, economic and cultural circumstances. In Spain it started later than in most of Europe. Slowly at first in the 1950s, off the back of reprisals and divisions after the Civil War. But the process has accelerated in the last twenty years. The building boom of the 1990s and early 2000s, concentrating almost solely on the touristic coastal regions, followed fast by the crash of 2008, as destructive in Spain as Greece and other countries, all aggravated rural decline. The Spanish central plateau has some of the lowest population densities in Europe, comparable only to the Scottish Highlands.

But there is one crucial difference here in Spain. Passing through and stopping, sometimes staying over, in small places you know when it's the weekend. Suddenly the empty villages are busier. Spaniards, resident in Madrid or Barcelona or Valencia, are hardwired to their ancestral village. Among my acquaintances I can't think of anyone who calls themselves a *Madrileño/a*, *Barceloní* or *Barcelonina*. A *Pamplonés/a* or *Alacantino/a*. Three or more generations removed, they're still from 'their' village. Devotedly. They go back for family anniversaries, for local fiestas and saints' days, Christmas. As many weekends as they can. 'A Spaniards' first loyalty,' Gerald Brenan wrote, 'is to the village'.

My friend and colleague, Ana Zabalegui has retired from a life in the arts in Pamplona to live between there and Monreal, her village. She talks with such affection about the place. But she also points out that Monreal is only 20 kilometres from Pamplona. The villages furthest from cities suffer the most. People like Ana will add, eventually, to the ageing population of towns like Monreal. But they still bring vitality, and ideas, and younger people in their wake. The interior of Spain is, one way or another, nearly always remarkable – stark, or lush, towns high on rugged mountains or swathed in meadowlands, with ancient castles or secret histories.

Nava de la Asunción has a primary school, shops on the high street, a sports centre which we saw young people going to and fro from. But the playpark looked very overgrown. Our hotel was a little down-at heel and the food uninspiring. While we ate, the dining room filled up with men. Not a woman in sight. None of the usual Spanish clamour and guffaws. These men ate or drank silently. Some of them never took their eyes off the bullfight on the TV. There was a mood in the air of some unsettled argument; things that mustn't be spoken of. The wall of the sports centre had a poem inscribed on it. It took us some time to identify it. 'I'll Never Be Young Again,' by Jaime Gil de Biedma. One of the post-war poets. I knew of him, and it was good to be in the town of a poet's birth. But the piece selected for the wall seemed a little downbeat for a gym, and perhaps worryingly prophetic about the future of the writer's town and its youth: a mournfully entitled poem, lamenting that life's all about getting old and dying.

* * *

A strange education truly, this jumbled mixture of saints' lives and knight errantry!

Gabriela Cunninghame Graham,
Santa Teresa: Being Some Account of Her Life and Times

The road to Segovia city is fairly flat. Entry into the city itself is almost vertical. On cobblestones, tucking in from the traffic, round sharp bends, for about a mile. The view to our left of the castle sitting above us gave us the motivation we needed. I was the only one who had never been in Segovia.

Our hotel, right by that cathedral, was the best located of the whole tour. Smack in the main square, presumably originally an old grand residence. We were far from the deprivations of Laurie Lee now. *Two* nights of opulence and rest.

It had been a few days since we had busked publicly, and we'd decided we would perform again today. As soon as we were given our rooms, I went out into the square to watch a couple of seasoned street musicians. Two men, in their forties I guessed, probably Spanish though they sang songs from Mexico, Cuba, Trinidad, North America, as well as Spain. One or two pop songs in English. The singer played guitar and harmonica; the drummer had a puppet attached to his bass pedal that danced to the rhythm.

Listen and learn. Apart from knowing your material and playing it well, having a varied and likeable repertoire, these two offered another key lesson. Even when noone was listening, locals and tourists, lovers and families passing them by without a glance, they kept on performing with real commitment. They played at full volume, smiling, nodding, singing out like they were doing the Hollywood Bowl. Between songs they addressed the audience – an audience of either none, or uninterested pedestrians. Never a hint of annoyance, or embarrassment. Resolutely ignoring the reality that they were, often, talking to themselves.

Eventually, their geniality, their self-confidence and musical ability stopped somebody in their tracks. I remember this from busking years ago, once one person stops others nearly always do. The first listener gives you legitimacy. Buskers fluctuate between playing to crowds and being ignored. All day long. If I'm going to busk more here, with and without the lads when they're gone, then I need to do it with gusto. It's showbiz.

The only distinction this time round was that I/we weren't doing it for money. Which would cause me a problem later on. For most buskers – I imagine these two guys included – it's their principal source of income. For many people busking can be a desperate and precarious job. Think of the Eastern Europeans playing in every city in the UK these days. The horn-fiddle (properly a stroviol), accordion, occasionally a dulcimer. The level of skill is variable but generally these women and men are serious players. Years of practice, years of experience, and they're playing on Byres Road or Embankment Tube station for, sometimes literally, pennies. In some cases they're restricted – as I am – by a limited repertoire.

I remember being delighted when, writing all day in an office in Pamplona's Teatro Gayarre, a Romanian busker took up his position directly below my window. By mid-morning I had to go and balance my laptop on the dim back stairs. The same three songs, over and over and over... But he wasn't busking for fun, a little adventure. He was in his sixties too. But for him it was survival.

Our busk in Segovia was not of that ilk. It was essential we play here, it being a city where Machado, the original author of one of our theme songs, 'Cantares', had lived for many years. We located ourselves at the far, high, end of the aqueduct.

The Aqueduct, this... *thing*. We have seen so many beautiful cities and such seductive countryside on our tours in Spain, but the Segovia aqueduct is, without a moment's hesitation, the most perfect structure I have ever seen. It just sits there. As if it were still, for all it cared, in Roman times. You can walk its length, touch the stone – warm, like skin – take photos between its arches, lunch at either side of it, view it from above, below, close-up, from a distance. It doesn't care. It just *is*. And it is not yours.

A massive, exquisite, drystane dyke, the engineering is gobsmacking. The structure rises, a little wall, off a busy main road, bends melodically around some now long-gone obstruction, levitates up and into the old walls of the city. It disappears into the Moorish – wall like it keeps on going in some other dimension. Through rock and history, back through the Reconquista, Al-Andalus, into Roman times, reaching down to the graves of the people who built it, providing a bridge for them to return when the Fourth Watch of night, the Cuarte Vigilia, is over, and Segovia – *Ptolomea* – can return to its past. The ever-present Now, time and space intertwining in dimensions we can't grasp.

The perfect place to play 'The Irish Washerwoman', and 'Whisky In The Jar'? (Then again, pre-Roman, pre-aqueduct, Segovia's origins are Celtiberian.) We had a captive audience – choosing a position where the aqueduct meets the old city wall, a popular viewpoint. People stopped. Tapped their feet and clapped between songs. As ever, a little mystified as to what to do with their coins and – I noticed once or twice – notes. Notes for notes. Some of them were curious enough to ask *why* we were playing Scots and Irish songs with our cycling helmets on? (We had decided, some busks ago, that this would be our *look*, our USP, like mop-tops or the Gallaghers' anoraks, rappers' hoodies.) A reasonable question which gave us the opening we needed to tell our story. We chatted to a few tourists, to a local woman taking her out-of-town friend around the city. When they heard about our blog they signed up to it. A lot of folk did along the way. We talked to a man from Valencia, quick to tell us that Valencia's better than Segovia.

And then the Guardia came.

Sadly we had finished and were packing up. The Guardia looked disappointed too, no use in asking for permits now, or informing us that buskers are not allowed on the city walls. We'd been hoping we'd have another run-in with the police. We reckoned now we could handle the dreaded Guardia. In your sixties, it's good you can still bother the cops. These officers just gave us a disapproving look and went on their way.

I had planned to meet Robin Cunninghame Graham in Segovia. Robin's a teacher and couldn't get away until that evening, but he had given us some tips for where to eat. What *lechazo* is to Valladolid, *cochinillo* is to Segovia. Suckling pig. Another baby animal stretched out, slaughtered and skinned. But it's been a speciality in Segovia since Roman times and we were lunching, prime seats in the house, under the Aqueduct. The Aqueduct didn't care.

We met Robin in a more down-to-earth hostelry. They had a good selection of wines at affordable prices – Robin's something of an expert, his wife being in the wine trade. I'd met him several times over the years at various events celebrating the life and works of his great grand uncle, Robert Bontine Cunninghame Graham. This journey of ours has several ghostly Virgils. Laurie Lee, of course, Brenan, Rosalía de Castro, and Antonio Machado, whose statue here in Segovia welcomed us every time we stepped out of our hotel in the square. Soon, we would enter the land of Cervantes and Quixote. For me, Don Roberto and his partner Gabriela have been guiding spirits for many years.

Robin and his great grand uncle Robert look alike. That their two names are virtually synonymous is pleasing. Robin, Scottish and living in Spain with his Spanish wife, looks every inch the English gentleman. Tie, *americano*, loafers, bespectacled. Polite. The most famous images of Don Roberto on the other hand are quixotic, the great man in various fancy dress, particularly the flamboyant gaucho of the pampas. Nevertheless, he and Robin are clearly the same family. The legend of his antecedent hung over Robin's childhood. Not always helpfully – there was an expectation that he and his cousins should follow in his footstep and become as great, as bold, as globetrotting, as politically successful, as famous. Without the money, the lands, or the spirit of those times. Robin's grandfather was the political opposite of Roberto. An admiral, supporter of the Conservative Party, he always wrote "North Britain" instead of "Scotland" in his letters. Yet he still worshipped his Scottish nationalist anarchist ancestor.

As we chat, Robin tells us that he's an active member of an Evangelical Church. I'm not sure why this surprises me. Most Evangelicals I have known have been conservative, including in their politics. (Later, Robin told me that he is essentially Church of Scotland, and that the evangelical church he belongs to is as close a match as he can find in Spain. He tried Catholicism when he first arrived. It was the Mariology that drove him to change – personally it's one of the aspects of Catholicism I like, and miss.) Robin is culturally, personally and politically, forward-thinking.

Online and in person he speaks out against injustice and speaks up for equality and probity. There is a line I'd seen him use on social media: 'Christianity is about helping others and controlling yourself. When it becomes about controlling others and helping yourself, it ain't Christianity'.

Over a silky Rueda wine, Robin's recommendation, perfect for the sticky evening heat, we get talking about his great grand uncle's Spanish connections.

'Robert's grandmother was a Spanish-speaker. Her father was Italian and her mother Spanish. She grew up mainly in Cádiz. Her daughter, Robert's mother, Anna Elizabeth, was born on her father's flagship, HMS Barham, off the coast of Venezuela. She spent the first five years of her life in Caracas and then in Scotland and England. Robert himself spoke with a slight inherited Andalusian accent. Spain was a second home to him, returning here throughout his life. 'But he was a Scot first and foremost.' Like Robin himself, it occurs to me.

Don Roberto, the first British MP to declare himself a social-ist, became the founding president of the SNP in 1934. 'I want a national parliament with the pleasure of knowing that the taxes are wasted in Edinburgh instead of London,' he once joked.

Becoming an MP didn't temper his radical spirit. No sooner had he been elected, in 1886, than he joined a demonstration against unemployment in Trafalgar Square. Things got out of hand – they do when Robert's around – and the new MP was jailed for six weeks for fighting with police officers. Back in his seat he then got into trouble for using bad and irate language in the House.

Almost forty years before helping form the SNP, Cunninghame Graham had founded the Scottish Parliamentary Labour Party. Ultimately, he gave up on any parliament.

Robin quotes his great grand uncle: 'The enemies of Scottish Nationalism are not the English, for they were ever a great and generous folk, quick to respond when justice calls. Our real enemies are among us, born without imagination'.

The Spanish philosopher Ortega y Gasset said of Don Roberto: *'Un aristócrata de vieja alcurnia y socialista de nueva cepa'* – an aristocrat of the old school and a pioneering socialist of the new.

A group of *Segovianos* come in, work colleagues perhaps. They stand at the bar, order wine and tapas – olives, chorizo, artichokes. They laugh and talk and nod to us. We order another wine, a different one recommended by Robin. The four of us are talking again about the study of language itself. Liam mentioned Noam Chomsky's attack on simplistic behaviourist theories of language acquisition. Behaviourists maintain that we acquire language via conditioning, a process of stimulus/response and reward – which, apart from anything else, led to a lot of boring language drills for language students of our era. Chomsky argued that humans have an innate ability to acquire language, his theory of a 'Universal Grammar'. Steven Pinker's more recent work on language compares universal grammar to the hard drive on a computer: the particular language we each speak is the software. Pinker debunks myths about how language determines thought. The cliché that Inuit people think differently about snow because they have more words for it than in other languages. Or Scots for rain.

Eddie, Liam and Robin are all language teachers and broadly agree with another linguistic expert, Steven Krashen, that we learn a second language mainly by listening to it, so long as we have clues and connections to get the gist of what's going on. So if foreign students come to the UK to study, say, geography, rather than spend a lot of time in English classes, forcing them to speak when they don't want to, it's more effective to put them directly into the geography class with concepts and ideas they're already familiar with. 'My own experience,' Robin says, 'is that we learn through reading as much as listening.'

This is back on my daughter's territory. Emma's interested in Chomsky and his politics but thinks his ideas on language are masculinist. I had heard Emma argue that his theory of universal language fails to take into account gender, sexuality and race. And we're back to discussing whether or not a language can be sexist.

Language, how we use it, how it changes through time, what it says about us, cropped up over and over. Crossing from Galician speaking areas, through Leonese, Castilian Spanish, to the land of Valenciá, talking about Basques and Catalans, the words we use are endlessly political and sometimes divisive.

Spanish speakers can be magnificently athletic swearers. The things they can do to the chalice, or to a mother's milk, to all the saints of heaven, are imaginative to put it mildly. Translate them into English and they sound hideously violent and offensive. The C word in Spanish, *coño*, is relatively commonplace and generally socially acceptable, flung into sentences the way we might use 'well', or 'you know', a pause filler, a bridge between spoken ideas. This may, I admit, simply reflect the company I have kept over the years – no doubt some Spanish speakers would never use the word. But I haven't met many. In most contexts *coño* has, in Spanish, none of the misogyny, or bodily disgust that its English counterpart does. In general usage, the relationship with female genitalia is distant if not completely lost. I've heard, often, the steep hill in Arcos de La Frontera being referred to as *La Cuesta del Coño,* because the view is so breathtaking and beautiful from the top. Making it up the hill and seeing the view, people cry *'¡Ay coño!'*. Working class dialects across the UK – and, it seems to me most prolifically in working class Scotland – share some of that colloquial Spanish sensibility. Lots of men use the term as a phrase of endearment between themselves, calling each other '*coño*' (not in Spanish obviously, but while I can bring myself to type the Spanish form, the C word in English screams from the page). Libby, an actor friend of mine tells the story of going to play a part in a short film I had written. Arriving at the location, a well-known and much-loved industry driver gave her the lowdown on the rest of the cast and crew. Pointing from his cab Jas said, 'Him, he's an okay wee *coño*, Joanna there's a mad *coño*. And that's Colin – he's a bastard.' It was clear who she had to watch out for. The English or Scots rendering still feels more deliberately earthy than in Spanish. And gender runs deep and problematic in all language.

That observation seemed a bit full-on for a quiet drink under Segovia's aqueduct with the scholarly Robin. But I did tell this story: I was with my Auntie May, the least educated, and aware of it, of my gaggle of Maryhill aunts, at a funeral many years ago on a Glasgow day of sleet, hail, and snell wind. Walking along with the parish priest, hyper-correcting herself for him, May said, 'Dearie me, father, would you look at those *wholestones*.' Class, too, is linguistically complicated.

Tomorrow the three of us will be back on the road – further into the Castile of Machado and eventually Cervantes – so we finish our drinks and walk under the aqueduct with Robin. On the way, he tells me I'm right about Roberto living for a while in Vigo. We reckon the view from his house might well have been similar to ours from the hotel – and Laurie Lee's from the hilltop on his first night in Spain. I watch Robin walk back, homeward bound. A mid-tempo gait, looking around, interested in his world. In his early sixties now, gracious, but sharp-eyed. An Englishman, for having lived more than half his life there, but a Scot too, one who shares his ancestor's love for the country and speaks up for it publicly and astutely. And a *Segoviano auténtico*.

Don Roberto is getting a little more attention these days thanks to the efforts of people like Robin and our mutual friends in Scotland. But it has been Gabriela, Don Roberto's extraordinary wife, who has been more on my mind during this journey.

Gabriela

William Strang, the Scottish painter, used Robert Bontine Cunninghame Graham as his model for Don Quixote. Robert was up for it. The man loved dressing up. Part Spanish, he was a deal more handsome than Cervantes's hero, but his lean frame and long face fitted the bill well.

Now every Don Quixote needs his muse, his inspiration, his impossible, courtly love... his 'Dulcinea del Toboso'.

Despite young Robert's increasingly radical politics, he still liked to cut about Belle Époque Paris on his steed. One day, in the Jardin des Tuileries he almost knocked down a young woman. Or, rather, Lady. She turned out to be – wouldn't she just – Mademoiselle Gabrielle de la Balmondière. A Chilean lady of noble French descent. Two aristocrats looking for love, meet in the city of love. Dumas, Baroness Orczy, couldn't have written it. (But Robert might have!)

Gabrielle, it turns out, was, like Robert, another hopeful writer. Politically motivated, a woman who had travelled. A learned botanist, fluent Spanish speaker. The two of them were made for each other. He brought her back to Scotland, and they were married. From their base in Gartmore and the Lake of Menteith, the couple travelled the world together. Gabriela, as she became known later, hispanifying her name, was particularly active in local politics, becoming a popular and trusted lady laird. She wrote poetry and essays. And she travelled around Spain with just her Galician maid in the footsteps of the, equally extraordinary, St Theresa of Avila. The perfect, beautiful, intellectual, high-born but politicised couple.

Except...

Freewheelin'

When I was making a TV documentary on Cunninghame Graham with director Les Wilson ten years ago it was discovered that three years were missing in Gabriela's life. It took 100 years after her death for the truth to begin to emerge. This is what we knew at the time of making the programme...

Gabriela was *not* half-Chilean, half-French. She was *not*, as she had always said, a convent girl. She was *not* seventeen or eighteen when she met her future husband.
She was not Gabrielle de la Balmondière.

She *was*... Caroline Horsfall. A doctor's daughter from Masham, Yorkshire. Three years older than she claimed.

Dulcinea del Toboso was Quixote's fantasy from reading too many romantic tales. He built his vision of a damsel in distress around the far more ordinary, 'real' hearty rustic girl Aldonza Lorenzo. For the next few years the poor lassie couldn't get rid of the mad old knight in tarnished armor. And, of course, Aldonza was no more real than Dulcinea, both of them figments of the writer Cervantes's imagination.

Carrie was the second of thirteen children. She'd have spoken in an educated Yorkshire accent. Since childhood she'd been determined to escape from boring old Masham. Her niece later reported family stories about Carrie. 'A dynamic personality who delighted her siblings with stories. She was crazy to get on the stage, and ran away twice from home. The first time she was brought back in disgrace'. The second time... *'she's o'er the border and awa'*.

So, she managed her escape. But why hide three years of her life? How come she knows Spanish so well? Well enough to fool natural Spanish speakers throughout her life?

Robin and his cousin Jamie Jauncie, and Lachie Munroe

and others continue to research the Cunninghame Grahams' lives, unearthing new and fascinating material that I can't keep up with for this book. I'll stick to the little we knew at the time. Gaps in evidence allow for conjecture, other narratives. Carrie's younger sister, Grace, wrote a novel. Its heroine is Adelaide. A feisty girl who loved to tell stories and longed to be on the stage. She had 'a fantastic appetite for transferring herself into a heroine of romance or history – Heloise, or Lady Hamilton'. Adelaide runs away. But her plans don't work out. Before she is terribly shamed, she is run over and killed by – wait for it... a horse in the street. What could be worse than dying violently, young? In the nineteenth century, for a woman, social disgrace and ostracism.

Robert Cunninghame Graham wrote often – and with compassion and moral complexity – about sex workers. Almost certainly, he had some first-hand knowledge. Carrie had fallen on hard times and was a courtesan. Chances are she was in the employ of some minor Spanish nobleman – a Hidalgo, like Don Quixote – and lived in that country with him for a while, his concubine. Whether Robert bought her favours, or met her and saw immediately her intelligence and spirit and decided to 'save' her, is guesswork. Choose the story you prefer.

Did Carrie/Gabriela deceive Robert himself? It seems unlikely. Lady Polwarth, Robert's niece and biographer, believed that Gabriela was Carrie's stage name, and that Robert would have known that. But I prefer that they dreamt up 'Gabriela', and all the rest of it, together. Chile, the convent, her new age...

They were in love. They wanted to marry and be together. Yes, they were radicals, forward-thinking people, couldn't give a jot about the fusty conventions of the British upper class. But they had Robert's posh family to consider.

Gabriela Cunninghame Graham, as she now became, is most noted for authoring two books: *Santa Teresa: Being Some Account of Her Life and Times*, and a perceptive translation of St John of the Cross's *The Dark Night of the Soul*. Gabriela/Carrie, *fin-de-siècle* proto feminist radical, spending so much of her time thinking and writing about sixteenth-century Catholic mystics. (Kate O'Brien suggests that had Teresa been born 500 years later she'd have been a staunch supporter of the Republic during the war.)

To research her biography Gabriela walked in the footsteps of St Teresa, along the stony, narrow paths of Castile. She could have gone by train. But no, she travels around by horse. By all accounts a pretty pathetic creature – an old nag. Much as the saint herself must have done, three and a half centuries earlier. Or Don Quixote, around the same time, a little to the east, on Rocinante.

Gabriela writes in her biography of Teresa that as a young girl the future saint became a fan of pulp fiction: 'Books of Knight errantry took the place of the lives of the saints... the literature then so popular amongst all classes of society had not only a certain delicate flavour of idealism, but an unrestrained licentiousness of thought, together with a coarseness and brutality of expression... It is certain that they exercised a powerful influence on Teresa's intellectual development.'

The fallen woman, saved and restored to respectability. I think – despite the dangers, maybe *thanks* to the dangers – Robert and Carrie were having a grand old time of it. In public life, neither of them made much of the transfiguration of Carrie to Gabby. They didn't trade on it, it wasn't important to them in that sense. It was a way of freeing themselves from rules and conventions, allowing them to live the life they wanted and achieve the things they did.

Two writers, living their own fiction. Then again, how much of a fiction is it? What is *real,* and what's not? Maybe Gabriela *became* herself? She made herself up. She was *never* Caroline Horsfall. She just couldn't, no matter how hard she tried, *be* Carrie – daughter of middle-class provincial doctor, predestined to marry another, provincial doctor or lawyer or farmer. She *was*, always had been, in some sense, Gabriela. Intellectual, writer, mystic.

Gabriela wrote a poem once on the subject of Ovid's *Metamorphoses*. In response to his 'Happy is the man who has broken the chains which hurt the mind,' she wrote: *'The real, a lie – the unreal, the living truth.'*

Elsewhere she writes: 'We have denied the possibility of any other plane than that in which we live and breathe... But for all our physical senses can tell us, we may be moving at every step through invisible streets, passing invisible ships – surrounded by a stream of life, as keen, as ardent, as our own.'

Throughout their entire lives, Robert and Gabriela saw though fake boundaries, recognising possibilities, in politics, art, lifestyle. They fought laws and principles they judged false and tried to create the world anew, for themselves and others. In the words of another of her poems, 'The Key':

> *Thoughts moiling and toiling in the depths of me,*
> *Dreams of sweet passion, ecstasies of phantasy,*
> *Where is the golden key to set them free?*

Freewheelin'

The ideas, the ideals the two of them worked for. Social justice, solidarity, Home Rule – what is it, anyway, that makes a nation? How would they feel about Scottish Independence today? And how would they feel about the Catalonia question? About the very idea of Europe – a businessman's club, as unconcerned with the people as any parliament? Or a singular historical achievement thrown away? When is it justifiable, beneficial, to reinvent yourself, or your country, your continent? If your memories simply don't fit, get new ones.

Don Roberto: part Orwell, part Simón Bolívar, part Alan Breck Stewart. Gabriela: agnostic Anglican Catholic, feminist, revolutionary mystic. Quixotic characters, both. Long after his wife's death, Robert wrote: 'It is a natural desire in the majority of men to keep a secret garden in their souls, a something that they do not care to talk about, still less to set down, for the other members of the herd to trample on.'

Gabriela smoked up to 200 cigarettes a day. No surprise, then, but still a tragedy that she died young. Forty-five years old in 1906. The night before her burial, Robert dug her grave with his own hands, and lined it with heather. The following day, sending the mourners off, he filled it in. And he smoked the first of twenty-eight annual fags – he had promised Gabriela that he would return every year to her graveside, and smoke a cigarette in her honour.

I smoked one for both of them, a decade ago. While making the documentary, *The Adventures of Don Roberto*, Les Wilson and I sailed across the Lake of Menteith to the pair of graves, side-by-side, in the grounds of an ancient Augustinian priory, among gnarled Spanish chestnut trees. Gabriela, The Lady of the Lake.

The Plaque beside Gabriela's grave, a quote from Fernando Rojas's *La Celestina*, reads:

> '...*Los muertos abren los ojos a los que viven.*'
> *The dead open the eyes of the living.*

SOUTHERN DIVERSION

We arrive at who we are first by following, then by divergence
Andrew Greig, *The Loch of the Green Corrie*

At Segovia we leave the road that Laurie Lee had travelled. The decision taken months ago in the Trossachs, to cycle to Valencia, meant missing out the section of Laurie's route from Madrid through Andalusia. But this includes parts of Spain I've come to know well over the years.

Lee's description in 1935 of Madrid is recognisable to this day. He doesn't name specific bars but many of them sound like ones I know. In particular a restaurant in the Rastro, Madrid's Barras, which in the late 1970s sold only one red wine, one white, small *cañas* of beer, and one single dish. Behind the bar bubbled a witches' cauldron, massive, scorching, over an open flame. Snails in a hot paprika soup, served with bread. The place gave the impression of having been there for hundreds of years. I'd have thought at least as recently as 1935, in Lee's time. Back in Madrid last year, Moira and I went to find that restaurant. Casa Amadeo specialises in snails, is in the Rastro, and a sign says it has been there since 1942. I'm not convinced, though, that it is the same place. Amadeo serves other dishes too, it's smaller, cleaner, more upmarket than the place I remember. Then again, the Rastro itself has been gentrified, the once working-class area around it now hot property. And it's possible I've idealised the snail restaurant in my memory.

Although the Republican government had to move from the capital to Valencia as early as the end of 1936, the city itself held out to the bitter end of the Civil War in March 1939, bombed relentlessly the entire duration of the war, and suffering dreadful losses at the final Siege of Madrid.

Despite its history, the atmosphere, the drinking habits, the kind of food, the noise, the whole scene that Lee paints can still be found in less trendy areas of Madrid. The city of *Zarzuela* (musical theatre); of Golden Age writers Quevedo, Lope de Vega, Calderón de la Barca. Cascorro Square in the Latin Quarter. Sweeping, almost moving, statues. Real Madrid (the Cibeles Fountain) and Atlético Madrid (Neptune Fountain). A centre for flamenco, and bullfighting.

Lee stops next at Toledo where he meets the poet Roy Campbell who, at the time, enjoyed fame and respect, and was a friend of Elliot and Pound and other artists of the day. A South African, his father was an Ulsterman and his mother from Glenboig, in Liam and Eddie's Lanarkshire.

Lee met him with his wife, Mary Garman, and their two daughters – the beginning of the young traveller's convoluted relationships with female members of the Garman family. (He was lover to Mary's sister, Lorna, then to another sister, Helen. Later he married Helen's daughter, Kitty, who still lives in the Rose cottage in Slad with their daughter Jessy.)

In Toledo the Campbells were broke, Roy hiding from debts in France. But they were kind to young Laurie, feeding him up. They had left England after the poet discovered that his wife was having a torrid affair with Vita Sackville-West. Roy, a Christian, became ever more so. Not much later, dismissive of the attitudes of the Bloomsbury group's moneyed bohemia and other liberal writers and thinkers, Campbell moved towards Catholicism. Both he and Mary were formally received into the Roman Catholic Church – in Altea, a village 15 miles from where I am writing this in Relleu.

When the Civil War broke out a year later, Campbell supported the Falangists. He became the reverse of Ethel Macdonald (born in Bellshill, less than 10 miles from Glenboig, and who we shall meet shortly): if she was an early embedded reporter for the Anarchists, he was the same for Franco's Nationalists. He later claimed that he had fought for Franco in the war, but there is as little evidence of that as Lee's claims to having seen action fighting for the Republicans.

Campbell said that his commitment to Franco came from his abhorrence at the acts of the Communists and Anarchists and the violence of forces against priests and nuns. He claimed to have hidden some clerics from murderous Stalinist bands in Toledo. There were, indeed, numerous incidents of Catholics being rounded up and shot summarily, in public view. Making the documentary *An Anarchist's Story*, I asked Noam Chomsky about such atrocities: 'Yes, at the early stages of the Spanish Anarchist Revolution there were acts of violence – the killing of priests, burning down churches and so on – which were unconscionable,' Chomsky said. The incidents in Toledo were more likely to have been committed by Communist-backed militias, but I imagine Chomsky would stand by his thinking. 'They were a reaction of a very oppressed people to highly oppressive institutions which had been crushing them for centuries. And when people liberate themselves unpleasant things happen.'

Such killings and outrages were committed on all sides at the start of and during a profoundly vicious war. The Red and White Terrors. Paul Preston, in *The Spanish Holocaust*, lists, as a single example, twenty pregnant women dragged out from a maternity hospital and shot in the street by Falangist soldiers. When the war ended in 1939, the reprisals started. An estimated 100,000 republicans were executed, 35,000 more dying in concentration camps.

There is a story in the Spanish news at the moment. Román Morín is now ninety-seven years old and for the first time, thanks to the efforts of the Historical Memory movement, has told his story. A known Republican in Ciudad Real he was given a choice – either serve as a guard in the Nationalist prison in Real Ciudad, or face death himself. During his time, he was forced, including by the local priest, to shoot fellow Republican soldiers. People on both sides of that war have terrible stories to tell, vile memories to have lived with for so long, mostly in silence. Slowly, these legacies are coming out into the open.

* * *

After Toledo, Lee headed south, through Seville to Cádiz. I lived there for a year in 1978–79 and saw something akin to the Spain of 1935.

Spanish friends in Madrid had told me that flamenco was dead. That it belonged to the Franco era. I got off the train at 3AM (a *rápido*, of course – it was due to arrive at seven the previous evening) in San Juan de Diós in Cádiz. The first thing I heard entering the square was a group of teenagers clapping the most astonishingly intricate rhythms. Before any of them even sang you could hear in that clapping echoes of Morocco across the Strait, Jewish cantors expelled 500 years ago, murmurs of Al-Andalus from nearly 1,000 years ago, and the ancient origins of the Spanish *gitano* in Rajastan.

In my first month in Cádiz, between leaving a rented room in a *pensión* and moving into a flat (with a group of young guys doing their military service) there was a night unaccounted for. It didn't worry me. I was nineteen, I had some money, Cádiz was cheap. I had already found the cheapest bars in districts like Santa María (not to be confused with the prosperous town of El Puerto de Santa María, a pleasant boat ride across the water). I busked uptown – you wouldn't earn much in the crumbling areas where I took my earnings to spend in the old taverns and drinking dens. There was a *callejón,* or alleyway – now cleaned up – just off San Juan de Diós where every second bar was a pick-up joint or a brothel. The women used to stand in the doorways and ask passers-by in for 'a drink'. A percentage of them, it took you a moment to realise, were men in drag. Glasgow is a port city too, but I had never seen any drag queens there. Was Cádiz always a centre for gays and sexual freedom, or was it a reaction to the end of *Franquismo*, the rise of Almodóvar and a new confidence in being 'other'? I don't know.

That night in the barrio Santa María I came across an impromptu street party. It was hot, early September. A young man, a Che Guevara look-alike, was playing guitar while the rest of his family and neighbours ate their supper out in the cooler street. A woman, in her late sixties maybe, finished eating and, clearing up, began to dance her way into and out of the house. She was encouraged by others around her, with claps and cries *¡Dale! ¡Venga!',* so she began to perform. They had seen me, entering the street at the corner and stopping to watch. They didn't seem to mind. The woman grabbed her skirt between her legs and began to stamp and turn, moving her free arm in long swoops. I've heard the arm movement described as picking olives from the tree and putting them into an imagined basket on your other side. The woman had varicose veins, was wearing an apron, was short and stout. But her dance was fluid and sensuous. A man – her husband? – got up and joined her. Their dance was not a straightforward *Sevillana,* but something that looked, to my untrained eye, improvised, putting together strict rules and shapes in fleeting little creations. Che Guevara played louder. A younger woman began to sing, the sound like a fine and complex wine, notes of ancient rejection and expulsion, Jewish and Islamic tears. The *solera* system of Jerez wines involves adding fresh new wines to old, the casks never emptying so that in every glass there is a portion of wine decades and more in the ageing. The woman singing that night was young and she sang of the glories of growing up in an aged community, both poor and sophisticated. Her song ancient and dazzlingly fresh.

A man sitting near me pointed to an empty chair beside him. I sat down. They filled my glass, gave me bread and sardines. The group at the table wasn't fixed, some left and others arrived, changing places with other tables and groups in the street. They pointed at my violin, but I wasn't ready to play after hearing such artistry. We tried to converse but the Cádiz accent is notoriously difficult, even for other Spaniards. The Glaswegian of Spain. In this barrio the dialect was even thicker, almost secret. By the end of more than a year living there I still understood little of what was being said in streets like this. Eventually, when I reckoned that everybody had drunk too much to judge, and the echoes of the dance, guitar and singing had faded, I played a few tunes. Soft, slow airs – 'Fear a' Bhata', 'Ae Fond Kiss', 'Red Red Rose', 'Carrickfergus', 'Danny Boy'. I'd had enough to drink to think that the music suited the thinning night, the bow pulling in memories from across the dark Atlantic.

At some point I was invited in, the door of the house leading directly into the kitchen, and was given more to eat. Back out on the street more songs could be heard, but this time from off-stage, guitars and voices floating down like petals from rooms above us or further up the road. Every now and then someone – a child, a mother, grandad – would give a little spontaneous dance coming in or out of a house. When I left – to quiet good-byes, winks and slaps on the back – it was still dark. By the time I reached a bar near Carlos's flat, one that I knew opened early, the sun was beginning to rise.

Some months later, around the same area I saw, as I understood it, music being used in a way new to me. I was eating, the cheapest *menú del día*, mid-afternoon. A man in his fifties was at the bar, drunk. An unusual sight in Spain. A woman of about the same age appeared at the door. She shouted to the barman, but I didn't catch what she said. Then she began to sing. I thought perhaps she was busking. Would sing her song then pass around a hat or open the pocket of her apron for coppers. But halfway through her song the drunk at the bar joined in, sang a verse himself. She waited till he was finished, then she sang again. Slowly I began to think they were having a conversation. A kind of musical domestic.

'Get yourself up the road. Your tea's out.'

'Leave a man to drink in peace, woman.'

'It's your family's blood you're drinking, you good-for-nothing!' *¿Me estás oyendo, inútil…?*

And so it went on. Nobody else in the bar seemed to notice. Perhaps this was a regular performance. Eventually, she won the day. He emptied his glass, banged it down on the counter and went off down the road with her.

My year in Cádiz turned out to be one long celebration of Flamenco. It stunned me how poor people eking a living found the time, patience and commitment to learn to play such complex guitar, dance such intricate movements. The singing, on the other hand, seemed to come almost naturally, from some bottomless well of collective memory and pain. *Cante jondo*. Of course, that sound comes from practice and skill too. Lorca himself said that he is not an artist thanks to any god or devil, but because he understands what writing is and he works very hard at it. The same is true of *cantaores*.

In the late 1970s Paco de Lucia was erupting as an international star; Camarón de la Isla had been modernising the form musically and lyrically. El Lebrijano was at his height. Carmen Linares was pushing boundaries. The Montoya and (my personal favourite) the Morente families were laying down musical dynasties, combining Ladino and grunge and sacred song. My friends in Madrid were wrong, flamenco continues to move and adapt. From the classics of La Niña de los Peines and Antonio Mairena, both still listened to avidly, to Rosalía and Kiko Veneno… As the cry was back in Cádiz: '*¡El Flamenco está muerto! Viva el Flamenco!*'

I've never met a Spaniard yet who can tell me exactly who is and who is not a '*Gitano*'. There are some very identifiable Roma or travelling communities in Spain just as there are in the UK and Ireland. But people often call older, deprived areas 'Gypsy'. I've often heard, particularly in the South, people curse and scorn 'Gypsies', meaning those they consider beneath them or disreputable, and in the next breath proudly tell you they have *gitano* blood.

After our coast-to-coast ride I discovered another traveller-fiddler-writer who preceded not only me but Laurie Lee himself. Walter Fitzwilliam Starkie played and wandered through Spain a couple of years before Lee. Starkie was an academic, friend of Shaw and Yeats and O'Casey, expert in 'gypsy' language, culture and music. And a Catholic right-winger, supporter of Franco. His two books, *Spanish Raggle-Taggle: Adventures with a Fiddle in Northern Spain* (1934) and *Don Gypsy: Adventures with a Fiddle in Barbary, Andalusia and La Mancha* (1936) are firmly in the Spanish picaresque tradition – unruly, eccentric, funny, if often scurrilous. Starkie, amazingly, inveigled his way into the now fêted flamenco *Concurso de Cante Jondo* (Spanish Deep Song conference) at the Alhambra in 1922. Organised by the composer Manuel de Falla, together with the new sensation of Spanish letters, Federico García Lorca, it was the event that christened the most influential movement in Spanish arts of the last century, the Generation of '27. The rationale of the event was to celebrate *gitano* music and culture and find within it artistic expression for a new age. These were musicians and writers who had detected something ancient, noble and essential, not only in Gypsy expression but in the *gitanos* themselves. Not everyone gave them then, or now, the same respect. Or even recognised them as a people, or community.

The road that Laurie Lee walked in 1935 from Cádiz to Málaga I drove in 1979. Or rather, I was driven, by a flat mate, Llopis, who was taking me and Carlos and another, Madrileño, flatmate Juan, to Valencia to see the fiesta of *Las Fallas*. So it must have been March.

Lee writes of the section he walked from Algeciras – a town he judged to sport small-town, almost quaint, corruption, but which still feels to me downright dangerous – to Málaga: 'an exhausted shore, seemingly forgotten by the world…Estepona, Marbella, and Fuengirola.' A mere ten years later, Lee himself says those forgotten towns were fast becoming millionaires' playgrounds. Nowadays centres for international and political corruption.

I remember my Spanish flatmates being enraged, seeing a road sign in English rather than Spanish. I wonder what they must make of it now. Resorts with English, Dutch and Scottish bars, where nobody speaks Spanish, where they're drinking pints and eating McDonalds.

1979 was well before mobile phones, only slow mail and crackly *Telefónica* connections in provincial towns like Cádiz. But we were aware of the fall of Phnom Penh, Sandinistas overthrowing the dictator Somoza in Nicaragua, and a different kind of revolution in Iran. Back home we heard that the Scottish devolution referendum had failed to get the 40 per cent of the electorate needed. Spain held its first democratic election under the terms of 1978 Spanish Constitution. Rod Stewart asked if we thought he was sexy, and Gloria Gaynor proclaimed she would survive. I busked the Spanish translation of Chiquitita and everybody danced *Rock and Roll en la Plaza del Pueblo.*

Back on the road in 2019, south-eastwards from Segovia through Civil War battlegrounds, we got snippets of news on our phones and in hotel rooms: Bolsonaro elected in Brazil, Brexit dividing the UK ever more deeply, the steady rise of Vox, the Spanish acting Prime Minister making it almost impossible for anyone to form a governing pact with his Socialist Party. Rod Stewart back on tour; Abba too, in hologram form.

And the hardest hill climb was round the corner for us cyclists…

PROVINCIA DE GUADALAJARA /COMUNIDAD DE MADRID

There's no one thing that's true. It's all true.
Ernest Hemingway, *For Whom the Bell Tolls*

The Navacerrada Pass: approx. 1,900 metres; 6,250 feet; one and a half times up Ben Nevis; twice up Ben Lomond. In under 20 kilometres.

As well as the challenge, particularly on what turned out to be the coldest day of our journey, there were other reasons for climbing up through the Navacerrada Pass. In May 1937, exactly eighty-two years before us, the Republican Army mounted an offensive here in an attempt to stop Franco's troops advancing north from Segovia. International *brigadistas* were involved – and defeated, suffering huge losses of life. Through the Non-Intervention Agreement in 1937, the western democracies effectively supported Franco's nationalist rebels. But volunteers, determined to fight fascism, ignored it and were smuggled into Spain – as George Orwell was. The International Brigades recruited volunteers from many countries. Fifty thousand of them, with Glaswegian volunteers outnumbering volunteers from any other city, made their way to Spain – then a distant country. Over 500 British *brigadistas* were killed.

Moving up through La Granja to Valsaín you pass battle-grounds and strategic centres. There's an Education Centre, dedicated largely to ecology, flora and fauna. We got off our bikes and asked in the centre where we might see Civil War sites. The man behind the counter was less than forthcoming. Behind his desk he looked out plans of the grounds but was vague about the locations we were interested in. Another man came along – a friend of the official, though whether a colleague in the centre or not we couldn't tell. This man took the opposite tack. He gave us precise directions, was knowledgeable and pleased we had some knowledge of the conflict. We came across such contradictory attitudes throughout Spain.

About 100 yards from the Education Centre is an old sign, clearly marked *Paisaje De Guerra,* Civil War Area. There is a track leading to old bunkers and gun emplacements. Some of the trenches have been re-excavated. All this since the end of the Franco regime which did what it could to airbrush out memories of the war and the Republicans.

We couldn't venture too far in. The cold was getting to us, the sweat from cycling uphill in flimsy bike gear chilling us. We had a long way to go – we had only climbed a few hundred feet and at this point had no idea just *how* hard the rest of the hill would be, and how long it would take us. We were keen to perform, and record, some little act of commemoration of our own. We found a suitable spot and I fetched my violin. But the cold had done for it. The moment I touched it the bridge collapsed and two strings broke. We decided not to risk opening Liam's ukulele case. Laurie Lee's violin fell to pieces too, in Málaga, so he rightly attributes the cause to heat rather than cold. It was worse for him, being his only source of income. But here, where I really wanted to play, I had some inkling of how he must have felt.

We had hoped to play 'Freedom Come All Ye', to honour not only the fallen and the wounded, but for people with whom we have some kind of personal connections: Hamish Henderson, who wrote the song, never fought in the Spanish Civil War, but I knew him in the 1980s when he hosted events for Scottish veterans; Willy Maley, co-author with his brother of the play *From The Calton To Catalonia*, a tribute to their father and his comrades who went to Spain to fight; Mike Arnott, TUC Secretary in Dundee who has done much to celebrate the lives and deaths of the *Brigadistas*; Don Coutts and Daniel Gray – who I worked with on the STV series *Scots Who Fought Franco*, had spent years interviewing Scottish *Brigadistas*, and Daniel's book *Homage to Caledonia* is a fitting tribute to them all; and for Mike Gonzalez, lifelong friend, political activist, and important early influence on all three cyclists. Mike's father had fought Franco and escaped to London at the end of the war.

It was Mike who first told me about Ethel Macdonald. Ethel was an anarchist who reported the war from Barcelona – we'll hear more about her in a moment. I had made a BBC documentary about her, then later wrote a biography, *An Anarchist's Story* (Birlinn, 2009). Standing in that old battleground, I thought of the statue of La Pasionaria, Dolores Ibarurri, the great Basque Republican leader who first cried '¡No pasarán!' – they shall not pass! Ethel and Dolores never met, which is perhaps just as well, having very different stances on the Spanish Civil War. But both were thoughtful, courageous women.

There is a beautiful statue on the banks of the Clyde in the centre of Glasgow of Dolores Ibarurri. She stands, arms aloft, the embodiment of courage and hope. There are two plaques. One her own words: 'Better to die on your feet than live for ever on your knees.' (Yes, La Pasionaria said it long before Mel Gibson's William Wallace; she was most likely paraphrasing the great Mexican revolutionary Emiliano Zapata.) The other plaque reads: The City of Glasgow and the British Labour Movement pay tribute to the courage of those men and women who went to Spain to fight Fascism 1936–1939. 2,100 volunteers went from Britain; 534 were killed, 65 of whom came from Glasgow.

I'd like to think that, from the vantage point of eighty years since the conflict, with the right on the rise again, Ethel would be happy to see La Pasionaria standing guard over our river.

In the end we sang the 'Freedom Come All Ye'. Shivering, and badly, no doubt, but it felt right in that place. The trees themselves had the look of mourners, standing cold by a mass graveside and a lost cause. I like to think they nodded their consent, before sighing in the snell wind.

We carried on up through the pass, the sky getting cloudier, glowering with the long-held anger of injustices yet to be righted. Hitting the first steep bend and seeing the road fly up into the clouds I repeated my own version of Eddie's *Lizzy McKim Hamill Morrison* mantra, '*It is what it is. It will be what it will be. We'll get there*'.

We rode alone for most of the hill, going at our own pace, stopping when we needed to. Liam photographed each sign that announced another 100 metres up. I began to worry I wouldn't make it to the top. We had all agreed that this whole trip was about crossing Spain, not bike-club bravado about never getting off and pushing. In the event, I never pushed, but I had to stop three times to catch my breath and rest my legs. We climbed slowly into the low-hanging clouds, the temperature dropping drastically. On another day the scenery and the views may be better – we'll never know – but that afternoon it felt like the clouds and hills, the nearly perpendicular road, were closing in on us, ambushing us. José Camilo Cela, passing the surrounding peaks on a train in the 1940s names some of them: *La Maliciosa* (Malevolence), *Las Cabezas de Hierro* (Iron Heads), all of them covered in snow.

It was in the Navacerrada Pass that Ernest Hemingway set the final scene from his Civil War novel, *For Whom The Bell Tolls*. Robert Jordan, the hero, is wounded after blowing up a bridge to hold off the Nationalist army. He turns down an offer from a fellow-fighter to shoot him dead – the Fascists are likely to find him soon, and torture him for information. Jordan, being a typical Hemingway macho man, resolves to take one of them before they take him. We never find out – the book ends with Jordan waiting, probably to die. He *'could feel his heart beating against the pine needle floor of the forest'*. Every now and then we crossed little bridges over rivers, deep below in the ravines. I wondered if any of them, rebuilt, had been the one Robert Jordan blew up. Even though I knew he didn't exist, and never blew up anything.

It tells you something of our own heroic exploits that the bar at the top of the hill was a ski centre which had a temperature sign reading 2° C. It didn't *feel* like two degrees. Clearly it wasn't taking into account the wind-chill factor – it felt like -2° C. We got inside quick and ordered coffee, water, soup and sandwiches, walking around, rubbing our hands, desperately trying to warm up.

The good thing about any ascent, as every cyclist knows, is that it leads to a descent. Down the other side. The pay-off for all the hard work, the achievement prize. Not on this occasion.

None of us were equipped for cold weather. As we had on Misty Mountain in Galicia we took as many layers from our panniers as we could, until we looked like three toddlers happed up on trikes. We didn't have cold weather gloves, so our hands were freezing all the way down, worrying about frostbite. Even more worrying was that we couldn't move our fingers, so couldn't brake. Flying down round tight blind-corners, the gradient every bit as sheer as the climb up, we used the little technique we had to try and slow – leaning back on the bike, using your body as a windbrake, zig-zagging on the little bit of road we had without crossing the central line. The broken fiddle didn't seem to help much as a windbreak.

At the end of the day, safe and sound, Liam wrote one of his homages to Machado, poems in both English and Spanish in the style of *Campos de Castilla*:

Sierras de Castilla

Sierras de Castilla
Señorías, omniscientes, implacables
Pistas de belleza casi divina
Testigos de crueldades inimaginables

Mountain Ranges of Castille

Mountain ranges of Castille
Majestic, omniscient, implacable
Hinting at beauty almost divine
Witness to cruelties unimaginable

Ethel

'Governments will never save the people. They exist to exploit and destroy the people. There is but one force that can save the people – and that is the people themselves.'

A young woman walks, wide-eyed, down the Ramblas in the early morning. The sky's a lively, welcoming blue, the air balmy. She's been in Barcelona for only twelve hours; she has a notebook at the ready. She's small, quietly dressed, knows how to disappear into a crowd.

Freewheelin'

The flower-sellers are out in strength this morning, which surprises her, given the situation. It could be just another day in an ordinary city.

But this is the most exciting place to be in late 1936. Especially for Ethel Macdonald.

War is sweeping over Spain, and although the Catalan capital is preparing for battle, there's an air of optimism, exhilaration. The city is in the throes of the most profound revolution of the twentieth century. Workers run businesses by committee. The police force has been abolished. Two-thousand years of sexual politics overturned. Anarchism – not anarchy – for the only time in its history is the official state system.

Ethel jots down a few notes – she knows no shorthand, can barely type – but these observations will form the first of many despatches that will grow in import and drama over the next ten months.

'Birds were singing in the trees and the sky was the most beautiful blue I have ever seen. Civilian soldiers dressed in dungarees and little red and black "Glengarry" bonnets, smoking endless cigarettes, strolled casually in Las Ramblas, or chatted to the girl soldiers in the Plaza Catalunya. We had difficulty deciding which were young men and which were girls. They were dressed exactly alike, but as we drew nearer we saw that all the girls had beautifully "permed" hair and were strikingly made up.'

The first things Ethel would have sought out were the various military centres. The telephone exchange and Chamber of Commerce were held by the anarchists. The Socialists and Communists were uptown. In between, the P.O.U.M. - the Trotskyists George Orwell was fighting with.

What was a girl from an impoverished background in

Motherwell doing in Barcelona?

Ethel Macdonald was to become, for a few short months, one of the world's most famous voices. She was, perhaps, the first example of an 'embedded reporter', sending dispatches back from the Spanish Anarchist camp. But she made no pretence of 'impartiality'.

Ethel was a socialist – but with little faith in the Parliamentary system, and none in authoritarian Communism. She was utterly committed to anarchism and revolution. But these ideals were not comic-book clichés – her anarchism was in search of peace, reason, and liberty.

Working people don't leave much evidence behind them. History belongs to the rich and the powerful – they write themselves in, and airbrush out the irksome hoi polloi. Once in a while a single voice – quite literally in this case – makes itself heard. History belongs too, of course, to the victors. Anarchism's most glorious period was not to last. Forty years of Franco's regime has all but wiped out the memory of the Spanish Revolution. The Communists, too, who were soon to play a vital part in the ending of that Revolution, would prefer that we forget all about the Anarchists and their extraordinary achievements.

Of Ethel's time in Spain we know almost everything. She left behind her – in Glasgow's Mitchell library – articles and letters, and scripts of her radio broadcasts from Barcelona.

On 9 July 1937 newspaper headlines announced that Ethel Macdonald had been arrested and jailed in Spain and would soon be tried. In an article smuggled out of Barcelona she describes the scene of her arrest.

'One night at about 1 o'clock there was a thunderous knocking at the door. Assault Guards marched in and, without a word of explanation, ransacked every corner and

*every cupboard... They took me to the police station, and
left me there all night. They wanted me to sign some doc-
ument, but I refused. The next morning I was moved to the
Hotel Falcon – which had become a prison for anarchist soldiers. They took me in a motor-lorry that for all the world
was like the tumbrel of the French Revolution.'*

But it wasn't Franco who imprisoned her, and thousands of her friends. It was her erstwhile comrades – the
Communists.

Beyond Barcelona Ethel was dubbed 'The Scots Scarlet
Pimpernel'. Editors and readers demanded action, fearing
the worst. The girl from Motherwell had been imprisoned
by the very people she had gone to Spain to help, whose
story she was still determined to tell to the wider world.

Macdonald was part of a generation of dedicated people
– mainly men – who left their families, jobs, security, to
fight for an ideal in a distant country. Ethel was different
not just for being female. Her hopes for Spain were much
more radical than the Republican Government's or the
Communist- backed militias. Some might argue today, as
they did then, that those hopes were *too* radical, unrealistic.

But she was hardly alone – the vast majority of the Catalan
people not only shared her vision but had been carefully
making it a reality for two years before Ethel's arrival. The
men who came from Scotland, England, Ireland, Germany,
Italy and almost every conceivable part of Europe and the
United States fought alongside the Spanish people to halt
the rise of Fascism. The question was, and remains to this
day, what to replace it with? Many international *brigadistas* were inspired by the Communist ideal; others had no
notion that there were alternatives until they got there.
What was the point, Ethel and the Catalan people asked, in

fighting one tyranny only to replace it with another?

Finally out of Spain, having escaped Stalin's secret police, Ethel spoke to crowds in France, Holland, London and, on her return home, in Glasgow. These speeches are a record of a fundamental ideal that refuses to die. The notion of a truly democratic and just society, free of coercion and oppression.

Her story is also, of course, one of defeat. A personal loss and, more importantly a national loss in Catalonia and Spain generally. Fascism won out. But what the Catalan people achieved in the mid 1930s is a potent reminder of the politically possible.

Ethel lived on for another twenty-five years, working in a radical bookshop in Glasgow's east end, still dying too young. What she saw in Spain did not diminish either her resolve or her optimism for a better world. Far from seeing the betrayal of comrades and the triumph of the extreme right as a final defeat, she pointed to the profound changes that took place in Barcelona as proof of the need to fight on. In all her speeches and articles after the war, Ethel argued that what happened in Spain was a setback – a tragic and unnecessary one – but no more than that. Certainly not a final defeat.

A Scottish Anarchist. Ethel herself would not allow that term to be restrictive or sectarian. She saw herself as a radical, a socialist, a feminist. What mattered was working for a decent, free society, in that, she takes her place in a long worldwide, and Scottish, tradition.

From the Celtic Church, through the Reformation, the Enlightenment, the Red Clydesiders and the General Strike, Scotland has played more than its part in the struggle for egalitarianism and freedom.

> *'English-speaking workers! Why are you sleeping*
> *while your Spanish brothers and sisters are being*
> *murdered? Where are your traditions? Speak! Act!'*
> **Ethel Macdonald** (quoted in *An Anarchist's Story*)

LA MANCHA

Ours is a period of writing particularly devoted to facts, to a fond-
ness for data rather than divination, as though to possess the exact
measurements of the Taj Mahal is somehow to possess its spirit.

Laurie Lee, *I Can't Stay Long*

The next day, on the road to Alcalá de Henares, birthplace of Miguel de Cervantes, we began to channel his hero, Don Quixote, in ways we hadn't intended.

Only 10 miles out of Colmenar Viejo we could find no way forward without going back onto an *autopista*. After talking to locals, including more Guardia, we realised we would have to go off-road entirely and follow what looked, on maps and GPS, like a track that ran more or less parallel to the motorway and that should lead us to an A-road towards Alcalá. Our bikes, with hefty panniers were not built for such roads. But there was no other option.

We became proper Knights Errant, erring our way through lanes and woods and scrubland, tackling giants (boulders), muleteers (mountain bikers), castles (barns), enemy armies (sheep), and fording deep dangerous rivers (okay, streams…). All the while not at all convinced we were shadowing the road we wanted, or even heading in the right direction. Eventually, three gallant *caballeros* surmounted all the obstacles thrown in our way and, a couple of hours later than planned, we entered the city of Cervantes. (The hometown of his creation, Don Quixote, on the other hand, might be anywhere in La Mancha – every second town there claims to be the place *'cuyo nombre no quiero recordar'* – the name of which Cervantes didn't care to recall. Thus gifting the entire region tourist gold.)

In his home town the great writer is still very much part of the community. Statues to him everywhere, streets named after him and his characters. His house is a museum… although we didn't think there was a single remnant of the man himself there. Perhaps not even the bricks themselves.

Years ago, out of curiosity and being a fan of the book, I considered signing up for a 'Don Quixote Tour of La Mancha'. I read all about it. It took in the *actual windmills* that Quixote fought. Except that he didn't fight windmills, he fought giants. And anyway, he didn't exist in the first place. The Knight Errant slaying giants was the mad illusion of the hidalgo Alonso Quixano. Who didn't exist either, being entirely made up by Miguel de Cervantes… What a surreal idea for a tour. An inspired magical idea, or money-grubbing tourism? Certainly quixotic – dreams, lies, and fictions. Invented memories.

We had a night out with another contact of Liam's. This time the daughter of a friend who was doing a year abroad in Spain. Just as we had done, but forty years later. Claire is a lively young woman, her year abroad seemingly not dissimilar to ours. The same excitement, interspersed with moments of homesickness, quickly recovered from, and on to the next new friend and adventure. Claire's Spanish is already excellent, as is her local knowledge. She took us to a crowded eatery – popular with everyone, regardless of age, class, taste. They served a tapa with every drink, which got us discussing that other impenetrable Spanish mystery – when and why do some bars, in some places, sometimes, give free tapas? We've 150 combined years of eating and drinking all over Spain and we have never worked it out.

'It's an Andalusian thing, isn't it?'

'I don't remember free tapas in Cádiz.' Then again, perhaps that had something to do the kinds of places I could afford to eat in back then. 'I thought it was northern.' Robin in Segovia had told us that in Castile and Leon *pinchos* are smaller and free while tapas are always paid for. I'm not sure that distinction has always existed everywhere. If the old story of one of the Castilian kings being too ill to eat anything more than a morsel has any grain of truth, that would make tapas northern. And free. If you prefer the story of a barman in Seville covering glasses of wine with saucers to keep the flies out then the tapa, or *pincho*, is southern.

'I think,' one of us said, 'it's back into fashion. Tourists expect it.'

But we'd often been given tapas in out-of-the-way places where there were no tourists. Not just added into the price of the original drink but genuinely complimentary.

Later, we stopped to listen to a political debate taking place in a central square – just as Spain brings culture to the people, it also brings politics to the streets. The group hosting the debate were called '*Somos Alcalá*' (We Are Alcala), a rainbow alliance of left, centre, green, and liberals. Their discussion was about gay and transgender rights. The atmosphere was relaxed, good humoured. The audience a reasonable size – about 150 people. Then one young man, shoulders thrown back, crew-cut, sporting expensive shoes, strode confidently up between the debaters and the audience. He slowed and declared, self-possessed, for all to hear: '*¡Viva España!*'. Instantly, I was back in Franco's Spain.

That same day we heard a car driving round, festooned with Vox stickers and Spanish flags. The tune they were blaring out was *Y Viva España*. A Belgian pop song, originally in Dutch '*If you'd like to chat a matador, in some cool cabaña, and meet señoritas by the score...*' That's Vox's vision for a new Spain? The version Vox use is by pop-flamenco artist Manolo Escobar, a '60s star careful to remain non-political throughout his career, and a Barça fan. An odd choice for Vox's battle-cry. The audience, and the debaters, in the square in Alcalá just laughed as the ultra-right-winger marched off, satisfied with his work.

The night before we left Alcalá, a Sunday, we joined the evening *paseo*. Every hot Mediterranean country has this lovely tradition – *la passagiatta* in Italian, *o passeio* in Portuguese. Once the evening cools, locals don their Sunday best and go out walking, having a drink in one bar, then walking to another, greeting or meeting up with friends. Everyone *paseando* together, grannies, teens and toddlers. You could watch that same parade in any city in the 1970s and, I am sure, in the '30s, or Brenan's '20s. The styles have changed, but everyone is still dressed to the nines, fresh, starched, elegant. And in the midst of it all, three smelly cyclists in dirty Lycra studying maps of La Mancha at the feet of the statue of Miguel de Cervantes Saavedra.

Don Quijote de la Mancha

There's this guy nobody knows or cares much about – Alonso Quixano. A middle-aged 'hidalgo' from La Mancha. Or, if you like, a wee bourgeois from Glasgow. Either way, he reads too many books, fills his head with fictions and fancies. So much so, he gets the real world – whatever that is – mixed up with his fantasies, and heads out across Spain on a mad journey, on his old nag, Rocinante. Or his old Ridgeback Panorama touring bike.

Alonso wasn't that good at his job. Aye girning about man-flu, staying up too late with his stories. But when he takes to the road, becomes Don Quixote de la Mancha and dons his suit of armour – or Under Armour base layers – his life suddenly becomes meaningful. Full of colour and adventure.

Freewheelin'

There are giants to be slayed – or mountains to be cycled up.

Then there's poor old Aldonza Lorenzo, perfectly happy lassie minding her own business – like Moira, or Anne or Lizzie – who've got their own dreams to chase thank-you-very-much – when the Knight Errant decides *she* is the Lady For Whom he Battles, the perfect impossible courtly love. Dulcinea del Toboso he cries her – the sweetest damsel of all Toboso and Toledo.

Don Quixote thinks he's a dab hand with a sword. Or a fiddle bow. He's out to save us all from an evil wizard – the Sorcerer of Defeat. He fights the Humdrum tribe and the acolytes of Docility.

He sees life as a quest. The dull old existence of that bore Alonso Quixano was a spell and now he's free of it.

The evil powers want to make us believe we're ordinary, powerless, insignificant. Quixote knows the opposite is true – life is a constant challenge, a jousting match; it is big and bold and bloody and dangerous and exhilarating. And we, each of us, are the Knights Errant of our own Tales.

Out on our own roads, with our Sancho Panzas – the three of us here, of course, all think the other two are the Sanchos – on our steeds, saving the world, defending the meek, singing our heraldic songs.

While our brave chevalier is out on the road, freeing *doncellas*, chasing phantoms, battling ne'er-do-wells, the 'sane' folk back home are trying to save him. They burn his books, obviously. Stories? What good did they ever do anyone? Save fill up dunder-heads with unconventional, romantic – god forbid – and rebellious ideas. They bring in the priest and the doctor and, for some reason, the local barber, to tell mad old Quixote where he is going wrong.

Fill in the forms, save your pennies, mind your own

business, let the proper authorities deal with the world out there... Twenty years of schooling and they put you on the day shift... Leave the hills and byways to proper cyclists, and for heaven's sake let the real musicians do the busking...

Quixote/Quixano might have been daft, but he wasn't stupid. He listened to them. He saw the errors of his errant ways. And the first ever novel ends with the saddest ever chapter: Don Quixote gets down off his horse, takes off his armour, takes to his bed, and dies – in the real world. Except it wasn't real – it was all a fiction inside Cervantes' head.

And 400 years later, Don Quixote feels more real to me than a lot of people I actually know.

Ay Alonso, amigo mío - which world's sadder? Which world's madder? And which of us truly knows what's 'real'?

A final act of madness, coming out of La Mancha. We decided to sing and record another classic moment of art – 'Chirpy Chirpy Cheep Cheep'. Watching it now it's a surprisingly animated, belligerent even, take on a hit by a '70s Glasgow band. Our excuse being to show that we were, and had been for several miles, cycling free of traffic... in the Middle of the Road.

PROVINCIA DE CUENCA

Finally, from too little sleeping and too much reading, his brain dried up and he went completely mad.

Miguel de Cervantes, *Don Quixote*

We are cycling such beautiful roads, watching the landscape change from the misty mountains of Galicia to the flat arable fields of León, rugged Guadarrama tumbling down into the vast

Central Plain, the rolling expanse of the Alcarria and La Mancha.

The poppies grab your attention, but the more you cycle beside the hedgerows bordering almost every road, you begin to see quieter, coyer flowers. Cowslips and small, intense blue Pimpernels. Taller thistles blushing pale pink. Cela has a lovely line: *'los dorados botones del botón de oro'* (the budding gold of the Golden Button). Laced through them all, those poppies: blood red, like an artery, leading us through the heart of Spain.

Still, it was a hard, hot cycle. 'Heids doon, boots swingin' lads,' as Eddie put it. But we enjoyed ourselves along the way, rehearsing our repertoire, including by some haystacks a little off the road. Mid 'Whiskey In The Jar', perched high on a wall of haystacks, a jeep came growling down the track, creating a dust storm, like a scene from the Beverly Hillbillies. The – edited – conversation went something like…

'¡Coño! What the… hell are you doing?!'

'Em. Playing 'Whiskey In The Jar' on haystacks.'

'Are you insured?'

'For playing 'Whiskey In The Jar' on haystacks in Spain? Not entirely sure.'

'Well, *I'm* not insured. What if you fall off?'

'Sorry,' we said, climbing down. 'We did look for someone to ask…' And I wondered how we might have put that question had we found anyone.

'Sorry if we worried you.'

'Worried? I couldn't give a… (Spanish phrase that's best not to translate).'

There were two men in the car, probably father and son. They ended up laughing – at, rather than with us, I imagine. They asked about our journey and we asked about their farm. It had been a difficult few years since the economic crash, they said, but there were signs now that things were picking up. We did the selfies, and father and son waved goodbye to three Scottish eejits.

Mucking around had held us back again and we had another scare that we might not find a place to get water and provisions. So were relieved, 10 miles down the road, to arrive at last at a little village. The relief didn't last long – no bar, no shop. We saw only one elderly man, sitting in a bus shelter.

'Morning, sir. Is there a shop or a bar here?'

He shook his head. 'Sorry, gentlemen, I'm afraid not.'

'In the whole town? How do people do their shopping?'

'You need to have a car.' His tone suggested that he did not. 'There used to be a couple of bars. Several shops. Good ones too. A fruit shop, paper shop… Not now. The young ones, they've all gone. Who can blame them? I'd do the same.'

He looked up the road, seeing ghosts, hearing echoes of a lively town, not so many years ago.

'This is a good village, good people. But sorry, my friends, I can't help you.'

We thanked him and set off. We got the distinct impression that no bus was going to arrive, that he knew it wouldn't. He wasn't waiting for one. It was just a place to sit in the shade.

Our destination for the day was the larger town of Estremera. Not the prettiest of towns, but with good views over the *vega* – meadow-land – towards the *Sistema Central*, the mountains we had cycled over a few days ago. We found our lodging for the night, a house in a quiet old terraced street. The owner, Inés, told us its history.

'The whole row was once a convent.' Our rooms did have an agreeably consecrated feel. It would also explain the smallness. 'Teaching nuns. They used to be very important in this town. My great grandfather took it over when the order closed the school. At the end of his life he divided it up among his five children.'

So now it's a street of siblings and cousins. But most of them have left to work in Madrid, not that far away, or abroad. Inés has stayed and she and her husband have turned their portion into rooms for travellers. We couldn't imagine she'd get much business. There aren't a lot of reasons to go, or even pass through, Estremera.

I went off to make some notes, passing by the new education centre, named after José Camilo Cela. Whether in honour of his writing or his politics, it wasn't clear. Cela is a complicated figure. He fought for Franco, leaving his Republican district deliberately to do so, and he stayed in Spain throughout Franco's reign when many other writers fled the country. But his novels and his travel books are, contrarily, fiercely critical of the *Generalísimo* and his policies, of the social divisions they caused, the pitiless divide between rich and poor. He was also a key figure to many of the up-and-coming writers of the '50s and '60s, a literary godfather, helping even those openly critical of the regime to get published.

Reading his *Journey To Alcarria*, an area around Guadalajara we were only skirting, I'm struck by how *peopled* his country-side is. Everywhere 'the traveller' (as he calls himself, in the third person, throughout) goes in 1946 he meets farmers, carters, field-workers, wanderers, girls washing clothes in streams, women selling fruit by the roadside, people in transit from one village to another. Every one of those villages offers a choice of restaurants, shops, lodgings.

Eddie and Liam, going off down another street, met an elderly woman, María, who told the same story as the man in the bus stop, the story we heard all through central Spain. Estremera used to be a bustling town. Still can be at weekends and holidays when the young families come back. But usually, like today, it's dull.

In an impassioned essay on the destruction of village and rural life, Laurie Lee wrote: 'A decade in the country can slip down the gullet with the deceptive smoothness of an oyster. Yet the last ten years have marked rural life more than anything done to it for centuries.' He was talking about the Cotswolds, of course, but he was no doubt aware of the creeping loss of Spanish village life.

'Estremera is dying on its feet,' María said.

* * *

As I Walked Out One Midsummer Morning has Cádiz 'a rotting hulk on the edge of a disease-ridden sea.' Zamora, which we had found graceful, melodic as a lullaby, Lee judged rocky, decrepit and stern. His Segovia is carrion-infested. All across Spain he came across 'fat old crones' or women shrivelled as carob beans, men half-mad and vicious. Gerald Brenan describes the entire journey from La Coruña to Granada as monotonous, the landscape barren and broken, the people 'disappointing', squat and unfriendly. 'Harpies' in a Madrid boarding house demanded payment up front for meagre dinners. Both writers often retch at the food they are offered – rancid, foul-smelling, flavourless.

Neither can compete with the nineteenth-century traveller, Richard Ford. For him, Valencians are 'vindictive, sullen, fickle and treacherous', while Catalans are philistines and brooding discontents. Of Spaniards generally, Ford numbers the 'faults' of the race: 'Apt to indulge in habits of procrastination, waste, improvidence, and untidiness. They are unmechanical and obstinate, easily beaten...' He is talking, generally, about the common people. The higher classes he likes a lot more.

All three, ultimately, are hispanophiles in their own way. The moment Brenan arrives in his beloved village of Yegen in the Alpujarras, *South From Granada* is a lyrical elegy. Despite his misfortunes, and his exaggerations, Lee becomes obsessed with Spain. Both men kept one foot in England, another in Spain, for the rest of their lives.

Kate O'Brien, travelling from Ireland in the '20s and '30s is kinder.

Where the men saw laziness and fatalism, O'Brien sees dignity, courtesy, pride in country and culture, conviviality and hospitality. So far, O'Brien's Spain chimes with ours, but in *Farewell Spain*, she is gobsmackingly anti-Muslim. She sees nothing in the beauty of what remains of Al Andalus. Not the architecture of Córdoba or Granada, not the literature, the musical influence so crucial to the development of Flamenco and Spanish folk music. In this she is not only wilfully dismissive but transparently racist.

All countries can be stereotyped. Scotland, misty or murky, roaming in the gloaming versus Billy Connolly's nights fair drawing in; 'Scots Wha Hae' and *Trainspotting*'s 'It's shite being Scottish'. The old dialectic of 'shooting up or shooting grouse'. I tried to get a sense of what the poet Hugh MacDiarmid called 'Scottish anti-syzygy' in *The Pitiless Storm,* a play I wrote for David Hayman in 2014, 'Mad wee land of Covenanters and Catholics, Jews, Hindus, hippies, Muslims, Wee Frees, Big Frees, Middle-sized Frees, Buddhists and schismatics and socialists. Red Clydesiders rubbing boiler-suit shoulders with Armani yuppies... disputating to our hearts' content.' MacDiarmid's love of contradiction, in the tradition of Robert Cunninghame Graham, led him to be kicked out of the Communist party for being a nationalist and the National Party of Scotland for being a communist.

My youthful dreams of Spain wallowed in clichés too: Carmen the beautiful fiery *gitana*, guitars, *sol y sombra*. I picked up more when I actually got here: sensual Al-Andalus, the excitement of revolution, anarchism. There's no doubt that earlier travellers experienced a less developed country and an oppressed people, which I only glimpsed in the 1970s. There are still too many open wounds in towns and cities inflicted by poverty, crusted scabs from four decades of dictatorship. Over various cycles we've passed slums near Seville that are essentially *favelas,* and towns like Estremera with the lives sucked out of them. Still, Lee's,

Brenan's, Ford's and others' slowness to notice the diverse beauties of Spain suggests a kind of reluctance. Good tarmac and decent bikes, a healthy budget, all contribute to our more favourable impressions. For the next, and final, week of our voyage west to east, we had little but delights ahead.

* * *

If the *lentejas* in an unknown town in León will be the most memorable meal we had, Estremera to Huete will be the most memorable cycle.

It started well and ended movingly. We were out and about early, the morning sky like a daisy, petal rays radiating from a gentle sun. Kites, falcons, hawks, in every direction. I'm forever being accused of "seeing" eagles, but I'm sure I did that day. Much further down the line, talking to poet and naturalist Christopher North I described what I had seen – I had taken notes, and on this occasion did not lie, even to myself. Christopher thought it very likely we had seen a short-toed snake eagle. Or a Belloni's eagle, smaller than most eagles, they're relatively common in central Spain. Another, almost as large, bird swept down onto the road about 20 yards in front of Eddie and me. It had mistaken a pot-hole for a small animal. Swooped, touched down, bit tarmac and looked up at us as if it were our fault.

A day of one joy after another, the next was the best descent so far, one that seemed to disprove the cyclist's conviction that Everything That Goes Down Must First Go Up. We may well have climbed, but gradually enough that we hadn't noticed, distracted by the scenery. (In fact, we had gone up three Category hills: a 5, a 4, and a 2.) The warming morning was as fresh and cosy as newly baked bannocks. The perfume of the wildflowers, the pastures beyond them. Like a María Dolores Pradera song: *Ahora que aún se mece en un sueño / El viejo puente, el río y la alameda...*

a dreamy *muchacha*, hips swaying, saunters over the bridge and down the lane, wafts of jasmine and cinnamon in the air. There was a small incline, taking us to the top of the downhill. A view from a dream, La Mancha spooled below us for miles in every direction; and us, specks in the sky.

This descent had none of the problems of Navacerrada. The day was warm and the road was a series of wide bends, trafficless. There was a town below us that, from so high up, looked like a cluster of sapphires. It promised riches of coffee, *bocadillos* of tortilla, cheese, cold drinks. We skimmed down that hillside, leaning into the curves like proper cyclists. It reminded us of our first Spanish cycle as a trio, flying down O Cebreiro at 47 miles per hour. Whether we equalled that speed, none of us cared.

The nuggets of sapphire quickly became the town of Vellisco. Living up to our expectations that this would be a village with a bar. We bought what we needed for our picnic. Increasingly, due in part to so many villages not having amenities, we had been opting for lunching *al fresco*. Lumps of bread, a couple of tomatoes each, slices of cheese and ham. There is something satisfying, instinctive, about sitting by the side of the road or in a town *plaza*, biting into fresh tomatoes, necking water, closing your eyes.

Chema had the same idea. He arrived ten minutes after us. The other end of the cycling spectrum: a racing snake of a lad.

'Where you going, *chicos*?' *Chicos*. God bless 'im.

'Vigo to Valencia.'

'*¡Buen ritmo!*' A cyclists' phrase we'd heard before. Good rhythm.

'Today we're heading for Huete. You?'

'Cuenca.' We're taking two days to get to Cuenca, and he's doing it in one. 'I suddenly got a couple of days off, so thought I'd leg it,' Chema says, in a tangy, street-smart, Madrid accent.

He certainly was legging it. Over 200 kilometres in two days, given his route.

We offered him some of our picnic as he didn't seem to be carrying anything – no panniers, tiny backpack, no pockets in his aerodynamic shirt and shorts.

'I'm good, thanks.' He produced an apple from somewhere and necked his own water. 'Plan is, do the Alcarria but nip off every now and then. Some cool roads round this bit.'

He showed no interest whatsoever in where we were from. Perhaps our Spanish was that good now. Then again, he's a city boy. Has seen stranger sights than three old codgers lying around squares munching tomatoes. What interests Chema is bikes and speeds and routes. We chatted a bit about tourers versus road bikes. How far you can go with a load.

On routes he was useful. 'Don't take the A-road to Huete. Veer off left, just down there. It's a B job, good surface though. Tomorrow, when you get close to Cuenca, there's another trick. Back road out of Nohares.'

Chema. Happy in his own company. Happy to chat to whomever passes. Loving his days off. Stretching, yawning, smiling. He remounted and slid off into the Alcarria. Cheers, Chema – the perfect man to meet on that perfect day.

We had seen what looked like a great road from the hilltop and hoped that it was the one we were about to cycle. The only worry being that it looked from up there like a dirt track. It turned out to be compacted, hard baked earth. Bleached by the sun, reflecting the young wheat, the soft grasses in fallow fields. Fine for the bikes. The *amapolas* had taken the day off, not caring to disrupt the hushed water-colours, their red too vibrant for a quiet, sincere path like this. Lone creamy clouds tiptoed across the vast sky, dropping cool raindrops occasionally. From this low position we could see even further than from atop the hill. The early evening meadows lay like satin bedsheets, still rumpled and humid as if from an afternoon of lovemaking. The hills in the distance faded into the sky. All we could hear was the breeze, the odd raindrop dripping – whispers on the warm road. We had to walk a little away from each other. If you can't shed a tear in the face of such beauty, it's a crying shame.

The cycle of a lifetime eased off into the market town of Huete. A sleepy Tuesday evening, I went off to jot down notes, leaving the boys to their siesta of Arcadia.

I walked past an elegant sixteenth-century church, now a photography museum, closed like the town itself, until I found a bar. There's a Western on the telly, reminding me of childhood Sunday afternoons, watching John Wayne with my dad and brothers. Two guys sit at the bar, chatting sporadically to the barman, glancing between comments at the gunslingers. Two women walk in and, without them asking, the barman changes the channel to a Spanish soap opera. They sit and watch, ordering nothing. I like these soaps. My friend Nella Yanes wrote one of my favourites, a Venezuelan mini-series *La Revancha* (The Revenge) that I used to watch when I was teaching in Pamplona. I know the format and get into this new one quickly. A brother and a husband discuss the problem of their sister/wife. An elderly lady is stood up at some kind of meeting. The soap ends and the two women leave with a wave to the barman. The Western goes back on. Two more women come in, more animated. They order coffee, sit in the same seats as their predecessors a few minutes ago, and talk about what to do about some man. Maybe their husband/brother. A third woman comes in with a pile of envelopes, giving everyone, except me, one each. Lottery tickets? Adverts? Political pamphlets – the Euro elections are in six days' time? Whatever they are everyone was expecting them, but none of them open them. An old man, stooped, comes in, cap and stick. He has a little dog. I go to pay for my coffee as the old man is getting his. The dog, a cute mongrel, is the only one to look at me. What's a *guiri* (foreigner) like you doing in a place like this, dressed like that?

I ask, 'What's his name?'

'Fidel,' the old man smiles. He's got a great smile. I wonder, inwardly, if he's a Communist. The man, not the dog. Then again, *fidel* means loyal, and that wee dog looks very loyal indeed.

'Adiós. Gracias,' I say as I leave.

'*Caballero*,' the men all chorus. And I'm happy to have been called a gentleman.

Walking back to our *hostal*, the heat hugging me, I pass a gaggle of teens. That's a good sign – maybe a town the size of Huete has more to offer young families. They're friends, but they're flirting – *coqueteando*, rather than *ligando*. Teasing, not hooking up. They're about the same age Brendan and I were when we first came to this country. It's a happy memory, and it doesn't make me feel old. Just lucky.

Showering, I'm surprised how much dust I've picked up from the Beautiful Road, despite the drops of rain. It comes off me, gold in the water. Delicious days such as these, no matter how content you've been, bring a certain sadness in their wake. We're nearing the end of our journey, I'm aware of how important it has been to me. And, when we're done cycling, I'll be meeting up with my son and my nephew. We'll retell how my brother brought the younger me home, and we'll laugh. But I miss my big brother. And now I do feel old.

There is a family photograph, mum, dad, all my brothers and sisters. Including Brennie – a brother I never met. Brennie died two years before I was born. There's another photo, very similar, five or six years later. I'm there. Brennie's not. Presence and absence, in the 1950s. Everything leaves a trace.

Freewheelin'

* * *

On to Cuenca. Another lovely road. Maybe as lovely as yesterday's, with the misfortune to come after it, so it goes less noticed, lost in yesterday's afterglow. The poppies are back out in numbers and they lead us to another village and another old man lamenting the loss of family, friends and neighbours. For several miles we follow a train line, straight and flat. We only see one train all day long, cutting through the prairie – you almost expect to see Woody Guthrie or Big Bill Broonzy freight-hop down out a boxcar, guitar slung. *Let the towns drift slowly by / Listen to the steel rails hummin'... That's the hobo's lullaby.*

Each of us went at our own pace. The opium of yesterday's road leaving us spaced out, in our own little worlds. At one point, I find I'm cycling a couple of hundred yards behind Liam and Eddie. They're two abreast, talking, laughing. I ride, a few seconds behind, into the echo of their guffaws. And I have a rush of love for these two men. Decent, generous, brotherly. It's good to be with them, to share this journey. Friendship can be a difficult business. Spending an entire month together, the difference in physical strength, mental endurance, with all manner of challenges and chores: collaborating on blogs, breakfasting every morning and dining together every evening. Taking choices, making concessions. I don't mean to suggest that we were braving the full *Vuelta a España*, but there were trials and tests enough for me. And now we're closing in on our destination, and we've held it together as a group.

Chema was right about the road into Cuenca, although it turns out it was a road Liam had already identified. At the end of it, entering the city, we're greeted by another cobbled sheer hill like Segovia, up, up, up. Bump, bump, bump. Not much short of 1,000 feet, and, again like Segovia, another treat of a hotel, and the last posh one of the trip. As far as we can see, it's the highest hotel in the entire city.

I've got form in Cuenca, and it's on my mind as we pedal up. I left my violin here in 1979. A violin that had been in the family for generations. A bunch of friends, Glaswegians and Spaniards met up for Cuenca's famous *Semana Santa,* Holy Week. A few faded photographs survive. Moody and posed, they look like old LP covers...

The photoshoot for the 1970s Scots-Latin folk-rock band Adelante's first album, *Way Of The Stars,* shows a tight-knit group, leaning against old city walls overlooking a deep gorge. Lead singer Brandon Yew aloof, fiddle player Mario Dolido – a cross between Leonard Cohen and Elvis. Carmen and Mercedes, keyboards and vocals, smile Mona Lisa-like. Fergal, bassist, stares defiantly, drummer Jonny Gee thoughtful. Micki Roll-Morton, electric lead, hair down his back, gypsy rocker. Hard to believe that within a year the stories of excess and depravity would be hitting the headlines. *Way Of The Stars* received rave reviews, 'a sublime blend of folk-rock with gypsy overtones', and was reckoned to be a precursor of fusion music. The last album *Lies of the Land,* 'songs of regret, loneliness, trying and failing to escape the past...', is the ultimate break-up record. They're pictured in the shade, at the base of the ravine now, not the top. The battles, break-ups, drugs and alcohol, artistic differences, etched on ashen faces.

An alter-ego lonely hearts club band! There's a tiny grain of truth in that we did a lot of singing together in Cuenca, and it was a profitable time and place for busking. At the end of Holy Week, I had planned to return and left my violin with a friend. But I never did make it back, so the family fiddle never left Cuenca.

Brendan thinks that's not how it happened. His version is that I did take my violin back to Cádiz. Which would make sense – I would have wanted it to keep busking. He 'remembers' that I *did* return to Cuenca, and from there a few of us returned to Scotland in late summer. That was when I left my violin. There are problems with both versions – why would I leave a fiddle when I was going back to Scotland, with no plans to return to Cuenca?

Whatever, ten years ago two of the friends who had visited in '79 and I took a few days' holiday in Madrid. I persuaded them to take a trip to Cuenca, partly to revisit where we had been forty odd years previously, but also to try and find out what happened to the violin. Before we left I wrote an article for the two main *Conquense* daily newspapers. They printed them. Anyone with any news of my violin would know that I'd be at such-and-such a place at a given time. I gave as many clues as I could – first names of Spanish friends (I never knew any of their surnames) etc. When we got there, the radio interviewed me, and I saw that the newspaper articles had been fairly prominently placed. So my hopes were high.

I waited at the appointed place. For a couple of hours. Nobody came.

It so happened that I had been teaching regularly in Pamplona at that time and had a student who was from Cuenca. I'd agreed to meet him there, to discuss scripts.

'I saw your articles,' he said. 'I knew nobody would turn up.'

'Why not? I wasn't accusing anyone of stealing my fiddle. I really just wanted its story.'

'This is a conservative town, Chris. Those girls you knew back then, they're all mothers now.'

'Grandmothers probably.'

'Members of the local church, Union of Catholic Mothers. And the guys? Members of the PP.' Spain's Tories. 'No way they're going to make such a public show of their wild days with a bunch of Glaswegian lads. It was never going to happen.'

What struck me when I re-entered Cuenca with Liam and

Eddie was I had never realised how magnificent a city it is. In '79 I was too young. At sixty-one I now see it in all its glory. If the road to Huete was the best we had cycled so far, Eddie, who knows Spain well but was a first-timer in Cuenca, declared '*This is the most beautiful city in Spain*'. A cathedral that has sections dating back as far as the twelfth century, with additions and repairs, remodellings undertaken in every century since. A sixteenth-century bridge, over the most dramatic gorge that looks like it could have been gouged out by a comet. The famous *casas colgadas*, hanging houses, built in and up from the rock of the gorge. Walking around Cuenca's high old town you feel that *most* of the houses are *colgadas*, their rear ends tottering hundreds of feet over the chasm below.

The Sexygenarians busked in a little square, just up from the cathedral steps where I had tried my musical luck all those years ago. Passers-by seemed to like us, but were as confused as ever about buskers not looking for money. We played 'Ode To Joy'. Slowly, with feeling. We were only getting snippets of news, but the clamour back home in the UK for leaving the EU without a deal was growing. It's not only the actual leaving of Europe, it's the anachronistic dreams of empire, the curling up in a foetal self-obsessed British ball. The rejection of the bigger world – of my Paris bistro, of the Celtic connection with Galicia, Ireland, Brittany, of the Fifteenth International Brigade – seems a poor exchange for a sad isolationism, a misreading of the past. Sitting in that first bistro at sixteen years of age I'd have been amazed to be told that one day I'd have my name on an office door in Paris. In the late 1990s I worked as international consultant for UNESCO. Another occasion when the UK, following the US's lead, left a major international organisation. It would give present-day remainers hope that the UK rejoined UNESCO in 1997, followed by the US in 2003, were it not for Trump having taken the US out *again*, and people in Johnson's and Cummings' inner circle moving for us to follow them once more. Depressed by these thoughts of isolation we played 'Freedom Come All Ye', and reflected on the freakish irony that, for many, opting for Scottish independence is a vote against nationalism.

Over a post-busk beer we agree we shouldn't get too starry-eyed about the European project. It was Jacques Delors first standing up to Thatcher that made many people of our generation warm, for the first time, to the EU. But the idea that Europe has protected workers' and human rights sounds hollow after twenty years of ferocious deregulation. The demise of trade unions and ever-increasing privatisation across much of the EU played their part in the crash of 2008. The EU is as much about moving capital around as workers and students.

The following morning, the day we leave Cuenca, I sit writing in a bar by the quiet side of the cathedral where children are running around, all horseplay and laughter. Cyclists power by, practising on the hill. And, in the main square, a PSOE (Socialist Party) street stall, the first we've seen all the way through Spain. The European elections are two days away with Vox still on the rise and Podemos riven by division. An ex-pat couple, on a weekend away from their home of eighteen years in Alicante, came over to tell me that there was a better bar down the road 'where they speak English'. I like where I am. The noise, the families, the weans.

But it makes me miss my own family. I phone my son. I'm lucky to get him. He's taking time out from dealing with a psychotic young man in a mental health clinic. Daniel had stepped outside, trying to decide what to do, when I phoned.

'The system breaks down at this point. We can't keep the poor guy locked up, but we can't let him onto the streets either. He's a danger, to himself and everybody else.'

My daughter's up to her ears with the final draft of her thesis. Although it would make no difference – Emma's in Aberdeen, Daniel in Manchester, Moira in Glasgow – I feel I should be home. Guilty for sitting in this beguiling town, sipping Verdejo.

At least this time I was leaving Cuenca with a fiddle on my back. But by the end of this journey, I would abandon yet another violin in Spain.

PROVINCIA DE VALENCIA

Valencia, one of the sunniest regions of Spain. *València*, as it is in the local language, Valenciano, country of oranges, lemons, palm trees. We're not quite there yet but are riding into it. Can smell the sea, our coast-to-coast becoming a reality. Having confronted the mountains and mists of Galicia, the freezing peak of Navacerrada, the reward is Valencia at the end of May. Balmy, breezy, dry...

And so it started out. We were sad to say goodbye to Cuenca. Heading east and south the conditions appeared promising. We had seen the weather reports – rain, unsettled, temperatures falling. To Scots, to whom *temperatura en descenso* is good news in Spain, not bad. And we all like descents.

Despite having lost various items along the way – shorts, shoes, specs, chargers, adaptors, amongst them – our panniers seemed to be getting heavier. Still, we were all in good fettle. Eddie's knee giving him less gyp, Liam's foot behaving itself, my hamstring easing.

We rode through gaps between hills like extras in a cowboy film. Eddie had already claimed the name Rocinante for his bike. Liam's had to be Silver, the Lone Ranger's mount (because, really, he'd prefer to do this trail alone). So Scout might be good for my Ridgeback Panorama. Tonto's horse. There's a curious linguistic discrepancy in *The Lone Ranger* TV series. The Ranger himself is referred to as Kemosabe, apparently after the name of a place. But it sounds, in Spanish, very like *'quien lo sabe'* *(*the man who *knows)*. 'Tonto' we're told, means, in some unidentified Native American language, 'the wild one'. But *tonto* is the Spanish word for stupid. Even if unintended, 420 million Spanish speakers worldwide must associate the white man with knowledge and sense, the 'Indian' with stupidity. Riding through that Western landscape I rejected being Tonto to Liam's Lone Ranger. One of Buffalo Bill's horses was called Charlie; Bill himself was a friend of Robert Cunninghame Graham. So now our posse – Rocinante, Silver and Charlie – is galloping high on the trail through untamed rocky hills (on perfect tarmac).

We passed our 1,000-kilometre mark at a bus stop in a small town called Valeria. A very ordinary town, it could have been Fife or Lanarkshire, especially now that the day had become overcast. It felt right somehow, celebrating at a bus stop outside a closed electrical goods store.

A little later we stopped by the side of a road for a snack and a chat. The weather was indecisive, blotchy and argumentative, like a man waking up with a hangover and regrets. Behind us the sky was dark, moody. But we were moving southwards, so we reckoned we'd dodge any rain. I headed off first – they were both on form that day and I worried that, without a head start, I might get left behind, especially as there were a couple of hills to get over. Just 5 kilometres along the road, the clouds began to chase us. Valencia and it's going to rain? I hammered on trying to keep ahead of the darkening clouds. Then, in the distance, the first faint rumble of thunder. The boys behind me would be trying to outrun the rain too so I pedalled even faster. The thunder got louder. The first flash of lightning, behind a hill, maybe 10 miles away. There was a town ahead, but we had made no plans to stop. Liam had been reading up on what cyclists should do in a lightning storm. I had to avoid it like the plague.

A metal bike on an empty road, the rider sitting tall in the saddle, is a magnet for lightning. When the sign for Valera de Abajo appeared, I thought it best to wait. Just as well, by the time we found a café the rain had started. Just a smirr, but two minutes later it was lashing. Everyone in town was running for cafés or home. The bartender gave us piping hot coffee, let us eat our picnic indoors. After the first shot of caffeine it was *a cántaros*, bucketing down, outside. Then the thunder roared blackly. Day turned into night, and we found ourselves in the eye of the storm.

Our bikes were partially sheltered under the eaves of the houses on the street, but the more exposed of my two saddle bags might be the one that contained my laptop. I dashed out and checked the bike was the right way round, shielding the computer. It was. The whole operation took less than thirty seconds, but I was drenched through, head to foot. Drookit. *Calado hasta los huesos* (soaked to the bones). The road had liquefied into a river in spate. Hailstones as big as Spanish meatballs, but harder. Then the lightning reached us. Directly overhead. Bright, frequent, cracking as loud as Spanish fireworks.

We had to wait two full hours in that little caff until the storm abated and the thunder and lightning moved on, looking for less wary cyclists down the road.

It was late when we got to our stopping place for the night, pedalling first through rain and cold, then, the storm over, through rapidly rising temperatures. Motilla del Palancar is right on the edge of Valencia Province. Motilla del Palancar, fancy name, and, this time, moderately large. But in no way fancy.

That may be unfair. We arrived late and left early and didn't get to explore. What we saw was not so much a truck stop as a truck town. Cycling into it, we became aware of more and more lorries, articulated, with trailers, vans, car-transporters, heavy goods vehicles.

Freewheelin'

Probably because we were on an *autovia* – unlike the motorway proper they have no tolls, so cheaper for hauliers. Valencia is Spain's third biggest city after Madrid and Barcelona, and this road is a direct line to the capital and the north. Motilla clearly owes its existence to passing traffic. Flat as a pancake, it is lined on either side by garages, gas-stations, warehouses, industrial units, cheap eateries, amusement arcades with slot machines, motels… As though we had ridden forwards in time from the cowboy trails of the wild west to small-town American '50s of *Psycho*.

After checking in to our, well, truck stop, I went out for my usual note-taking. Anyone who knows the west of Scotland, or Lancashire, knows Motillla de Palancar. Peaked caps, bad teeth, inappropriate clothing, fags and ashen complexions, gravelly voices. A guy came and sat at the table next to me in the nearest bar I could find.

'Shite weather, big man.' It's a loose translation, but he had the lingo of hard-working, hard-bitten peoples everywhere. I am not a 'big' man, but he was what we'd call in Scots *shilpit*. Scrawny, T-shirt three sizes too big for him. Hems of his jeans still wet from the rain over an hour ago.

'Aye.'

'Just came up the road there. Baltic, *coño*.'

In his thirties, he ordered a beer and an *anís*. Hauf and a hauf.

'Divin' in here till she gets back.'

He got out his phone, gave me a massive smile. Conversation over, I got back to my notes, any threat of homesickness nipped in the bud.

That greasy spoon on truckers' highway was the only place that charged less than a euro for a coffee. Good coffee it was too – thick and black, strong enough, as Moira's granny used to say, to sink a battleship. Paying and leaving, the barman said, 'Mind how you go, chief.'

We didn't have high hopes for the evening meal. A big dark barn of a dining room, empty save for us. Then again, it might be like Hotel Bayona, Fany's place in Vendas de Barreira, back in Galicia. Chips and egg, hamburgers – pedallers' grub. Then the owner came out, teacloth over his arm, bearing menus. He was about five foot four – maybe a medium-sized man round these parts. Pudgy, balding, perfectly creased trousers.

'This is a special place,' he said, in English.

We glanced at the menus and saw immediately what he meant. Sophisticated dishes, with prices to match.

You'd never discover these restaurants yourself unless you'd lived forty years in Spain, or had friends who knew where to find them. A lot of excellent restaurants are in the most unlikely of places in Spain, often for some reason, next to petrol-stations. Bernardo Atxaga, the Basque writer, had taken Moira and me, years ago, to a place just like this near Vitoria. Our friend Rafa in Sanlúcar, and my colleague Ana Zabalagui in Pamplona, similarly.

The owner took us through the menu, explaining each dish, like a chef-de-cuisine in a top Paris establishment.

'These are mushrooms, but not ordinary mushrooms. *Níscalo. Tipo de bitorquis. Très délicates.*' He used Spanish, English, French and Latin to describe each dish. '*Farci.* With garlic, *jamón de cebo...* Parfait!'

He had real pride and absolute faith in his dishes. Our only concern now was the price, and our appetites. Our budget was holding up as well as our legs, but we didn't want to blow the remainder on one meal. A more general problem across all of Spain is the late hour of dining. Normally an enjoyable part of the culture, but when you're getting up early in the morning to cycle, a hefty meal before early bedtime is not ideal. And it was late now, by our standards.

We ordered the mushrooms, and stuffed artichokes. One of each, each. They were truly *très délicates*. As we ate, the little chef

– or perhaps it was his wife in the back doing the cooking – came out every now and then to parade fresh lobsters, still moving, thin-cut carpaccio, 'best of tenderloin, messieurs', cheeses, dessert wines.

We disappointed him by ordering the bean stew, the least complex, and cheapest, thing on the menu. Then an apple tart to share between three. They were both just as delicious and we told him so, but the gleam had gone out of his eye. He seemed to be having more luck with the middle-aged couple who came in after us and switched his attention to them.

The problem with such fare is that a certain kind of Hispanophile – Hispanophiles like us – has a fetish for *cocina casera* – old-fashioned home cooking. It's partly nostalgia for when we first came to this country and could only afford down-market restaurants. But Spanish food is often at its best when it is the diametric opposite of French haute cuisine: no creamy sauces, no garnishes, no *farci*. Places where when you ask for fish, you get A Fish. When you ask for meat, you get A Meat. Order a salad to go with it, and it'll come first. Or after. Another of Spain's mysteries.

Over coffee we congratulated each other. Two more rides to go. Tomorrow medium-hard, the following day long but mainly flats and downhills, a victory lap. Nothing that will cause us a problem. Our sexagenarian bodies had made it this far, no reason why we couldn't handle the last two days.

'Looks like we're going to make it boys.'

* * *

Hoy, tú, mañana, yo.

Marcos

The cycle to Utiel looked fine on paper. 70 miles, two Category 5s. But on cycling sites you get pictograms of the actual lie of the land, and this one showed a very definite V shape about halfway along. Category hills take into account length of climb as well as height gain. That means, if a hill isn't long enough, no matter the gradient, it doesn't get categorised. Which, in turn, means that the most difficult hills, so long as they're short, don't show up.

We'd hoped the first section of the ride would be easy enough and we'd have the legs for the nasty V ahead. But it was still cold, and the wind was against us all the way. For the last week, the fiddle on my back hadn't been acting as a sail, quite the opposite. No matter how I tried to position myself on the bike, the wind caught the case and acted as a drag. Or a side-gust threatened to topple me. *It is what it is. It will be what it will be. We'll get there.* And another old mantra from walking with my brother Paul: 'Don't let the uphills ruin the downhills.' I repeated the phrases over and over as the road dipped and then started to climb. Haruki Murakami in *What I Talk About When I Talk About Running* has a mantra of his own: *Pain is inevitable, suffering is optional.* Eddie would be doing his *Lizzie McKim Hamill Morrison*, or perhaps on this occasion opting for intercession by reciting *Hail Marys.* Liam probably wasn't noticing there *was* a hill.

Whatever our strategies, we all made it. Plain sailing from here on in. At this very moment Moira and Anne were on a plane, coming over to cheer us over the finishing line. Liam and Anne's sons were booking a restaurant for our victory celebration tomorrow evening. We could smell the *paella valenciana*, taste the Champagne (Cava, as it turned out), feel the sea salt in the wind on our skin.

And the rest of the road into Utiel was smooth, flat, the wind abating, the poppies as excited as us. I was ahead again. As ever, I had worried about the V-shaped hill, so I'd had set off first after a snack break. Eddie would catch up any minute, stay with me for a bit for chat and songs then speed ahead.

But he never did. I stopped a couple of times. Still no Eddie. My cycling had improved over the month, but so had Eddie's. I knew precisely what had happened, though. They had stopped to take pictures. Maybe they had met someone and were chatting. Then a darker suspicion: they'd taken a break to have a bite to eat. They were carrying the picnic provisions – I should have known that was a mistake. Worse, they had stopped to have a coffee in one of the villages I had whizzed past.

Even given all those things put together, 10 miles on, Eddie would still have caught up. I tried texting a few times. One of us had no signal. I carried on towards town. Finally, a text came in.

LIAM KANE:
We have a wee problem and will be delayed. N3 all the way to Utiel and hostal el vegano.

I know Liam Kane too well. 'A wee problem' in his language is more than it sounds. Again, I thought I knew what had happened. The nineteenth cycle out of twenty-one and we hadn't had a single burst. This was probably more serious. A simple puncture wouldn't be a problem at all in Liam-speak. Snapped chain? Brake wire frayed? Problems we couldn't fix on the road, that needed a cycle shop. Then my text buzzed again.

LIAM KANE:
Chris. Eddie has fallen and hurt his ribs. A kind man is giving him a lift to Utiel. The plan is to drop the stuff at the hotel and take Eddie to a medical centre. So if you're at the hotel and can watch out for them that would be great. I'm back on my bike and about 20k away. Real shame!

I got the story later. They'd both got over the V-shaped hill. Eddie had cycled ahead. Me still in his sights. The road at this point was wide, very few cars. There was a slip road coming down from the right, widening the space even more. The last place you would have a fall. Eddie said he had veered out from the side of the road, safely, towards the right, the slip road being clear. A momentary lapse of concentration. In the junction between the main and slip road there was a lump of dried concrete, presumably not cleared up from some maintenance work. Only a couple of inches high, but his wheel hit it at exactly the wrong angle.

Eddie was thrown clear over his handlebars. He did a full somersault, landing badly, on his front and side.

Nothing that will cause us a problem.

He shouted, screamed out at me, still just ahead but I heard nothing. That'll bother me in days to come.

We've made it this far, no reason why we can't handle the last two days.

Eddie told us later he'd kept shouting, worried he'd lose consciousness. The pain in his chest and sides was searing and at this point didn't know what harm he'd done himself. He was lying on the road, just beyond a blind bend. Cars were few, but they were fast.

He managed, after the initial trauma faded, to pick himself up and was trying to get back on his bike when Liam caught up. Even if Eddie could have ridden, his front wheel was buckled beyond repair. What to do? By this time he was putting a good face on it, saying he'd be fine, just a fright and a few bruises. Even if that had been the case, they now only had one functioning bike between them. They were miles from any kind of habitation. They'd have to wait, try and flag down a car, take Eddie, and his bike, to the nearest village and call a taxi from there.

Intercession came in the form of a thirty-something chap in a jeep. I met him later: sturdy, dusty, fair haired, serious eyes. Marcos. He drove down the slip road that had caused the problem. They hardly had to flag him; Marcos stopped as soon as he saw something was wrong. The right driver in the right vehicle – his estate could take both Eddie and bike. He drove Eddie, not to the nearest village, and he had a choice of several, but to our destination, Utiel. He stopped, passing me, so he and Eddie could update me on what had happened, then he took Eddie to our hotel. He got the bike out and into a secure place. He took Eddie on to the Medical Centre in town and waited there with him. When Eddie realized his E11 European Health Insurance card was in a bag on his bike, he phoned me. Marcos came back to collect me and the card, and drove back me to the Centre. On the way, we passed a warehouse.

'That's my wine there.'

Another vintner, like the man back in León.

'It's good wine. You should try it.'

But we drove past too quickly and I never got its name. We have no address for Marcos, no photo of him – no way of thanking him.

By the time we got to the centre Eddie had been told he'd need to go to the bigger town of Requena for an X-ray. Marcos offered to drive, to wait, but we managed to persuade him it was all right. I was here now. Liam had arrived at the hotel. Eddie was very sore, but unlikely to be in danger. The Medical Centre – every bit as helpful – would get an ambulance to take him to the hospital. Trying to thank Marcos, offering him money to give to his two little daughters, Marcos just shook his head, and shrugged: 'Hoy tú, mañana yo.'

You today, tomorrow me.

Four words that struck us as wise and human, the basis of a progressive political theory. Four words you could base an entire civilisation on. Words that are being ignored by our leaders today. Words that reminded us all of Visi, Visi, Visi; of others we had met along the way, of people back home. People no longer with us.

Not that Marcos's actions were that remarkable. Many people would do the same. It was the easy way he went about it, never checking his watch, asking unnecessary questions. This is how it works, plain and simple. The right man in exactly the right place at the right time, with the right attitude, in the right size of motor.

The X-ray showed that Eddie had fractured at least two ribs, and badly bruised most of the rest. With Liam at the accident site, then later with me at the medical centre, he wondered if he might just be able to do the last run. Tomorrow was all flats and downhills, wasn't it? There was a bike shop in town – probably a case of a brand new wheel. Dose up on paracetamol and ibuprofen and anything else we could get our hands on. Spanish pharmacies give out more liberal doses and some stronger painkillers, so he'd take whatever he could. Liam and I would find a way of taking his panniers. But the doctor who explained the X-ray to him said, 'No cycling – for three months'. In Spain they give you the X-ray to take away with you. It's bad enough trailing behind Eddie, his butt in mantyhose directly in your eyeline, now we had to see *inside* him.

Liam's son solved the transport problem. Although it would take us a full day cycling, Utiel was, in fact, only a couple of hours from Valencia on the motorway. Duncan hired a car big enough to take Eddie and his bike into Valencia.

Doped to the eyeballs, a tonic Rioja to wash them down, Eddie recovered enough to have some supper while he tried again to figure out what had happened, how he'd come off his bike at such an unlikely place.

'I've been thinking this for a few days. We're physically stronger. But this trip's taken its toll. I was just really tired.'

A few weeks later Chris Froome, on a practice run, blew his nose and snuffed out his chances for a fifth Tour de France win. Road-biking needs a lot of concentration, particularly for amateurs like us. Cars, potholes, slip roads, cambers and kerbs, unexpected lumps of concrete. Making sure you're drinking enough water, eating correctly for the day's ride. Listening to our (ageing) bodies and making allowances. On this particular trip the blogging, busking, practising, interviewing, editing, and the dynamics of three friends together for a month. Keeping your dodo, or gecko, at bay. And all that *remembering*.

The final of the Copa del Rey – a major event in football-obsessed Spain – in Utiel had to compete against a big-deal bullfight in Madrid. There were two TV sets in our hostel bar, one for each event, even though it was the local team, Valencia against the (increasingly not-so-) great Barça. Valencia, against the odds, won. But the bullfight still edged it on numbers of viewers. It's purely anecdotal evidence but the difference in behaviour between the two sets of fans was conspicuous: the football watchers cheered and jeered, commented on play and refereeing decisions; some women watched and joined in. The *tauromaquia* buffs, on the other hand, watched in silence, like they had in the bar in Nava de la Asunción, even if they were sitting in groups. Not a female amongst them.

The three of us were chatting later over coffee and brandy and I asked Eddie where his interest in Spain and Spanish started.

'All the fault of a teacher at my school. Roger Kennedy. Just stepping into his classroom was magical. The walls were covered in exciting images of mystical Spanish places, from Granada to Córdoba, Barcelona to Madrid. And there were flags of every nation of the Hispanic world. I found the whole thing uplifting, mesmerising... And Roger was ahead of his time in teaching methods. He focused on real communication, not dry grammar. He had an infectious ability to bring the subject alive.

'When I went to university, though, English literature was still my main interest. Then I found out that, if I did Spanish too, I'd get a year abroad out of it.

'I got sent to Santander.'

The most unfashionable town in the equally unfashionable

northern region of Cantabria.

'I fell in love with the place. Even the rain – it helped with the odd bout of homesickness. And that was it, addicted, infatuated. Spain was in my blood.'

Conversations, like memories, meander strangely. Eddie remembered, from childhood holidays, postcards by Donald McGill. Being from good Catholic families we were (or pretended to be, even to ourselves) scandalised by their vulgarity.

'Then I read Orwell's essay "The Art of Donald McGill",' Eddie said. 'I was about seventeen. Orwell makes the connection between the lewd cartoons and Don Quixote and Sancho Panza. Two sides of the human spirit: "Noble folly and base wisdom".'

Eddie has a keen memory for poems, speeches from plays, quotes. Passing a field of horses one day in León he was reminded of Philip Larkin's poem 'At Grass'. He recited it there and then, word for word. 'Do memories plague their ears like flies? / They shake their heads.' Retired stallions, living quietly in their pasture, great pasts behind them. It's precisely a year since Eddie retired, so the poem had been on his mind. On another occasion, along one of those perfect La Mancha cycles, he gave us his 'Ernie The Fastest Milkman In The West.' His timing was perfect, a silly song for high spirits, and as frowned upon by our parents as saucy postcards. There's some kind of art for every occasion.

At the end of the evening, Eddie's ribs are causing him pain. We realised that if Duncan was coming to get Eddie in the morning, he could take our luggage too. Liam and I could cycle without panniers, fiddle, uke, or laptop. The only downside: I couldn't now tell the world that I shouldered my fiddle, *à la* Laurie Lee, all across Spain. When morning came, and with it the prospect of an unburdened cycle into sunny Valencia, I dumped the thing in the back of the car.

Eddie was a sad sight in the morning. Joking and downplaying his injuries, he hadn't slept a wink. We all agreed it was a shame but could have been worse. Any one of us could have come off our bike on the first day. There was no lasting damage, he'd be back on his bike well before three months, knowing Eddie. We'd see him later in the afternoon and we'd all cross the finishing line together.

* * *

The two of us hurtled through the first 10 miles. An early start, a crystal morning, past vineyards, olive groves, *masías* – old Catalan country houses, often built on ancient Roman foundations, local stone that blends into the terrain. And there were our faithful poppies, our Ariadne's thread showing us the way.

We stopped for a coffee, a quick hit of caffeine and sugary buns – cyclists' speed and blow. Then back on the bikes, eager for the next stretch. It looked like all the predictions were right – plain sailing and downhill towards the sea. We'd reckoned a 3PM arrival, but now calculated we'd be there earlier. Let the brass band and cheerleaders know.

Then we hit the motorway. Again.

Service roads are a mixed blessing. Similar roads exist everywhere, designed for deliveries to motorway facilities; in Spain they're often much more extensive and can run alongside a road for tens of miles. Cars aren't allowed on them, at least not for any distance. The surfaces tend to be reasonably well maintained. The problem is they sometimes leave you no other exit but onto the motorway itself. Which is what happened that morning. Fitting, I suppose, the last ride recalling the first. Up from the Galician coast onto a six lane highway, and back down another towards the Valencian shoreline.

But today was Sunday, and election day, so the motorway was comparatively quiet. We saw, frustratingly, the service road we'd been on, reappear on our right. Stopping to peer at screens in the sunlight, we found our way, finally, back on to the service road. This time, it should last a good 15 kilometres and lead onto the

A-road we needed.

What GPS, Strava, Map My Ride and other devices don't tell you is the quality of road surface. This service road had been ripped through, like a torn strip of frayed cloth. And for miles. Getting over one blockage just led to another impasse. Under the crumbled, at points non-existent surface, there were boulders and rubble. Roots of trees protruded. A scene from a dystopian future, the world in tatters.

Adding insult to injury, we were hugging the motorway – which was perfectly flat – while this gouged track had more ups and downs and twists than a roller coaster. We were on and off our bikes for the best part of 5 kilometres, us carrying them rather than the other way round. We were relieved, at least, that Eddie hadn't attempted this. He wouldn't have been able to lift his bike let alone carry it and, on the odd stretch of rideable surface, we were using more upper body strength and movement than at any time in the trip.

Eventually, we got past the broken roads, and onto proper ones. The rest of the ride, until nearer the city, was what we had hoped for. Rolling hills, lots of Sunday cyclists.

Despite the delays of the ruined roads we were still making good time. We'd be crossing the Turia over to the Torres de Serranos, with any luck, in time for a late Spanish lunch. At points the road got more complicated than we had expected. We needed to stop and check turn-offs and directions. The afternoon heat was intensifying. We send an update: an hour later than last reported.

For ten golden miles, nothing but oranges. We were truly in Valencia. Thousands and thousands of trees, each one a Van Gogh painting. Low, green-bushy, the little suns of the fruits themselves brightening further the already bright day. The smell of them, stronger than a phial of essential oil, beyond sweet, minty, almost erotic. Grove after grove, orchard after orchard, filling the air with golden balm and incense.

The groves stopped as abruptly as they had appeared a couple of miles before the city limits, and our faithful poppies took their place, like someone had opened a bottle of pink Champagne. They had all turned up for the final furlong. Waving, cheering, calling on their mates to come see. Six lines deep, like we were passing royalty, they sang red as a bell, jumped and laughed us all the way into town.

Joining up with the Turia – once the semi-dried-up river that ran through the city, now a jewel of architectural and city planning, 5 miles of cycle paths, running paths, gardens, bars, shady arbours – we heard a penny whistle. We stopped, listened. It was in the distance, but definitely a whistle. We were half a mile short and ten minutes ahead of the agreed – post-lunch – rendezvous point. The whistle was, unmistakeably, playing Raglan Road, one of our standard busking tunes. We looked around. It must be Eddie, but where was he? We checked our phones – no changes of plan. We couldn't figure it out. We carried on to the dedicated meeting point, slightly spooked.

From there on in, a cycle track, 4 miles directly into the city centre, then the Torres de Serranos. A fourteenth-century gate, pinkly new-looking, at the end of a sturdy old bridge. Sun bright but not burning. The welcoming party had acquired bunting for a finishing line, poppers, Cava and (plastic) glasses, water, confetti. Even an extra bike, a stand-in for Eddie's busted one. Cameras flashing. We had texted Eddie earlier to tell him to walk over the bridge and come in with us. There he was. We crossed the line together, the three of us.

Ten years after our first cycle together. Over forty years since we first met. It was fun. And it was moving. I hadn't seen Moira in a month. Anne was there, as were Kevin and Duncan Kane and Duncan's partner Nadine. Lizzie had been with us all the way.

On the day of our first Galician hill Eddie texted Lizzie's sisters:

Girls,

Was cycling up probably our toughest hill to date, today. My thighs were burning, sweat dripping onto my handlebars and the only sound you could hear was my asthmatic wheeze. I looked at the interminable incline ahead and I knew I was going to struggle.

My thoughts turned to Lizzie and the day she said to me, "I want to go to the toilet. Don't help me."

I watched her for the next seven minutes make that journey from her bed to her en-suite. Step by step, inch by inch. Her face etched with the fear of failure. She stopped half-way to rest and lean on the windowsill, ostensibly to admire the garden. "It looks beautiful, darling," she whispered, then continued her journey and when she reached it, she turned and smiled triumphantly and closed the door.

I sat on her bed and wept with pride.

I wiped the sweat and the tears from my face, looked up and I was at the top of the hill...

When Chris joined me, he said, "Bloody hell, Eddie. What are you on?"

"Angel's wings," I said.

* * *

So far, Cuenca had been voted our favourite city on the route. Valencia is different in every aspect. Bigger, a coastal and shipping town, southern-feeling, while Cuenca looks north – historically and culturally. The first time I was here, in 1978, I didn't take to Valencia. The name conjured up visions of orange trees in little squares, exotic taverns. In fact, it felt too much like non-Glaswegians' idea of Glasgow: big and dirty and, I thought, threatening. Now, it boasts one of the most innovative and successful city-planning projects in Europe. The River Turia used to flood badly, with great cost to life and livelihood. A massive engineering project in the '60s redirected the flow of the river, making the city secure from flooding. It wasn't until the mid '80s that they started on the Turia Gardens.

Valencia is widely recognised as a culinary centre. These days it's competing with Barcelona on all kinds of levels. Its team beat Barça in the final of the King's Cup last week. Valencia's old town can rival its northern neighbour (the silk market, the palace, the railway station...) while the daring new architecture by Calatrava and others is its answer to Antoni Gaudi's Sagrada Familia. It would be reasonable to assume that, sharing similar histories and languages – Valencianos like to tell you that *Valenciá* is the older and purer form of *Catalán* – they'd be brothers-in-arms. In some respects they are, but there's a feeling among some in the southern city (Valencia) that the northern city (Barcelona) thinks it's a cut above and, should Catalonia ever get its independence, they'd make a bid to seize Valencia, city and province.

We had our victory meal at The Bodeguilla del Gato, a restaurant booked by Liam's son, Duncan, who knows the city and its restaurants intimately. The three cyclists, Moira, Anne, the Kane boys and Nadine. There was craic, and songs, and stories to tell. And conversation, catching up on what had been happening in the outside world beyond our saddle bags.

Looking at the UK from Valencia, and from a month's distance, the political contortions seem all the more bizarre. On an immediate level why do so many people back home want to distance themselves from *this*? From Valencia, Spain, Europe. They'll still come here, of course, but the political ties irk them, a feeling that not only the EU but *Europeans* themselves have somehow hoodwinked them, while feeling all the while that Brits are, in some vague way, better. Deserve better. We wonder if, had we been voters in Sunderland or South Wales mightn't we have voted Leave? No change is the worst option when you have no work, either no house or a damp one, few amenities and fewer prospects. Anything different couldn't be any worse, could it? We'll hear a Spanish version of that line of thought later tonight. We roam around the subject. The intransigence of the 'Troika', prepared to see Greece's people suffer. But aren't those policies – austerity, slashing social and cultural budgets, bedroom taxes – the very same ones that most political advocates for Brexit would *support*? The 'Eurocrats' of Brussels seem to have a lot in common with those who despise them.

The results of the Spanish European and local elections were just coming in. The Vox vote appeared to have declined. PSOE, despite their lack of visibility in the streets, were set to be the larger party, in a stronger position to assemble a coalition without resorting to the PP or Ciudadanos or other right-wing parties. The Podemos vote, on the other hand, was crumbling, weakening their hand still more in any future pact negotiations. Meanwhile, all the supposedly centre and centre-right parties were striking deals with Vox.

PSOE's relatively strong position is a result of them taking the centre ground. There would be no radical policies on the economy, unemployment, the environment. But at a moment in European history when populists from Farage to Salvini and Le Pen are out to destroy every social contract, ignore climate change, and provoke an atmosphere of racial fear and bitterness, Spain seemed to be holding on to more reasonable values. Perhaps, having experienced the extreme right so recently in their history, they know the reality of those choices.

The dishes kept coming out of the Bodeguilla's kitchen, our favourite way of eating – *raciones*. Of *morcilla de Burgos* (best black pudding in Spain, if not quite Stornoway class), *pimientos de padrón* (the peppers from Galicia which have the doubtful fame of one in every five – or eight, or ten, depending on who you ask – being spicy). A little elite of our own, commenting and opining on the world beyond this cosy little restaurant, the Valencian night waiting for us outside. *Pulpo a la gallega* (Galician style octopus), *jamón de cebo, boquerones al limón...*

Later we wandered round town, a coffee here, another there. The number of tourists and visitors feels about right. Enough to help the economy, the restaurants, bars, hotels, and the theatres, I hope. It has so much to show off, Valencia. But to date they have escaped the nightmare of stag weekends and hen parties. So far, Valencia hasn't brought in either the Magaluf 24-hour party people or the Ibiza ravers and trip-hoppers.

We settle for a last coffee in a quiet little square under Nadine and Duncan's flat. Both Kane boys play football and one of their teammates and his partner joined us. Young, bright – they spoke very good English and were keen to practise it, though neither of them had spent much time in an English-speaking country. Both with careers and an enviable lifestyle. When the conversation touched again on politics Jaume said: 'I voted Vox.'

A moment's silence.

'Why?'

'A kick up the ass to everyone else.'

'A protest vote, then?'

'Exactly.'

It wasn't our place to argue with him. This is his country, not ours. But we were interested and asked him about his decision.

'The corruption in this country, you wouldn't believe it.'

Spain has been beleaguered with corruption scandals for decades. Scandals involving prime ministers, in all the major political parties, mayors of cities, the Pujol family in Catalonia, even the royal family itself. We weren't sure how Vox could be the antidote to that.

'It's the establishment here. They're the worst.'

The two most prominent figures of Vox – Ortega Smith-Molina, and Abascal Conde – are from upper middle-class backgrounds.

Best schools, well connected families. Abascal Conde is a dis-affected ex-member of the People's Party, just as Farage is an ex-Tory. So here in Spain, too, there are competing establishments and competing interpretations of what the establishment is.

'Why not Podemos? For your protest vote.'

'I've voted them before, but now Iglesias has got himself a big house with a swimming pool.'

Hardly multi-million deals involving state property and ser-vices, or spiriting away public money in offshore accounts. But no doubt a political mistake by Pablo Iglesias, Secretary-General of Podemos.

'And anyway, they fight amongst themselves. You don't know what they stand for now.'

Jaume is right, the group of dynamic, young, witty people who formed Podemos a decade ago have splintered and the press publish whatever they can of the internal arguments. As the conversation continues, amiably and relaxed, over another brandy, about political parties and philosophies, I think about Ethel Macdonald, and the conflict-within-the-conflict of the Spanish Civil War. The Communists insisting on unity and dis-cipline, the anarchists on seizing the opportunity for a more radical revolution. One side believing you need unity and order to defeat the old order. The other worrying that that just leads to more authoritarianism. Hemingway, a vocal supporter of the Republican movement and aware of the work of Soviet-style *chekas,* the Republican political police, asked fellow American writer John Dos Passos why he wasn't more fully behind the Republic. Dos Passos answered, why defeat one authoritarian government only to replace it with another?

We asked Jaume about specific Vox policies. No, he had no problems with the gay community, with women's rights, with ecological change – all things that Vox campaign against.

Immigration he reckoned could be problematic – sitting at a table with six Scots and one German – but it wasn't a major concern. Quite a few young, educated people – a community hit badly by the banking crisis of 2008, with youth unemployment still unacceptably high – were voting Vox. None of them, Jaume included, ever wanted to see them in power. Only four years ago that same community had voted Podemos, or its local allies, and did hope to see them in power. Perhaps this is the generation that *is* young enough, never having known Francoism or war, that doesn't base decisions on such 'ancient' events. Remembering and forgetting.

We drank and discussed and laughed and talked as the square around us emptied.

The city of the Borgias, before they went off to Rome to infiltrate and conquer the Renaissance world, insinuating themselves at the highest levels of ecclesiastical, political and royal power, and creating family scandals that still thrill and appal us.

* * *

We had begun our mission on the beach at Vigo. 1142 kilometres in all, over sixty Category hill climbs, reaching an overall height of over 11,000 metres.

The next morning saw three sexagenarians, one of them holding his sore ribs, paddle-deep in Lycra, helmets unfastened at jaunty angles, singing, seemingly to ourselves, playing uke, whistle and violin to the rhythm of the Mediterranean waves. We play our usual repertoire, with an extra musician, Anne, replacing me in the band. We also play a bit of an old pop song, 'María Isabel.'

In his book ¿*Qué Me Estás Cantando?* (What Are You Singing? Memoir of a Century of Songs) journalist Fidel Moreno places pop songs in their historical context. He tells the story of 'María Isabel', a 1969 pop hit. A few months after Manuel Fraga – one of Franco's closest allies and founder of the Spanish Conservative party, the PP – announced that the Spanish Civil War was officially over. Across Spain, men who had been in hiding came out from caves, underground hideaways, basements and lofts. Pale, skinny and fearful. Meanwhile Fraga was also pushing the policy of making Spain a holiday destination. Los Payos were a pop group from Seville and their song became the first of decades of *canciones de verano* – Spanish summer hits. *'Coge tu sombrero y póntelo, vamos a la playa calienta el sol'* (Grab your hat and put it on, we're going to the beach, now the sun is out). Spaniards themselves were copying tourists, lying in the sun and bathing in the sea. 'En la arena escribí tu nombre…' I trace your name in the sand, María Isabel. The following year Los Diablos released 'Un Rayo de Sol', the next big summer hit, and the record my sister Liz had brought back from her first ever Spanish holiday.

Sitting at twelve years of age, watching the single spin on the old Dansette turntable playing the song over and over. Almost fifty years ago. At that age I'd still have been serving early Mass at the convent. From the altar I watch my mother kneel in the little chapel she cleans from top to bottom, including the stained-glass windows. She closes her eyes towards the Queen of Heaven, milky light beyond. Her first dream of the day.

Our second time busking on a beach was more successful than in Vigo. Several people stopped. One or two clapped. Nobody tried to give us money. It was only when we played back a video that we noticed a young woman had interrupted her shoreline run to slow down momentarily and dance a little dance. When we finished our set a lady clapped. We gave a final bow. We had done it – coast-to-shining-coast.

PART FOUR

Full Cycle

ALICANTE

And suddenly I'm on my own. Moira and Anne back to Scotland, the Valencianos back to work. We had boxed up our bikes, Liam and Eddie taking theirs home on the flight. I had mine couriered back.

Catching the bus to Alicante early on a Friday morning I feel not so much lonely, but a man misplaced, in the wrong time frame. There had been so much to do and prepare that I hadn't managed to get my hair cut before leaving Scotland. I'm waiting for the bus now with a fiddle tied to a rucksack, an old pair of trainers with holes in them, hair and beard a cross between Don Quixote and Janis Joplin. Sad old hippy. And I really miss the bike. After a month's cycling I identify now as A Cyclist. But now without wheels to prove it.

Still, it's exciting. Going to see Ana Eiroa, Brian Hughes' widow, in Alicante. Apart from one brief meeting more than twenty-five years ago, I haven't seen Ana since those first trips to Galicia in the 1970s. After catching up with her, reminiscing, I'll be going inland, up into the Alicante Mountains to try and make sense of all these experiences. Finally, Málaga to Almuñécar, end this adventure where Laurie Lee did, and where I'd meant to as a teenager.

The bus from Valencia to Alicante takes two hours, passing through places whose names I know from tourist brochures. Denia, Calpe, Benidorm. There weren't many, if any, tourists on board. Local people, visiting family, a man next to me talking quietly, business-like, into his phone. A young woman behind me made a call and spoke, loudly, in Russian. For some reason I got the idea she was speaking to her father, possibly because she kept saying '*Da, da*'. I had read only a day or two before that the largest foreign community in the Alicante area was North African, and the second,

Russian. The young woman – she *sounded* young; sitting directly behind me I had no real idea of her age or her appearance – made another phone call. This time in English. In both calls she sounded relaxed, her English good, apart from those tricky prepositions that trip everyone up in all Romance languages.

'Yes. I go back in my town. All is very good. Thank you.'

She is talking loud enough to make it impossible not to eavesdrop. I can't concentrate on either the view from the window or my book, re-reading Brenan's *South From Granada*. The middle-aged lady next to me reacts by looking more intently at her phone. I don't think she speaks English though, so the conversation behind us is not quite so disruptive for her.

'Yes. That is what they say, and it is fine. I think everyone is very happy. Thank you.'

It's her tone, too, that holds my attention. Still relaxed, but keeping it formal, very purposefully. For some reason I feel she is talking to someone who is closer to her than her words or her tone suggest.

'There is one question that I must ask to you.'

The person on the other end talks a lot, judging by her silences.

'Yes, what I said. Everyone is fine with that. But this question –'

' _ '

'Before we leave speaking I would like to get answer. So, if you please –'

She listens for quite a long time, responding with the odd Hm, and Uhu.

'Please. I will ask this question –'

' _ '

'Okay. Now I ask. If a man he proposes marriage to me, do I accept?'

The woman at my side definitely doesn't speak English – there is no reaction to this. The businessman across from me, I think he caught it. He closes his eyes, but sits up straight, leaning ever so slightly over the aisle to hear her better.

The unknown party on the line speaks for quite a long time. The woman answers 'Yes' and 'No' and 'Of course' intermittently.

'I ask the question one more. Will you answer?'

' _ '

'Wait. Wait a moment please. May I ask –'

' _ '

'So. You think me a rubbish? You think I am a rubbish girl?'

Despite the words her tone is still even and calm. But there is something, her voice dropping a little, a shade more apprehensive.

' _ '

'Okay. That is fine.'

' _ '

'I told you already. That is fine too. Now, please. My question.'

' _ '

'If a man, I know him. A good man. He will look after me. If he propose a marriage. Please tell me, do I say yes?'

' _ '

'Please. I do not love him. What do I do? Yes or no. Do I tell him Yes or No?'

' _ '

'Thank you. Goodbye.'

She hangs up. Whatever the answer was, I don't think it was the one she was hoping for.

Later I discover that sex work is a major black-market industry right along the holiday coastline, from the Costa Brava to del Sol. That human trafficking is a worsening problem and that some Eastern European sex workers have been murdered in the last decade. It feels like an unsubstantiated judgement, though, to decide this woman is being prostituted. She sounded, throughout her conversations, resolute and in control. Many circumstances could lead to such a conversation.

The closer we got to Alicante the more I recognise the names of holiday destinations. Signs off to Oliva, Altea. We pass a rock formation that, from the perspective of the bus passing fast, looks like the sculpture of a female goddess in a shrine. Gigantic, commanding. As we pass the shape changes, from the side it looks more animal-like, a female Seth, horse-headed. An elderly woman somewhere in front is shouting into her phone – '*Cariño!*' '*Te amo!*' 'Darling!', 'Yes, pet.' 'I love you!' 'I'll be home in half an hour.'

We pass close by Jávea and Benissa. I get my first glimpse ever of Benidorm.

The story goes that this massive mishmash of high-rises and amusement centres – from the road above like the contents of a gardening rubble sack – was 'invented' by a man called Pedro Zaragoza. In 1952 Zaragoza was an ex-banker who had been appointed mayor by local Francoists in the once small fishing village. *Benidorm* in Spanish sounds like it means 'sleep well'. In fact, it comes from an older Arabic name, from Spain's Islamic days. When Zaragoza became mayor it was both sleepy and on its uppers. An economy based on tuna fishing, they had overfished the waters and people were going hungry. Resorts elsewhere in Spain had begun to appear, a result of the Francoist Manuel Fraga's policies, frequented by well-off sun seekers from colder countries. Zaragoza, from a fishing family himself, had an idea.

One day, they say, in winter, he got on his little Vespa scooter, stuffed newspapers up his shirt (not having a proper leather biking jacket) and rode to Madrid, 500 miles away on bad roads. Arriving at Franco's residence in the Pardo Palace, he asked to see the *Generalísimo*. He was laughed at, told you don't get to see the *El Caudillo* just by knocking on the door. Who was he anyway – the mayor of a tiny, unknown village? But he persisted, telling anyone who would listen that he had the answer not only to Benidorm's economic problems, but the whole of Spain's. Eventually Franco, intrigued, gave the upstart a few minutes of his time. Zaragoza, his trousers black and tattered from exhaust smoke and engine oil, went to work on him.

Mass market tourism. Cover the entire length of Benidorm bay with affordable hotels. He had noticed, reading about international banking, that tourism and holidaying were becoming major industries. And not just for rich but for the growing lower-middle and middle-classes, with two weeks' holiday a year and a disposable income. Benidorm was the perfect place to trial this new business model. Build high, not deep, so that everyone could see the sea. The bay is 3 miles long – that's a lot of hotel rooms. Get private interests to invest in the building, for good returns. Market the idea particularly in the UK, where companies like Thomas Cook and Travel Club were beginning to charter aeroplanes, making foreign destinations accessible.

Franco thought about this for a few minutes. Nobody else had a plan for developing the Spanish coastal economy, and Zaragoza was persuasive. The mayor went back to Benidorm with Franco's blessing to start raising money and finding investors. However, before the two men parted, Zaragoza had a final condition.

'Bikinis.'

In some versions of the tale, Mariá del Carmen, Franco's ultra conservative and staunchly Catholic wife, was at the meeting. And was outraged. Semi-naked women? Over her dead body. Franco seemed to think, if necessary…

No doubt the story is more complicated, but the legend of Pedro Zaragoza has both a grain of truth and is revealing in its own way.

When my bus pulls into Benidorm all the Spanish speakers alight and their places are taken by, mainly, English speakers. Off to Alicante for a day's shopping, or back to the airport. We pass the tallest building in Benidorm, the Intempo tower. M-shaped, it was built just before the crash of 2008. A modern folly, it broke the backs of banks and individual investors and remains empty to this day. There is always talk of new investors getting on board and finishing it, but for now it stands as an emblem of the Spanish building mania of the early twenty-first century, brutally halted by the banking crisis. It dominates the town. Two lanky arthritic legs with the gold M on top, it looks like a pasty Brit walking to the sea in a tight pair of Speedos. Whatever Pedro Zaragoza's vision, it has been buried under decades now of cashing in, building sprees, and the devastation of bust.

Half an hour later we pull into Alicante and I see the Russian woman behind me for the first time. In her early thirties perhaps. Maybe younger – she's carrying a lot of weight. Inexpensively but tastefully dressed. I think I detect a hidden smile in her expression. The family of the older Spanish woman who has been telling them she loves them for most of the journey are there to welcome her. As if she had returned after thirty years in Cuba. My guess is she left last week to see her sister or cousin in Valencia. '*¡Mamá!*' '*¡Mami, has vuelto!*' You're back!

I haven't busked yet on my own and think I have to do it quickly or I never will. Ana is not expecting me until two o'clock and it's only midday. She's told me to get the bus or tram from the city centre, but I decide to walk. It's hot and I'm carrying too much stuff, and awkwardly. At least I have GPS – unavailable to Laurie Lee. I wonder if the existence of such new technologies has put paid to just wandering and seeing where you end up.

Crossing the first large street and alameda, I arrive at a little park area called Plaza Galicia. Where better to busk? It feels like a good omen. There are one or two people sitting on benches, a few passers-by with shopping bags. I'm never going to make much money here. That's not what this is about. But I'm interested to see if anyone does give me anything. If they don't then I can blame the pitch.

Without Liam and Eddie, the fiddle solo sounds friendless, forlorn. I try a faster tune – 'Whiskey In The Jar' always worked before, a tune most people half-recognise. No matter how hard I bowed and how much I upped the pace, it still sounded funereal. Then a guy dropped a single euro coin in my open violin case. He didn't stop, or look at me, listen, or say anything. He did it surreptitiously, like it was something shameful. Still, I had earned my first solo donation, so I played another tune. A slower one, giving in to my mood. I try to remember the buskers in the square in Segovia, playing for all their worth as if in front of a huge audience.

A couple of kids run by hardly glancing at me. They go off to play on the swings and roundabout a couple of hundred yards away. I can hear them laughing, and I'm pretty sure they're laughing at me. A woman passes by, in her fifties, she smiles at me, nods, but puts nothing in my case. Then one of the children runs up and drops a couple of brown coins in – about 15p.

'No, no. Here, take it back.'

The little boy, around ten or so, lifts his coins back out. Then a girl, his sister I imagine, comes over and tells him to put it back in.

'It's fine. Children don't pay.' I give them the euro coin too. The boy is delighted.

'Gracias!'

And I suddenly worry if it's foolish to play so close to a playground. The worst paedophile strategy of all time, playing foreign airs on a violin in the middle of a small square, but potentially a strategy all the same. A problem Laurie Lee never had to worry about. Then again, the treatment and condition of children he comes across in *Midsummer* is horrific and abusive. The boy shows his sister the euro coin, and she waves at me. They run back to the park area, and she turns and shouts:

Full Cycle

'Keep playing!'

But I'm worried now and want to move on. I've made my point. I've busked alone, if only for about ten minutes. Before I can finish the tune a man who I think might be the dad steps towards me. I get ready to defend myself. But he listens to the end of the song, gives a couple of short claps, and nods his head.

'Not really the right place to play,' I say putting away my violin. The guy shrugs. 'Quiet around here.'

I head back over towards the main street and the little girl calls 'Bye' after me.

My first solo busk in nearly half a century. Ten minutes. Broke even. Didn't get arrested.

* * *

Alicante held out against Franco's troops and their German and Italian allies until the end of the war. The Fascist Italian air force had been bombing Republican-held areas indiscriminately for a year. Franco mounted a final attack in March 1939. The result, in Alicante, was that many thousands of refugees, displaced by the conflict or in hiding, were rounded up by Spanish and Italian troops. An agreement had been made between the Nationalists and the Republican government to allow the rescue of many of these men, women, and children. At the last moment the Nationalists decided to ignore the agreement. People in Alicante, to this day, tell terrible stories of inhumane treatment and outright murder of innocent people. One British ship, the HMS Stanbrook, under the captaincy of Welshman Archibald Dickson, managed to save a few thousand lives. Most of the rest, tens of thousands, were imprisoned in the infamous Campo de los Almendros (The Almond Orchard) and other concentration camps. Dozens took their own life rather than face the cruelty of Mussolini's and Franco's men.

There is a simple plaque there now. It's in the opposite direction from Ana's house so I can't go today. I'm not sure if I ever want to go. It smacks of 'Dark Tourism'. My colleague at Glasgow Caledonian University, Professor John Lennon, would defend not only these sites but the reasons for visiting them. It's a form of witness. Cover them over, and you allow governments to rewrite history.

'In these days of fake news,' John says, 'such places are hugely important. Having them in the open allows us to remember, and potentially to understand the past better. Selectivity in our understanding of history is dangerous. What is conserved and what is ignored tells us a lot about a state and its relationship with the past.'

Spain's unofficial 'Pact of Silence' is coming undone. That little plaque, and those like it – the faded wooden sign at La Granja at the foot of Navacerrada, for instance – are becoming more evident, and more politically charged.

Only months later, war with the Axis powers imminent, the British government worried that all Italians, Germans and Austrians living in the UK were potential spies, supporters of Mussolini or Hitler. The Italian community had been settling in Britain for several generations. Few had been to Italy or could speak the language. While there was the odd show of support for Mussolini when he first came to power, the majority of British Italians knew little of the dictator let alone supported him. In 1940, the war going badly, the worry became an obsession and hundreds of thousands of Germans and Austrians – including Jews – were rounded up. Italians, too, though Britain was not yet at war with Italy. Churchill is reported to have ordered: 'collar the lot!'

The Canadian government agreed to take a number of these internees for the duration of the fighting. The Arandora Star liner left Liverpool for St John's, Newfoundland, on 1 July 1940. It was torpedoed and sunk by a German U-Boat, within sight of the Donegal coast, out from Gweedore. 865 died, nearly all the Italian and German internees.

Full Cycle

My mother, originally from Donegal, had lied about her age, emigrated to London and talked her way into training as a nurse. Many of the survivors of the Arandora Star were hospitalised at Mearnskirk, Glasgow. They desperately needed more nurses... Which is why my mother came to Scotland, and why I am here at all.

Ana's house is in San Vicente de Raspeig, a town in its own right, just north of Alicante. It's a hot and sweaty walk but I get close with a little time to spare, so I wander into the campus of the university where Brian Hughes, my friend Brendan's brother, became Professor Brian Hughes, chair of the English Department, Vice Rector in charge of the university's international projects. The grounds remind me of Stirling University's campus. There's a statue at the entrance of a huge white stone hand with pen poised. There are a few students walking, unhurried – this isn't term-time. Cafés dotted around. Later, I'll discover that Brian's old office is still there, named after him, a portrait of him at the door. Setting off towards his house I try to imagine him walking around this campus, through these streets, between home and work, for years.

Within minutes of that house, I'm still a little early. I'd like to cool off, hot and red and sweaty from the walk through town. There's a park area just along the road, gardens with modern sculptures. I find a seat in the shade and close my eyes for a few moments...

In 1974 Brendan and I travelled from Paris to La Coruña by train. Despite the *pichet* of wine and bloody steak *frites*, the real romance lay beyond the Pyrenees.

We crossed the border at Hendaye (France) and Irún (Spain) and boarded a Spanish *'rápido'*. A standing joke that the 'rapid' train was tortuously slow. But there was always a carriage where an entire family meal was being set out – *bocadillos* of cheese and tortilla, salads, the *¡glúp!* of a wine bottle being opened – which they always shared. We were on those trains for the best part of twenty-four hours, going from family to family, sleeping intermittently. The trains may have been slow but they were, or felt to us, stylishly old-fashioned. Like the Orient Express, carriages out of '40s movies. Compartments, with sliding doors, upholstered benches facing each other, enough to seat four passengers either side. But much more comfortable if you get the whole place to yourself, and could stretch out on the benches. Having secured a compartment, when we pulled into a station Brendan and I protected it by opening the window and, contorting our faces into twisted smiles, beckoning new arrivals to come and join us. It worked, they gave us a wide berth.

Smiling at the memory, I get up from my shady seat in the garden in Raspeig and turn onto Ana's street.

Brendan and I arrived in La Coruña mid-morning, and made our way, following pencilled directions, to Brian and Ana's flat, just behind Riazor beach.

I find the house number, ring the bell. Waiting for Ana to answer, I notice, just beyond the gate, a riotous bougainvillea bush, purple and orange, in full bloom…

It was Ana who opened the door in 1974; and it's Ana who opens the door again now. She talks and smiles and hugs all at once. As ebullient as the bougainvillea, as persistent as the waves on Riazor beach.

In 2019, of course she's older, but she has not changed in any important way. A grandmother now, recently retired, she's as warm and effervescent as ever. First time round she ushered us in, poured us a drink, found some cheese in the fridge, told us the bags could wait. This time she pours a beer, tells me to throw my stuff wherever, finds some cheese and ham in the fridge. She talks as she does it, asks questions, throws in comments on politics, the weather, her family, eyes gleaming. I hear you're a writer now. We talk about Brian. At sixty-one, Ana gets a little upset, at sixteen, he arrives. And, he can talk as much as she can, talks over her, so she talks louder, over him, the two of them arguing, agreeing, demonstrative with each other, physical. Here, in Alicante, Sean their son arrives. He doesn't strike me, at first, as being Brian-like. Then *he* starts talking, books, ideas, jokes. And *she* starts talking over him, and they hug and push and pull at each other... No time has passed, the same energy, the immediacy, words, ideals. Forty-five years later I'm in Spain, with the Hugheses again.

Sean has a son, two years old. Physically, the boy is more like Brian, fair haired. Sean looks more like his mum. But as we talk, in English – both are completely fluent – over gazpacho and cans of cold beer, I can hear Brian in him. And *see* Brendan. (Months later, back in Glasgow, Brendan reminds me that I had met Sean before. Brian and Ana brought him when we all met up in Cuenca, in 1979. Sean would have been about the same age as his son is now.) The subject of bullfighting comes up, mum and son disagree.

'Ach what do you know? You're a northerner, a *Gallega*.'

Sean has lived all his life in the south.

'It's got nothing to do with being a northerner. I just don't like it.'

'You're just an old leftie.'

'That's true.'

Brian was, and Sean is now, a lover and teacher of literature. The *corrida* plays a big role in Spanish culture. Not just the voyeurism of foreigners like Hemingway, but in key Spanish texts. Lorca's Lament for Ignacio Sánchez Mejías, one of the most important, and beautiful poems, of the twentieth century. Blasco Ibañez writes about this very region, his novel *Blood And Sand* a fiery depiction of the *corrida*. I mention that the great Scottish writer A. L. Kennedy wrote a wonderful little book about bullfighting. For years I enjoyed the sport, went to a few *corridas* in Cádiz. It just felt so intrinsic to Spanish culture. It's hard to understand flamenco music and dance, much of the literature, and the Spanish take on the world at large without it. The *corrida* is often thought of as being defended only by right-wingers – which it often is – but, as with flamenco, the situation is more complicated. *Matadores* like the legendary El Viti, a thoughtful progressive, are friends and collaborators with writers and painters and musicians. Manolete, considered the greatest *matador* of all time, despite Franco's efforts to co-opt him distanced himself from the regime, supporting Republican refugees in Mexico. The art of such greats as De Falla, Picasso, Goya, would be incomprehensible without some idea of *tauromaquia*. In the current elections Vox are weaponising it, turning it into a symbol of Spanish machismo and pride.

I comment that over this cycling trip, we watched quiet men turn in on themselves staring at the bullfight on TV. The blood on the screen and how the odds are stacked so impossibly against the bull, I can no longer defend it. The Catalans banned it in 2010. We discuss the danger of the entire world being forced to align itself with a particular set of middle-class, first world, market-friendly attitudes.

Sean's little son has two names, or rather a Scottish and *Valenciá* version of the same name: Jamie/Jaume. I remember a daft wee song his grandfather sang back in the flat at Riazor. It's stayed with me for forty-five years:

I love a sausage
A bonny heilan' sausage
And I put it in the oven for my tea,
I went out to the lobby
To fetch my uncle Bobby
And my sausage came after me!

It's the only song I ever heard Brian sing that you could possibly repeat to a child. He had lots of ditties and mad poems, most of them outrageous, some self-penned, and always performed hilariously by, at the time, Tolstoy-bearded Brian, intoning operatically.

Brian Hughes and Ana Eiroa

The Hugheses, like any Scots-Irish family of the time: Catholic parents and school, Mass on a Sunday, the Clancy Brothers, Celtic football Club, distrust of the host community and terrified of Scottish nationalism, mother hoping one of her sons will be a priest, Frank O'Connor stories, single ciggies from the shop across form the primary school, the Catechism ('This likeness to God is chiefly in my soul'), fathers dying of heart conditions, the Singing Nun *'Dominique-nique-nique, s'en allait tout simplement…',* big families and limited funds.

Ana's family: Franco and the shame of him being a fellow *Gallego,* Galician sun and showers, *'Black is black I want my baby back',* Georges Moustaki, Catholic parents and *Misa* on a Sunday, fiestas, bagpipes, big family and an old house…

In later photographs of him, Brian is clean shaven. In my mind he'll always be bearded. Ana, on the other hand, hasn't changed apart from those tell-tale signs that affect us all. Thought lines, worry lines that, as it turned out, Brian never had to worry about. *Brumas,* Ana used to call him: Misty. Man from the cloudy country.

Ana and Brian spoke each other's languages well. When I first knew them, they would swap between English and Spanish for no obvious reason. Both linguists, they threw in Gallego, French, Scots expressions. I loved that dance of language, the facility they had for it, the joy of improvising, like jazz musicians.

Ana's family had a large house further north in Galicia, in

Xubia. Hers was a family of seven sisters and one brother. If the individual notes of the Hughes family sounded like The Firebird Suite, the Eiroas I heard as pipe band. Pipe major was their father who sat at the top of the table when we were invited to eat at the old house. I remember him talking and Brendan and I not understanding a word. Apart from once when he leaned over and shouted, '*¿Franco? Una bomba. ¡Una bomba!*' Successful as the family were – they produced a gin, for one thing, famous at the time – the family despised Franco and all he stood for.

Brian was always... combustible. He could flare up over an opinion, or an awkward piece of machinery. In 2019, Sean tells me he remembers his dad taking a screwdriver to his PC, wrecking it, even though it was a power failure and hardly the computer's fault. But generally, Brian was the joker, an extremely erudite joker, turning conversations and situations into absurdist comedies, contriving daft poems and songs on the spur of the moment.

The newly married couple moved from Galicia for teaching jobs, first in Benghazi in Libya, then in the Alicante region. After living in villages, Brian was offered a post lecturing at the University of Alicante. His doctoral thesis on the poetry of Seamus Heaney was judged to be of the highest standard and is still in print. He is acknowledged as the person who introduced Anglo-Irish literature not only to Spanish academe but to the Spanish world. A noted Hispanist in his own right, his speciality was the poet Luis Cernuda. (Cernuda, from Seville, in exile from Franco, ended up in Glasgow – a city he hated with a passion.) Brian was involved in setting up the Erasmus project, now so fundamental to European and global academic exchange. And under serious Brexit threat in the UK.

Full Cycle

Ana worked in schools, then followed Brian into academia. She has translated some of the most difficult writers into Spanish, including Henry James. But she also liked to translate popular fiction – her house is a shrine to the best of the *novela negra (*crime fiction). Many of the books on her shelves she translated herself.

One evening in 2003, Brian said he wasn't feeling well and went to bed. He never woke again. He was fifty-two years old.

The rector of Alicante University, at the celebration of Brian some months later, called him *'Sabio y culto'* (wise and cultured). But also *'jovial, cordial y alegre – un hombre bueno, bueno, bueno.'*

The shock was as immediate in Glasgow. I remember Brendan phoning me. Though Brian was far away, and I hadn't seen him in years, his death felt to me like a colour being lost forever.

Ana and I sit up late and talk. She shows me some of Brian's work, gives me a lovely edition of his translation of selected Heaney poems, and her own translation of *Retrato de una Dama*, Henry James's *Portrait of a Lady*. We get to talking about La Coruña in the '70s.

'It's a richer town than it used to be.'

'Great.'

'You've heard of Inditex?'

'No.'

'But you have heard of Zara? And Pull & Bear. Massimo Dutti. Stradivarious? They're all owned by Inditex.'

'What's the connection with La Coruña?'

Ana explains that Zara's first shop was in La Coruña. Started up by Amancio Ortega, a local tailor, and his wife, Rosalía, a

seamstress. Now they employ half the town. At one point he sur-
passed Bill Gates as the richest man in the world. 'You can't say a
word against Amancio in Galicia. They all love him.'

'Sounds like with good reason.'

'He gives a lot of people jobs, all over the world, and he helps
schools and small businesses in Galicia.' She pauses for a moment.
'Some people, though, would prefer that he just paid his proper
taxes rather than trying to dodge them.'

'Ah. That old story.'

I tell her that I can remember minute details about her and
Brian's flat. The layout, the kitchen, where the olive oil was kept,
Georges Moustaki record lying on the old record player – a
Glasgow-made Linn, in my memory. I can remember so many
unimportant things, the orange-coloured suite. In the midst of
this Ana happens to mention two names. John and Laura.

'Who?'

She told me their surnames.

'Who are they?'

'What do you mean who are they,' she laughs. 'We were sharing
that flat with them.'

'But not while Brendan and I were there.'

'They were there the whole time.'

This is astonishing news to me. It wasn't one of those occasions where, after a moment's thought, you get some kind of faint
memory. There was nothing. Gone.

She describes them to me. She tells me that their bedroom was
next door to where I slept. Not only have the two people gone but,
despite my belief that I had remembered *everything* about that
flat, actually I've missed out an entire room. Including the door.
When I try to imagine where it is all I see is a blank wall.

I feel bad about John and Laura – apparently I got on well
enough with them. But I have edited them out of my story. I have

no idea why. My own jump-cut. They didn't fit the narrative in some way, so I've obliterated them.

And then another, shocking, revelation. We text Brendan in Scotland to say hi from Alicante. He's been thinking – always a worrying thing – and doing the math. He's worked out that we couldn't have been sixteen when we first went to Spain, but seventeen. After much debate and calculation, he's right of course, and the story I've been telling myself all my life is fundamentally flawed. Well, I did say I have a tendency towards mythologising. We are our past, and the past is never reliable.

Ana just shrugs – it's only a matter of months, but I feel as fraudulent as Amancio Ortega. She searches her house to find pictures of our time back in La Coruña. She can't. Neither Brendan nor I had a camera back then. So there is no pictorial evidence. I don't think I ever wrote home at that time, so there is no written confirmation, either. We left not a trace.

Facts are not truth, though they are part of it – information is not knowledge. And history is not the past... It is no more 'the past' than a birth certificate is a birth, or a script is a performance, or a map is a journey.

Hilary Mantel, The Reith Lectures 2017

RELLEU

You've listened long enough. Now strike your note.
Seamus Heaney, *Station Island*

Basta ya
de escuchar. Que suene tu propia nota.
(Translated by Brian Hughes)

Christopher North and his Alicantina wife Marisa run the Almàssera Vella, a writers' retreat in their home in the village of Relleu, 25 miles north of the city. Sean gives me a lift to the local tram station. I change in town and catch another tram to Vilajoiosa – 'La Vila', I discover it's known locally. I'm surprised at how much tourism there is along the Alicante coast. The tram passes resort after resort and there are as many English and Dutch speakers aboard as Spanish or Valencian.

Christopher has texted to say that we will meet in Café Carlos, near where the tram stops in La Vila. I'm over an hour early, so I have no excuse not to busk again. But nor do I have time to find an ideal spot, not knowing the area. There's a little square just down from the tram stop, a few people passing through it. That's probably the best I can do – at least there's no playpark.

I play for about five minutes and nobody passes. Until a mother and daughter come over to me. I'm playing a jig and the woman dances with her four-year-old just in front of me. They're blonde and look dressed for holidays so I assume they're tourists. Another woman, possibly a local, stops and watches them dancing. At the end of the tune I say hello, and play another tune. The Spanish lady moves on just as an elderly couple arrive, again probably tourists. The little girl gets fed up dancing and her mother gives her a two euro coin to put in my violin case. They wave and walk away.

'You Irish, then?' the older man says in a London accent.

'It's an Irish tune, but I'm Scottish.'

'There's a Scottish guy with a guitar plays down by the beach.'

Two teenage boys stop, keeping a few yards' distance. Looking up, I realise I have a small audience dotted around the square. One of them, a guy in his twenties, dressed in classically Spanish hippy style – loose, faded but once highly coloured harem pants, cheese-cloth shirt, long hair tied in a ponytail, beard and shoulder bag – catches my eye and comes over, stands quite close to me. An English woman in holiday mood, tells me I sound 'fab' and leaves a fistful of copper coins and totters off, for her next *sangría* or G&T. There's a café at the far end of the square and the few customers sitting outside are drinking *cañas* of beer. I think, that'd be a good place to play, you could pass a hat round the tables. What I really want is to meet people, payment in stories and memories. Still, when I hear someone else drop a coin or two into my case, it's a good feeling. The afternoon is hot and my violin goes out of tune easily. I have to adjust my fingering and avoid open strings. A very elderly man, with a walking stick, shuffles past, just as I finish a piece. I say good afternoon to the old man.

'Is there a song you'd like me to play?' This is a risky strategy as I have a limited repertoire and I'm not good at picking a tune out the air and playing by ear, without prior practice. But he doesn't suggest a song anyway.

'I used to sing.'

'Great. What kind of singing?'

And he sings me a verse of something I don't know. A *jota* perhaps. His voice is frail and parched, I can only make out the odd word. I think a sad tale of unrequited love.

'That's lovely. What is it?'

But he just laughs, says goodbye and shuffles on. Before I can start a new tune, a middle-aged Spanish-looking guy walks past and places several coins carefully into my violin case, doesn't just drop them. The guy in the harem pants steps towards me, so I don't have time to see how much the older man put in. Maybe three or four euros. And I'm not sure he actually heard me play. I'm about to joke to the hippy guy that that's maybe my best strategy, just stand, violin in hand and case open. Actually playing seems to bring in less money. But I don't get a chance to say anything.

'You got a licence?'

This is not what I expected. And I realise for the first time he's not been happy about my playing.

'No. I'm just passing through.' I haven't been anywhere long enough yet to request an official licence. From what I've gathered there's no nation-wide system. Each region, or city, has its own regulations.

'I'm going up to Relleu in an hour. I'll be there for a bit, so thought I'd apply there.'

'You should have a licence.'

'You're right. Sorry. Is this someone's pitch?' I'm wondering if it's his, though I can't see an instrument.

'If you want to play, you have to go to the police. The station's just over there.'

What he's saying and how he looks are completely mismatched, like the wrong soundtrack. I tell him, thanks, it's okay, I'm moving on now anyway. And I pack up my fiddle. Shame, this busk was beginning to work out. He watches me sternly as I pack up. I try a couple of friendly questions but he's not up for them. He stands firm and makes sure I leave, watching me walk right through the square. I wave. He doesn't wave back.

Sitting waiting for Christopher North in Café Carlos I remember rumours from Glasgow, that busking pitches are gang controlled. I have no idea if that is the case either there or here. I count my takings – 14 euros and 50 céntimos. Not bad for twenty minutes' work, rudely interrupted.

A week later I take the bus down from the village to Alicante to try and get a busking permit. I make a guess at asking first in the town hall. The lady at the desk is very helpful and directs me to another building a ten-minute walk away, the office of the *Vía Pública* – everything to do with street and outdoor regulations. I get there and have to wait for about an hour before another very helpful woman takes me into an office. There, I'm given a three-page form to fill out, and told to go to yet another building, ten minutes away. On the way, reading the forms, I realise that you have to apply at least a month in advance, that there's a test you have to take (which I worry I might not pass) before you are allotted two locations in the city and two time slots. So just turning up, playing and moving on, like Laurie Lee, like I used to do in the 1970s, is no longer possible. Or legal, at least. I reckon it's still worth it as I'm going to be here for another two months. But at the next office I'm told that the licence only applies to the city of Alicante. If I want to play in Relleu, even though it is in the same province, I'd have to apply to the town hall there. My plan had been to play in various mountain villages, but if you have to apply, pay, and risk being turned down every time...

Relleu is a case study of coastal Spain's relationship with tourism. Where I'm staying is 100 per cent Spanish, or rather, Valenciano. The other end of town is 90 per cent English and Dutch. Mainly ex-pats, or second-home owners, very few of them speak Spanish, and seldom venture beyond the far square where their bars are. Their houses are either the new-build blocks at the edge of town, on the road down to La Vila and Benidorm, or more expensive ones with private pools outside the village itself.

On the one hand, tourism saved this town, like so many others, from dying completely. On the other, an old way of life is endangered.

I'm based down the hill from the main square, the church and the shops. My friend and Scottish writer David Simons was in the area last year and visited the Almàssera Vella – Old Olive Press. Linda Cracknell, another friend and writer, has stayed here. The house still has the original olive press – a beautiful thing but no longer in use. Christopher and Marisa have converted the large five-bedroom house into a space for writers and retreats. They have a smaller property directly across the road, divided into apartments. I'm in the smaller flat at the top. All I have to do is cross the road to use the extensive, cool and quiet library they've built up over the years, and the swimming pool and orchard and olive groves (they still make oil from their olives, though they're pressed elsewhere now). The village lies on the lip of the Marina Baja mountains.

There's a three-minute walk from my door to a little balcony overlooking a valley and the hills beyond. A landscape that's at once spectacular and soothing. Like a giant has been called away from his pudding, great spoonfuls scooped out of the flan-coloured hillsides. Birds of all stripes strafe the sky around the rock face. Chris Lambert, who I met through Christopher – which would get confusing, with three Chrises – is a geologist who, having been the chief engineer of major projects internationally, has retired here with his Dutch wife, Tineke Vlijm. Chris can read the mountains like a history book; the rocks being starkly exposed he can look right back to the Jurassic and Cretaceous periods. He can see clear evidence of the meteor impact that wiped out most of earth's dinosaurs. The Spanish peninsula is, to simplify massively, the result of continents crashing into each other, tectonic plates colliding. That's the reason Spain is a series of horizontal, east-to-west, mountain ranges, crushed and corrugated by colossal forces. Starting with the Pyrenees and the Cantabrian mountain range in the north, down through the *Cordillera Ibérica,* the *Sistema*

Full Cycle

Central to the Sierra Morena and where I am now in the *Cordillera Bética*. The entire landmass is one huge crinkle-cut crisp. At some point or another in our travels, Liam and Eddie and I have cycled over, or through, all those ranges.

On my first morning in the village I go up to the central square, take a seat at Bar La Plaça and order coffee and toast. Served the old-fashioned way: milky, lukewarm coffee, a small baguette cut in two, hardly toasted, and a cruet of oil, vinegar, salt and pepper. There's no mention of butter or jam, or even tomato. This was the breakfast norm of my days in Galicia and Cádiz. This morning I was the first to sit outside at the back of nine in the morning and made the mistake of taking a seat at the middle table. Within minutes the local retired men sit at either side of me. They talk loudly over me. Pepe, the bar owner, brings one man his breakfast – same as mine, but with a serious measure of what looks like *anís*. An old lady, passing, berates him:

'Oy Mano, drinking already?'

'No. Breakfast.'

Something else that hasn't changed since my first days in Spain. In Cádiz, more often it was a mix of brandy and *anís*. Gerald Brenan reports on exactly the same breakfast, cheap booze included, not far from here, in 1919.

The guy at my ear shouts to the one at my other side:

'Think this guy's a poet, eh?'

The Old Olive Press has been a centre for poets for fifteen years, so it's a reasonable conclusion. And I am writing, taking notes. Long hair and, I admit, somewhat unkempt. They assume I can't speak Spanish let alone Valenciano, but I can understand enough of the latter to get the gist.

'S'pose somebody has to be.'

They all laugh, and Mano shouts in to Paco in the bar to bring him another *anís*.

That evening there's a baptism in the church. Christopher and Marisa tell me that the majority of the Valencian population of Relleu is a complex intertwining of four or five families. The square becomes ever more active, kids running around, cousins and friends kissing, calling and shouting. In the side streets, trestle tables have been set up for outdoor dining later.

I walk up to the top of the town, three streets away, where the ex-pats are gathering to watch the football in an English bar. Liverpool v Tottenham in the final of the European Champions League. The average age is blotchy late-fifties, a gallery of Lucian Freud portraits. Lumpy gents, arms, legs and shoulders prickling red from the sun, No. 1 haircuts, like a row of King Edward potatoes. But the atmosphere is relaxed and there are a few jokers in the crowd to make everyone laugh. They drink pints and eat crisps and chips.

The two communities rub along together well enough. But at a distance. The incomers take in very little to do with Spanish life. No interest in the politics of the country, changing under their very feet. A good number of them are vocally pro-Brexit, though they live here year-round. (There is a Brit bar in the neighbouring village of Finestrat where they refuse to serve you if you're a 'Remainer'.) What they *do* know is that Spain needs their money and will do everything it can to protect their rights. Some are even excited by the idea of a no-deal Brexit, though it's hard to imagine that that won't be anything but detrimental to their situations. The triumphalism of hope and glory over prudence.

Talking to one avid Brexiteer couple I get the feeling we are both living through Shakespearean dramas. Just, theirs is a History and mine a Tragedy. Theirs is a glorious battle against European adversaries, *'we happy few, a band of brothers'* standing firm, dreaming of a great British, or more specifically, English triumph, *'Once more unto the breach, dear friends... Or close the wall up with our English dead'*. While for me, a tragic flaw, a terrible waste is leading us all, ever more clearly, unavoidably, towards our collective catastrophe. We scorn help, or expert advice, *'throw physic to the dogs I'll none of it'*. They're in the Henry plays, I'm in Macbeth and Lear. *'Oh let us not be mad, sweet heaven...'*

Any other community would be condemned – including by some of the people here – for coming to a country with no job, never learning the language and benefiting from the State. The difference, of course, is that these displaced persons have money. But they haven't, psychologically, left home. The meals offered in the three English bars are curry, pie and chips, burgers, meat-and-two-veg.

There are different kinds of incomers of course. Tineke is Dutch but has lived in Spain for years and speaks excellent Spanish; Ton, a Dutch photographer, has a long history in Relleu, once trying to set up an animal sanctuary here, he knows everyone in both communities.

The football is dull, so I go for a walk over to the complex of houses, currently empty because their inhabitants are watching the game in the bar. A few blocks of flats stuck together. They don't look happy, their facades blank, giving no clue as to the lives within their walls. No tended gardens, no pot plants, they look awkward and temporary, like they're not sure how they ended up here.

* * *

Every dawn here I'm greeted by swallows, martins and swifts, heavenly music. *'Crazed with morning,'* as Christopher North has it in one of his poems. I've never seen so many birds, filling the sky. In the salty evenings they fall into group formations above the square and circle the spire, an air display show, lending the church another kind of transcendence. Swifts plummet from out of thin air like miniature birds of prey, swallows skim and sip from swimming pools and fountains. The tiny serins can be mistaken for butterflies. There's a lullaby every night – after the town crier has made his rounds and told us what's on tomorrow – of frogs, owls, the gurning of nightjars, dogs in the distance barking either listlessly or expectantly. A couple of cockerels declaring twenty different dawns each day and night. As summer hots up the cicadas join in, a rhythm section to nature's erratic ensemble. I'm told that, just out of town, you can see, regularly, golden orioles, bee-eaters, hoopoes, huge eagle owls and tiny scops owls.

The Marina Baja mountains are a cyclist's dream. Hard hills quickly followed by dazzling downhills, no section more than 20 kilometres from a village with cafés, seats, fountains to fill your water bottles from. The roads quiet and in pristine condition. I'm filled with envy every morning watching groups of riders stopping to rest in the Bar Balcón, wishing I'd brought my bike with me. It looks like hard work, but with well-earned payoffs. Instead of cycling I go back over notes and video and sound files from our trip, enjoying writing them up and organising them.

There are two recordings of Joan Manuel Serrat's version of Antonio Machado's 'Cantares' (from a section of his book, *The Fields of Castile, Songs and Proverbs*). One we recorded in Glasgow before we left, and another we filmed at the end of our journey in Valencia. It was a suitable venue, I now realise. As Franco's Nationalist Forces took over more and more of Spain, Machado had to run from his beloved Castile which had fallen early in the war. He lived in Republican-controlled Valencia for two years until that fell too and he had to escape to Barcelona, and finally France where he died before the end of the war.

Watching the videos and reflecting on our adventure I worry that I'm flouting what Machado meant by his poem. Essentially, don't look back. Go (in my own translation) *'wherever your*

footprints lead… behind you the road you'll never tread again…
Nothing but the wake o' the water, ebbing.' I've been consumed
these last months with looking back, but I tell myself it's to see
the past in the present, and the present emerging from days and
deeds gone by.

The appeal of Joan Manuel Serrat's pop version of the poem is
down in part to the beauty of his voice. But I think Liam sings it
well, too. Making the song his own. Serrat's original is a big production affair. Full rock band, horn section, strings. A massive hit
in 1969, it was still criticized by some for losing the intimacy and
tenderness of the original. Liam's version restores it. Eddie has a
keen ear for poetry and a perfect voice for reciting. It is, in the
end, a fitting anthem for us.

Years later, singing the song to a huge audience on a high stage
in Madrid, reaching for the crescendo, *'¡Golpe a golpe, verso a*
verso!' (Step by step, word for word, One by one we make our road!),
Serrat fell off the stage. He was uninjured, but perhaps Machado's
spirit had its moment.

In Relleu, I'm still in touch with Liam and Eddie on social
media. Spanish friends have joined in the debate on the Catalan
question, which fills up every newspaper and all the radio and
television news here at the moment. It's hardly a new issue
but it is coming to a head, perhaps partly by missteps on both
sides. Jamie Jauncey, a Cunninghame Graham, cousin of Robin
in Segovia, published an article in which he quotes his great-
great uncle in 1906: 'As to Catalonia, your correspondent may
be sure that if, in the long run, she wishes to be free she will
gain her independence, for the whole trend of modern thought
and economics is toward the evolution of small states and every
great and unwieldy Power, our own included, is on the verge of
a break-up and a return to its component parts.'

A friend from Cantabria says that the *transición* after Franco's death feels, to many, like an imposition. That the 1978 Constitution (which was given a linguistic polish by José Camilo Cela himself) was drawn up largely to maintain the status quo. The loudest voices, including the Francoist Manuel Fraga and members of the centre-right UCD party, out-muscled the only two left wing members on the seven strong committee. Some say that the creation of the Autonomous Regions, including Catalonia, was a step in the right direction, but outlawing any future vote on further devolution or independence was both a mistake and undemocratic. The Catalan movement has grown stronger in the twenty-first century, but Madrid has refused to engage with it, exacerbating the problem. Until the illegal, according to the Constitution, referendum of 1 October 2017 and the Spanish State's heavy-handed response to it brought the matter to where we are now. In the coming months the courts will sentence democratic leaders to up to twelve years' in prison each – and for many Spanish people that is lenient. In Catalonia the sentences and accusations of sedition feel dictatorial.

Other friends disagree. Like Ángel and his group in Valladolid, they think that the transition was correctly and democratically undertaken. Discussed, considered, changed and voted upon. (As a memorable pop song of the time, 'Libertad Sin Ira', had it: 'Freedom without anger / enough of fear and rancour / if we don't have freedom now, we very soon will.') These people believe the Constitution is binding. They disagree strongly with the Catalanist position that Spanish corruption extends to the justice system itself or is in thrall to Madrid's political power. And what about the corruption scandals in Catalonia – the region can hardly take the high moral ground. The sad fact that leaders in Barcelona and Madrid cannot speak to one another, negotiate, is at least as much the fault of the Catalan nationalists as the Spanish government. Under the Constitution the referendum of October 1st was clearly against the law and when the law is broken castigation must follow. If, as these friends see it, the Catalan nationalists consider the Constitution flawed then they should stand for election on that basis and argue to change it.

We cyclists are lovers of Spain, and Catalonia, but we make no claim to be historians or authorities on the constitutional matters of a country that isn't ours. We take part in the debate by asking questions and drawing comparisons with Scottish Indyref and Brexit. The Catalan situation is different from the Scots one in various ways. Catalonia is richer than Scotland – if it secedes the rest of Spain will be poorer, and that could be a disaster for working people in Andalusia and other less wealthy regions. Is the argument not against nationalism – Catalan or Scottish – but between *nationalisms*? Catalan v Spanish, Scottish v British. One as bad, or as valid, as the other? Some of those against Catalan independence think that the whole country, as it now stands, should vote on the question of secession, not just Catalans. That argument was around in the 2014 Indyref too. And the Conservative party have renewed that call in the event of a second Scottish Referendum. But in that case, no smaller country would ever be able to secede, being always massively outvoted, which can't be democratic?

A few weeks later a young Catalan friend and fellow writer, Dania (who gave me permission to quote her), wrote:

'The transition to democracy was rushed and the context was less than fair. Certain conditions were approved under the veiled threat of a regression to a military regime. We were sold the narrative of a "war between brothers", which means that no one answered for forty years of fascist dictatorship. Thousands of dead bodies remained in ditches, stolen property went unreturned, people who had spent years in prison were never compensated and those who had been in power simply remained under a new disguise. The ideas that had held Francoism together were not fully contested, but brushed under the carpet, where they festered.

'The referendum in October 2017 was, indeed, illegal,' Dania says. 'But justice doesn't exist in a vacuum; laws are made and interpreted by members of society, with their own ideology and prejudices. There have always been unfair laws and, often, they have been forced to change via civil disobedience. It's hard to understand that police brutality and jail are the best strategies a democratic State can come up with to respond to three peaceful forms of political dissidence.

'I think that, at the point we are now, it is a mistake to reduce pro-independence to nationalism. The three parties that most visibly represent the movement roam in wildly different areas of the political spectrum. Importantly, they are not the only agents in play. There are civic associations, there are activists. A good example is "*l'acampada a Plaça Universitat*": young people, mostly students, occupied University Square for twenty days, until they were forced out. They talked about being "a generation without a future", about the precariat, climate emergency, violence against women, racism, repression. I would say that the sentences handed out on October 14th was the straw that broke the camel's back. There is a general feeling of outrage towards a system that keeps squeezing, and not only us.

'The cry, "*a por ellos*" ['let's get them', a slogan often shouted at Spanish national team football games] 'in 2017 was meant to cheer on police repression against pro-independence Catalans. It still echoes. On election night, it became the victory chant from the far right (now the third force in Parliament)'.

All these people are friends and colleagues. They are thoughtful, informed, and well-intentioned, but arrive at very different versions not only of the present situation, but of the 'facts' of the past.

While this debate goes on, we're seeing videos of mass marches in both Barcelona and Scotland. Both sets of independence seekers flying flags. Flags frighten me. For me, they're reminiscent of

Full Cycle

Nuremberg. Of Tricolours and Union Jacks vying for attention in the streets of Belfast, and at Rangers v. Celtic games. I've seen Stars of David flying provocatively, like jabbing fingers at Palestinian areas and towns. St George's flags outside Westminster, wielded by red-faced men, spitting mad. The sickening black flag of Isis; white supremacists wrapping themselves in the Southern Cross. The politics of identity are in the mix somewhere, and on all sides. It comes down, again, to what stories we tell ourselves, what we choose to commemorate, and fight for.

Dania signed her post off with: 'Anyway, that's my opinion. But, as the journalist Hibai Arbide Aza says: "less than five contradictions is dogmatism".' Antisyzygy clearly isn't a purely Scottish phenomenon. It strikes me again that not only individuals but groups of people – three guys cycling, families, nations – might suffer complexes and internal turmoil. Are Scotland and Catalonia undergoing some kind of dissociative personality disorder? Feeling ignored or misunderstood by the failing 'parents' of the UK and Spain? The latter feel that the EU is an enforced asylum they need to escape from; the former see it as another kind of asylum, benign, a place where siblings can find refuge and common cause in one another. One trapped in fantasies of individual past greatness, the other in dreams of utopian harmony.

The debate about Catalonia and being in touch with friends there reminds me of Antonia Fontanillas. Ten years ago, making the BBC documentary about Ethel Macdonald, I went to France to meet Antonia – survivor not only of the Civil War, but of the Spanish Revolution. Antonia passed away not long after I met her, but the impression she made on me is indelible. Her concerns, both as an elderly lady and as a young radical, had little to do with nationalism. She spoke in a mixture of Catalan, Spanish and French, and what she remembered was the hope, the plans for a brighter future. And the sense of loss when it all ended badly.

Antonia

Dreux is a shabby town west of Paris with a high percentage of North African immigrants. It has come to international attention only once, when France's National Front Party won elections in 1983, seizing control of the city council. It is home now for ninety-year-old Antonia Fontanillas. We sit in her tiny kitchen, her window looking onto a dilapidated swing park where North African, Pakistani, French, and Chinese children play together amid uncollected rubbish and broken glass. Antonia shows me photographs of a young, bright-eyed, dark-haired girl. In some of them she wears the red bandana of the anarchists. Despite the passage of seventy years, the girl is immediately recognisable as the elderly lady sitting across the table from me.

'What was important to us then was loyalty – that's what lay at the heart of anarchism. It was about breaking down barriers, not to be subservient, to fight to become decent people, for dignity.'

Antonia lived at a time when women's education and the role women played in political organisations and movements were pitifully undervalued. 'The girls where I worked started wearing hats to work. At that time only well-off middle-class ladies wore hats. Really, it was all a big change.' *Mujeres Libres* was an anarchist feminist organisation fighting for women's rights, running classes and workshops for other women. They also challenged language, ditching the word 'wife'. 'What *Mujeres Libres* really wanted was to encourage the ordinary girl,' Antonia says. 'Show her she had a role in society. We were women, but first we were individuals. You have the right to choose your own life. You were no longer condemned to stay at home.

You didn't have to become a mother. You had the right to be whatever you want to be.'

The Republican alliance was already beginning to disintegrate at the end of 1936. The POUM, whom George Orwell enlisted with, had fought alongside anarchist militia without many problems; in the early days of the war both fought side by side with Communists. 'There were never any problems in the factory where I used to work. I never felt there was a difficulty in the committee because members were of one organisation or the other.'

My friend back in Glasgow, Willy Maley, whose father was a *Brigadista,* concurred: 'I never heard my father judging whether anarchists, POUM, the socialists, and so on, were right or wrong.' Antonia Fontanillas in Dreux can't recall a single incident or argument around sectarian divisions.

Antonia's smile fades when she remembers Franco's nationalists entering Barcelona. 'To this day I hate to think about it. I was in the workers' solidarity office. A colleague, Hieres Núñez, came in and said, "It's all lost. Whoever wants to escape there's a truck leaving this afternoon." When I got home that evening, I told my family, "Let's go". But my father wasn't well. He couldn't leave.' A little later, stuck in Barcelona and hiding from nationalist troops and policemen, Antonia went with her mother to the cinema. 'My mother said "Remember, we'll have to raise our arms in their salute. Otherwise they'll find us." I said, "I'm not going to raise my arm!" When the moment came, my mother stood up to salute. I stayed seated. A man behind me shouted, "You! Stand up!" If I hadn't, they would have put me in jail. It brought tears to my eyes.' It still does.

Antonia would have been pleased to hear that Spain is now seen as leading the way in making femicide a specific crime. In 2004 the PSOE government passed a law and set up a network of courts dedicated to domestic and gender-based violence, backed up by a series of measures to support survivors. But she'd be horrified to know that in June 2019, while we were merrily cycling through central Spain, the 1,000th female victim of domestic abuse since records began in 2003 was murdered at home by her partner.

* * *

Visiting Christopher's library, across the road from my writing den in Relleu, he shows me the original olive press, cleaned up, in his house. Belén, their housekeeper and friend, a woman several decades younger than me, remembers the press actually working, coming with her uncle to have his olive harvest turned into treacly gold. She now keeps the machine pristine. I mention something of my project to Christopher, who recognises the name Brian Hughes. Then he remembers, he was at Brian's memorial event at Alicante university. Terry Gifford, fellow poet, naturalist and climber, was friends with Brian. Christopher had never met him, but Terry suggested that he come along to the celebration, that he'd like Brian's work. Both Christopher and Ana fondly remember Terry closing the celebration by getting everyone to sing 'Will Ye Go, Lassie, Go'. Rummaging around his library, Christopher finds two books published by the University of Alicante in memoriam for Brian. *Thistles 1* is a collection of some of Brian's work on Heaney, Irish writers, thoughts on translation. *Thistles 2* is work by academics and writers who knew Brian and who contributed work that touches on his interests. We are, it's true, only 25 miles north of Alicante but the connection still delights me. I end up writing a book, which begins with Brian forty-five years ago, in an old olive press that houses two of his books.

Full Cycle

Christopher's library takes me back to another library, the most important of my life, in Partick, Glasgow. Its cream stone muddied, it was brighter on the inside. Crossing Dumbarton Road from primary school, two abreast, in lines. Saturdays with my sister Maggie, swapping *Black Beauty* for *Treasure Island*, *Alice in Wonderland* for *The Hobbit*. Conquering the castle together.

Writing about our coast-to-coast ride, I realise there's another unconscious connection with Brian. One of our busking tunes was 'Che Faró Senza Eurydice', the aria from Gluck's opera *Orpheus and Eurydice*. Researching Brian Hughes's career, especially his involvement with the early days of the Erasmus project, the student international programme creating links and supporting student exchanges between European universities, I remember that Eurydice is an extension of that programme, researching ways of enriching both students' and academics' study across Europe. And now the very notion of Europe is under attack. Orpheus the poet and musician is silenced by the loss of his muse. In a few months' time Nigel Farage and his Brexit party MEPs will turn their backs on 'Ode to Joy' in Brussels.

*　*　*

Relleu is overlooked by the remains of an old Moorish castle. As an experiment I walked out early on a now genuinely midsummer morning and headed up the hill it sits on. I find a small blanket in my flat, take my violin out of its case, wrap it up and take it with me, just like Laurie Lee used to do. He must have had a system – I try every configuration and can't stop the blanket coming loose at one end or the other or unfolding completely. I almost drop and break the fiddle several times. The bow slips out repeatedly. How did he manage it? How did he carry anything else?

The road leads up past the old washhouse, in use until only a few years ago. (In 2005 Christopher was showing some writers the

lavadero: 'I was just saying "Of course it's not been used for years".
And as we went in two elderly ladies were deep in conversation
as they did the family wash.') I expect to hit compacted earth, a
country lane, once I'm clear of the houses. Relleu is in the heart of
a network of tracks and paths, over terraces, connecting villages
deep into the hills. The kind of trails and byways Laurie would
have walked. Well-trodden, the compacted earth is warm as skin,
dusty-smelling, softer on the feet, except for the odd stone that
stubs your toe. But the road to the castle turns out to be decora-
tively pathed with mosaics most of the way up.

At night they light the old castle, so that it seems to float and
glow ghostly in the dark sky. Villagers are proud of their ruin now,
but throughout Franco's regime there was a concerted effort to
wipe Al Andalus from the collective memory. Deny 900 years of
history. Even now, talking to people of my age, educated during
Franco's time, some have very little knowledge of a fascinating part
of their history. It's now a cliché that Africa begins at the Pyrenees.
As Laurie Lee puts it in *Midsummer*: '...where Africa and Europe
touched finger-tips in this merging of day and night'. Relleu itself
was once an almost completely Muslim village. Built on a hillside,
its streets and wynds could be in Palestine or Morocco. There is
acknowledgement of the Islamic past in two plaques on the way
up to the castle, but what brought it to an end is very much more
on show. The parish church, in the heart of the town, is named
after San Jaime – Santiago.

One Sunday I go to Mass. No longer a Catholic, churches and
services, hymns, still hold a fascination for me, reconnecting me
to an earlier time in my life, to people in my family. The parish
priest here is Fr. Juan Berchmans, from the Congo originally, the
only black man in town, popular with everyone. In the streets he
can be seen day and night, laughing and talking, surrounded by
people from all the communities. He speaks to them, as much

as he can, in their own languages – Juan speaks Kinyarwanda, Spanish, Swahili, French, English. On the altar he's more serious. He says Mass in Spanish, I imagine because his Valencian isn't good enough. But to speak in Spanish here is a kind of political statement, whether intentional or not. Many years ago, in the Basque Country with writer Bernardo Atxaga, we were out walking, conversing in Spanish, when Bernardo saw some neighbours approaching. He said quickly to Moira and me, 'We have to speak in English now.' To be heard, in *Euskadi,* speaking Castellano would be seen as a kind of treachery. The sense of national and linguistic difference in the Valencia and Alicante regions is not nearly so strong, nor the anger against the notion of 'Spain' and Spanish. Still, there is a local language, and it's not used at Mass here.

I don't notice until we get to the part of the service when the priest says, *Daos fraternalmente la paz* (Let us offer each other the sign of peace). While I'm shaking hands with the parishioners in the pew in front of me I look up and realise that the centrepiece behind the altar, pride of place, is a statue of St James, on horseback, spear raised to kill a second Moor, the first one dead under his horse's hoofs. Santiago, *Matamoros* – Muslim killer.

'Santiago, and close Spain!' is a rallying call for Spain's far right, and has been for over a thousand years. It was the plea made to the spirit of the apostle: that he materialise and help defeat the Saracens at the ninth century battle of Clavijo. Vanquish the infidel, then close Spain's borders for evermore! Obligingly, the saint turned up, in his distinctive sea-shell armour, astride a white horse.

Christopher told me that the Equestrian figure in the Church has an interesting history. 'When Marisa and I first came to Relleu in 1998 the mounted Santiago was lifting a sceptre in an acclamatory gesture – the horse rearing on a sward of grass. We were told that the grass was painted over a row of severed Moorish heads. Seven years later, after the arrival of Padre Juan, we went to Belén's wedding in the church. During the service I noticed that the Santiago's sceptre had been replaced by a sword and a recumbent Moor had appeared. There'd been protests in Alicante at the time decrying the *Moros y Cristianos* festivals as insensitive. There was also a kerfuffle in nearby Orcheta – a Muslim couple living there were offended by the appearance of a similar depiction of *Matamoros* in the church there, a church also in the parish of Padre Juan. I've never talked about it with him, but the church here was repaired and redecorated under his guidance.'

The *Moros y Cristianos* street theatre can be seen in various parts of Spain, but its heartland is here in the Valencian Community. Like re-enactments of Bannockburn, citizens get together once a year and dress up either as a fifteenth-century Christian, or his mortal enemy, a Moor. They are fantastically colourful displays, sometimes with the Moors on actual elephants, Christians on horseback. The Moors, to be fair, are every bit as colourful in their dress and actions. It is far from a dishonour to play a Moor rather than a reconquering knight. The owner of a restaurant in a nearby village showed me twenty years' worth of photographs, he himself proudly 'Moorish'. Strangely they sometimes have the entire Moorish army smoking cigars – something more frowned upon in Islam than in Christianity. An example of Orientalism, perhaps, focusing on imagining exotic eastern sensuality. On a TV set in a bar in town they're showing highlights from this year's *Moros y Cristianos* in Alcoy, the local capital. Verging on Brazilian-style carnival they're the sexiest, and most sexist, Moors and Christians I've ever seen, dancing in short tunics. Truly shockingly, some of the women have been blacked-up. By chance, I'm re-reading Thomas Hardy novels – another re-visitation to teenage infatuations – in the evenings here, and discover that, in *The Return of the Native,* Hardy has Eustacia Vye, in the 1870s, dress up like a Turkish knight in a mummers' play re-enacting, and distorting the history of, Crusader victories. Orientalism has smudged our festivities for a long time.

The road up to the old Muslim castle in Relleu has been made into a Calvary, a series of Stations of the Cross. Another statement of historical remembering and forgetting. I like walking around the Stations of the Cross when I visit churches. They're a canvas on which artists can interpret a powerful story. The Stations can have a healing function, provide a conduit, a way of dealing with suffering. I have a half-written play somewhere that I was preparing for Glasgow's Oran Mor when David MacLennan died. David, a towering figure in Scottish theatre, founder of the hugely successful lunchtime dramas, A Play, a Pie and A Pint, is another hole in so many lives. I don't think my *Via Crucis* piece would be of any interest to Oran Mor now, but I think of David as I walk up my own little Way of Sorrows. The Stations on Relleu's *Calvari* have distinguishing features. They go in the wrong direction. You begin with Christ crucified and entombed at the bottom and go back through time, uphill, with him through his stumbles, Veronica wiping his face, his condemnation and Pilate washing his hands. Odd, to travel Christ's *Via Dolorosa* in the opposite direction from him. The fourteen stations include, unusually, depictions of the Nativity and the Annunciation, at the top of this Spanish Golgotha. A final, worrying feature is that somebody has systematically scratched the faces off all of Christ's Jewish captors. One or two Roman faces have been scrubbed out too, but it seems to be the Jews who inspired the vandal's attack. A show of anti-Semitism in a religious garden. Later, Christopher told me that tiles were defaced by 'an odd elderly lady. Significantly, no one has sought to repair them.' Kate O'Brien might have approved.

* * *

Not only are the social changes caused by mass tourism on show in villages such as Relleu but also that other process, depopulation.

There are now more expat restaurants serving food regularly in Relleu than there are Spanish. The crisis of 2008 hit this region as badly as anywhere in Spain. Prices have risen, so it's not as cheap to eat out as it used to be. And there are fewer people to do the cooking. One of the bar owners told me, and this is typical across rural Spain that, when her mother died, she didn't want to take on the huge amount of work of providing lunches and evening meals six days a week. The meagre profit doesn't justify the workload. The younger generation have either moved away or have no interest in running village restaurants. The ex-pats, by contrast, find it reasonably cheap and have retirement funds to spend. It's an adventure to open up a bar or restaurant in Spain. Mum and Dad have the cash and the time, and the kids fancy the change from Slough or Maastricht.

But keeping themselves to themselves leads to the ex-pat community missing out on aspects of Spanish village life.

In Valladolid they brought art to the people, in Alcalá de Henares, political debate, and in the Valencia area they bring sport to the streets. Relleu hosted the finals of the *Pelota Valenciana* 2019 cup. *Pelota* rules are a blend of handball and squash, teams of five a side. The buildings and all their features – balconies, roofs, doorways and guttering – become part of the court. The pitch here, *Carrer Major,* the High Street, presents another obstacle: it's on a steep slope. Each team takes a turn at playing from bottom up. The street is lined with residents sitting watching, or hanging out their windows, standing in bar doorways. That ball is a small, hard bullet, and the players hit it with all their might. It's a dangerous spectator sport.

But the ex-pats, more by chance than design, had chosen the

same day to have their karaoke party. MC'd by two Scots, performing another brand of busking, everyone seemed to be having fun, singing along to Queen and Take That numbers. 'This next song,' one of the MCs says, 'is for Steve the golfer,' before singing a Neil Diamond song. Both groups of people were having a day out, but their backs turned to one another.

The grand final of the pelota was a showdown between Benidorm and Parcent, a village north of Relleu. The majority of the crowd were supporting the smaller village team, but Benidorm, as a place, is popular with everyone here. Sean, in Alicante, told me that when he was younger all his friends went to Benidorm for the music, the clubs, the *movida* – the scene. My parents-in-law used to come in winter. They were ballroom dancers and, since the closure of places like the Plaza in Glasgow, Benidorm was a haven for them. On the other hand, there's an item in the newspaper today that Paul Gascoigne – once the best football player of my lifetime – was seen singing sectarian songs in a Benidorm bar. Migrants carry their problems and their divisions wherever they go. And they continue to age, despite the dream of life in the sun: elderly retired British people, often women who have outlived their husbands, their pensions running out, find themselves isolated in Benidorm high rises, not speaking the language and becoming sick, creating a burden for Spanish social services.

Parcent won the *pelota* on the day, and we were invited to join the victors, losers, and fans of both teams for an all-village paella, made in a *paellera* as big as a swimming pool. Moira had come over to visit at the time and, as far as we could see, we were the only foreigners at the banquet.

Relleu is a surprisingly musical town. I first heard the local band on Corpus Christi when I followed the statue being carried through the town's streets. Later they played in the main square for people to dance to and sing along with. They gave a concert in the town's little auditorium. On this occasion, a series of medleys of '70s rock music, brilliantly arranged and played with vigour. Later that night, I was awoken at 3AM, the band having reassembled outside the auditorium. Uninvited I went out to see what was happening. The young band members were throwing a party, playing Valencian tunes and songs, everybody singing along, dancing, drinking beer and caring not a jot for the noise they were making – louder, even, than during the performance. Forty-five years ago, Brendan and I would have been part of that *juerga* (revelry) – in Galicia. Now, at sixty-one it was quite enough to see it, to know that I had once had nights just like that. I went back to bed and listened happily till 5AM when either they called it a night, or I dozed off. The next day there was not a word of complaint. The people of Relleu are profoundly proud of their band. And anyway, they had nights like that too, in their youth.

The local kids love Padre Juan and he does what he can to connect them to the church. Everyone knows his story. Trained and ordained in Rwanda he saw first-hand some of the terrors of that civil war – and it gives him an insight now, he says, into another community still living with the fallout of their own civil conflict. We have a long chat one evening, over a beer in the square, just at the door of his church – a church that, when he arrived thirty-five years ago, was falling to pieces and which he began to rebuild with his own hands. No wonder he's popular. Juan is angered by the way the Rwandan war is represented in the West, as some kind of senseless blood lust between the Hutu and Tutsi peoples; that they just hated each other for no rational reason.

'This is not the case,' says the priest. 'A complete misrepresentation. The cause of the war was the economy. Poverty. And the lust, in the West, for cheap minerals. Especially coltan, used in computers and the like. Look there to find the cause of the war. And the continuing suffering of people in Africa.'

Full Cycle

I ask him about Liberation Theology, once a major force for change in the Hispanic world. Padre Juan shakes his head. 'After Popes John Paul II and Benedict? That's gone.'

Juan Berchmans is small and quietly spoken yet he seems to take up the entire village square. Everyone wants to say hello to him, Paco from the bar anxious to serve him what he wants. As he speaks, of secular subjects, there is still something of altar-movements in his gesticulations, his eyes severe as cassocks.

'I cannot go home to Congo. My family are split between three different countries and cannot visit one another.' When he finds the time, Juan goes to Uganda to work with refugees from the wars in central Africa. He has managed to get his parishioners interested, and to donate to his work.

'Look at the amount of puppet presidents and dictators in the region. Most of them supported by one or more of the big western powers. The Russians and Chinese are both moving in, building power and economy bases across the Continent. There is no real democracy anywhere, and the people are ignored. And hungry. These false leaders are put there so that the developed nations can buy coltan and other minerals cheaply. They are stealing from us.'

He has to stop and have a conversation with one of his, elderly, parishioners. Afterwards he says how hard it is here in Spain to get any of the younger people to take an interest in the church. We talk about falling congregations throughout Europe for a while. It's clear he likes the local kids immensely; he goes to their concerts, parties, sports days, the *pelota* matches. They like him immensely too, but they don't return the favour by visiting his church. Except on the big high days and holidays when the church becomes the focal centre for family and community fiestas. Before we part company, we get back to the subject of Africa for a moment.

'Look at the recent histories of so many African nations,' he says. 'Libya, Mali, Sudan, Burundi, Rwanda... We are suffering a new colonialism, and I cannot see where the solution is. I do my work in Uganda, and I pray. It's the best I can do.'

And he's whisked away by a group of townsfolk who he makes laugh immediately.

SOUTH THROUGH GRANADA

Yo voy soñando caminos
de la tarde...

Antonio Machado

Here I go, in the evening,
dreaming roads...

Organising three guys to cycle across Spain for a month proved easier than organising three others to walk and take buses for just 50 miles for four days. Admittedly two of the cyclists are retired, and we had a coordinator par excellence in Liam Kane.

Merely escaping Relleu without a car has its challenges. There's only one bus, leaving in the morning and returning late evening. I boarded the little ten-seater with standing room at the back to find that Gema was already on it. Gema is a stalwart of Padre Juan's church – just as my mother was in St Peter's, Partick. Gema cleans, organises Juan, knows everyone in the village, and sings in – essentially *is* – the choir. She's in her sixties, with the energy of a teenager. There's a certain kind of Spanish hymnody, steady and sharp, to my ears somewhere between plainsong and Scots Gaelic psalm-singing. Gema's voice is perfect for it, filling the quiet church like a bell. Gema introduced me to everyone in town, kept me up to date with local news, made sure I was invited along to any gatherings or events. This morning, on the bus to Alicante we made an unannounced stop. In Aigües, a young lad got on at a stop next to a café and spoke to the driver. I couldn't hear what they said, but the engine was turned off, the boy went and stood at the back, and we waited for a full fifteen minutes. Gema was with three other ladies; two men of my age sat behind. Nobody complained or asked for an explanation. Eventually, a teenage girl came out of the café and sauntered on. A local Dulcinea del Toboso. Young and fresh as morning coffee. The driver started up and we pulled out. As the girl made her way to the back where her friend was Gema gently stopped her.

'*Oye, guapa*. Hey gorgeous, say thank you to the driver.'

It was clear now that the boy had asked the bus to wait while the girl finished her breakfast. The girl half-turned towards the driver and half-heartedly waved her thanks.

'Now say thanks to us.'

She declined to go that far, but the bus burst out laughing, uniting us all. Glancing behind, the girl giggled at her companion, satisfied she'd caused a bit of a stir.

The next bus, out of Alicante, heads south-west, through Murcia city, where Moira had spent her year abroad in the late '70s, and out into the fertile valleys of the province. There are orchards of every type and on every side, oranges, lemons and limes, but mostly, olives. The first olive groves we saw during the coast-to-coast cycle were north of Madrid. From there down, through Cuenca to Jaén, you realise how fundamental the *aceituna* is to the Spanish economy. So many of them are grown on terraces first laid down by the Romans but extended and improved by the Moors. From the Almàssera Vella in Relleu you look out over *bancales* built and cultivated by the Moors over a thousand years ago. I've been gifted locally made olive oil by Christopher North and by José and Ana who run the shop (which acts as the unofficial centre of Relleu's social life). Both oils are deep and sweet, like the accidental eroticism of a chaste kiss on the lips. You'd think that it would transport you to Al Andalus. In fact, I remembered meeting Donald S. Murray in the Wild Olive Café in Nelson Mandela Square, where this whole escapade began.

Spain hasn't benefitted from its olive production as much as it should have. After Alicante city was taken violently by Italian forces, General Franco, as a way of thanks to his fellow-dictator Mussolini, gave him more than half of Spain's olive production in perpetuity. In Italy it was repackaged as 'Italian' olive oil. A lot of the expensive, high-quality oil we have been using in the UK is not Italian at all but Spanish. The 'deal' – Trump would have liked it – lasted throughout Franco's reign, and beyond and it's only now that the industry is beginning to recover. *'Los olivos / están cargados / de gritos...* (The olive trees / are loaded / with screams).' – García Lorca.

From Murcia the bus heads south and west towards Granada.

'Give him alms, woman, because there is nothing sadder in life than being blind in Granada', reads a plaque on the Alhambra. *'Leave me in Granada in the middle of paradise where my soul wells with poetry',* wrote José Zorrilla, betraying his hometown of Valladolid. Surely one of the most magnificent European cities, though tourism eats at the very structures of the Alhambra, the Generalife, the delicate, fading, memory of the Emirate of Granada. Coming in by bus from the north people must wonder what all the fuss is about. There is no sign anywhere of the beautiful architecture, of ancient Albaicín, or the old Jewish quarter Realejo. Instead, shabby suburbs and an even shabbier bus station.

We head south again, and downwards towards the sea, skirting Gerald Brenan's beloved Alpujarras. Brenan was the age I am now when he got round to writing up his youthful travels. Published in 1957, his journey began in 1919. Manuel de Falla's *Three Cornered Hat* was a musical sensation; so-called 'Spanish flu' became an international pandemic; the League of Nations was founded. On May 29th, almost exactly 100 years before I got on this bus, a solar eclipse demonstrated dramatically the theory of relativity and an obscure German physicist Albert Einstein became a superstar. Space and time are, we learned, deeply intertwined. But our everyday notion of 'time', a ticking clock, a reliable metronome, is really nothing more than a construct, a way of dealing with staggeringly complex concepts. We don't really know what time *is*. What happened when, at a deep structural level, remains mysterious.

In *South From Granada* Gerald Brenan peers at the strange Spanish species as through a microscope. With one or two exceptions, his visitors from the UK – Bloomsbury luminaries such as Virginia Woolf and Lytton Strachey – get a much better press than his native neighbours. (The only Scot in the book gets an even worse write-up, Brenan attributing to him offensive 'Scottish customs' I've never heard of.) He regularly disparages Spanish cuisine, 'deplorable', beliefs and customs. Yet – and, significantly, not reported in this memoir – his relations with local women were rather less pernickety.

Brenan had a daughter with a fifteen-year-old girl from Yegen, most likely one of his servants. He's quite open about it in his autobiography, *Personal Memoir*, published twenty years after *South From Granada*. He records the 'arrangement' he made with Juliana in 1931: 'I make it a condition that when the child has been weaned you hand it over to me to bring up in England'. He paid her a thousand pesetas.

Juliana gave birth to a girl, whom she named Elena. Brenan changed it to Miranda Helen and sent her, as per his plan, to England to be educated. She never learned Spanish. Juliana, for her part, pined for Elena until both their deaths, taking trips to Granada to look for young women who might be her daughter.

Brenan's own relationship with Miranda was unhealthy, writing about her alarmingly erotically.

Although Brenan called his later book *Personal Memoir*, it is really an autobiography. *South From Granada* is the true memoir. 'A memoir,' Gore Vidal wrote, 'is how one remembers one's own life, while an autobiography is history, requiring research, dates, facts double-checked.' In his other two great books – *The Spanish Labyrinth* and *The Literature of the Spanish People* – Brenan is far more generous and insightful on Spanish politics and culture. What he chose to record and discuss in *South From Granada* is, among other things, partial and deliberately distant.

The bus arrived in Málaga long before Mike's and Daniel's planes were scheduled to land, so I found the flat we had booked. My daughter, Emma, had tried to join us, but was at a critical moment in her academic career. Moira, my wife, is a teacher – working with refugee and immigrant children – so couldn't make it, it still being term time. My nephew Mike was keen to come but, as it turned out, he made perhaps too much of an effort.

Mike is an electrical engineer, and he gives up some of his time, on a regular basis, to help bring sustainable power to villages in Gambia. He had been working there only a few days before he was due to accompany my son and me to Almuñécar. This time he returned with a nasty stomach bug. Inadvisably, as it turned out, he made the journey to Málaga anyway. He wasn't just suffering physically, the poverty he had seen in Africa had hit him harder this time than usual. His descriptions of what he had seen echoed Padre Juan: millions of people worldwide living against the odds – odds laid down by powers far beyond their shores and lightyears beyond their influence.

When he arrived, we went out for a beer, the night being hot, and the streets calling. I realised even before we got to the nearest bar that the man wasn't well. We go straight back to the flat and

Mike goes to his bed. He'll decide in the morning whether to fly back home again. Daniel's plane from Manchester is delayed. So I'm left alone with my memories.

I had no special relationship with my brother Paul, Mike's dad, before leaving for Spain as a teen. He was, for one thing, fifteen years older than me. Two different life experiences: the younger unconsciously wishing to distinguish himself, failing and needing the older sibling's help. Later in life, we were as close as brothers can be. Whatever caused me to halt my journey forty-five years ago, running out of money and luck, the appearance of the debilitating dodo, a sudden bout of homesickness, it was Paul who got me safely home. In years to come Paul would delight in ribbing me about it, but at the time he knew what to do. The precise details of how I got in touch with him and how he arranged things are misty to me now, but he must have told me he would make a phone call and that I should go, the next day, to the British Consul in Vigo. This was before I even knew what credit cards or money transfers were.

I have a hazy memory of playing a couple more times in the street to get the money to return to Vigo. In mizzling smir, as if preparing me for Scotland. I hitched from a village somewhere near the Portuguese border. I remember the driver saying, when I told him I was abandoning my trek to Almuñécar, that I was making the wrong decision. When we reached the city and I got out he leaned over and said: 'Never go back. Keep going!'

On the day, decades later, that Liam and Eddie and I scouted around Vigo looking for the place I had busked to mock-up the photo, I thought I saw the street where the consul's office had been. Another little crumb of defeat that tempted the dodo out so recently? I can't remember the consul's name except that I thought at the time it sounded fictional. St John Montague. Cecil Montgomery. Reginald Bose-Sinclair.

A Spanish woman behind a desk told me to wait, that the

consul would be with me when he could. She looked me up and down distastefully and never acknowledged me again. Admittedly I must have looked exactly as she had expected. Rumpled, hairy, tattered backpack, violin case. At least back then I had the advantage of youth. I was made to wait for a long time. Eventually, a small, old (he was probably about forty) pudgy consul led me into his office. Dressed in white linen, crumpled and creased after several days', maybe weeks', wear in a relatively hot country. A fan turned limply above his desk, blowing up the corners of documents as though looking for one in particular.

'So. Señor O'Dolan. Talk to me.' I remember him calling me O'Something, though he had my details in front of him.

'I think my brother spoke to you?'

'I have had a communication with… someone, in your home city of…' he looked through his notes. 'Glasgow.' He said it like it was a private joke, a smile on his clammy lips. He looked at me, and then nodded at my violin. 'Can you play that?'

'Enough.'

'Can you play, for instance, Bartok?'

'If you could just let me know what I have to do to get home, I'd appreciate it.'

'Why such a hurry, Mr O'Donovan?'

I genuinely didn't know the answer to that.

'Girl trouble? Or, I don't know, these days, *boy* trouble?' The wet smile returned. 'Is it safe to let you go? Will there be people looking for you if I sign this? Will they come after *me*? Do you owe money?'

'No.'

'Have you committed a crime?'

I could see what looked like RENFE train vouchers on his desk. All he had to do was get me to sign something saying I'd pay the money back.

Full Cycle

'Passport,' he said, clicking his fingers. He signed several papers on his desk that couldn't have had anything to do with me.

'Repatriation is a serious business, young man. Do you understand what is actually happening here?'

I said I did, but really I had no notion. I had lost, somehow, all claims to being British and it was only through the inexhaustible generosity of the British state, and of course their important consul, that allowed me this single, munificent, opportunity to become a tiny part of the Empire again.

'Perhaps you have learned a lesson, Mr O'Doyle. This is a tricky country. The Spanish character can be, how shall we say, unaccommodating. You should be thankful there is a British diplomatic bureau here. Had you been in, say, Andalusia...' He made it sound stranger and further than Xanadu.

He picked up and put back down the vouchers several times as he continued his lecture. The foolishness of leaving home without the necessary finance. The idiocy of wandering about playing violin in the streets. People like me, with no connections, no access to bank transfers and funds, people from *Glasgow*...

Finally, he stamped my passport – a hallmark of shame and defeat – and gave it back to me, along with the vouchers, almost throwing them at me. 'The train is for 8AM tomorrow morning. Are you capable of rising in time for such an early departure? I hope so. Miss that train and your tickets will not be valid for any other train. 8AM, or it's back on the streets with you, *laddie*.'

I was given no subsistence allowance. I found the cheapest *pensión* nearest the train station and busked till I had made enough money for a cheap *menú del día* and to buy snacks and drinks for the two-day journey back to Glasgow. I was about to pack up when I saw the consul's secretary come down the street. So I played on until she passed. She stopped and looked at me, with even more distaste than before. I played faster, tried to work the audience a little. I got some claps and laughter, a moment of fun, and the lawyer's receptionist moved off, looking the other way.

Paul's then wife, Anne, still a close friend, not long after my return gave me a couple of LPs by a singer-songwriter I had only faintly heard of, Leonard Cohen. All these years later and I'm still listening to him. One song in particular has grabbed my attention, up here in Relleu – Leonard Cohen singing about a manual for living with defeat.

Paul

Halfway up O Cebreiro in 2000 snow starts falling fast and, at this altitude, it's lying. Soon we're knee-deep, barely able to see through the fog of fat flakes. My brother is a step ahead of me, head down, kicking the snow, leaving a path behind him. Frances's voice, only a couple of hundred yards ahead, ethereal. Billy and Neil's laughter behind, making us smile.

War baby to his boomer baby brother, we inhabited two Glasgows. Paul's: Churchill and rationing, 'Wild Rover' *('And it's no, nay, never / No nay never no more')*. Responsible elder. Mine: The Beats and Dylan *('I'm bound to get lucky baby / or I'm bound to die tryin'')*. Youngest sibling people-pleasing, trying to distinguish himself. Paul was rugby and due diligence. Tackle hard, try hard. Party hard after. Keep things as they are. Intensely private, for Paul all information and experience was classified. I don't have the clearance needed for revelations – I can still feel your hand on my shoulder: 'That's not how it happened.'

Forty years of arguing, drinking till the sun rose, I never managed to change your mind about anything. Never got you to read that book or listen to that song. For that matter, you seldom changed mine. Quits. Except in my head, the discussion continues every day. We travelled such different roads, not even parallel ones, yet always within sight of each other, all The Way…

Before the snows melted, before they bombed the Alcalá to Madrid train, before Europe began to disintegrate. Walking slow, always careful, always attentive, through Spain and life.

And here there *is* photographic evidence: you making everyone laugh, on Cruz de Hierro.

Everything passes. Everything remains.

Mike hadn't recovered by the following morning and took the sensible decision to return home. Daniel and I set off early, down to the port, the length of the beautiful Alameda, along the *paseo marítimo*, an esplanade skirting the beach for miles. Laurie Lee's Málaga is nothing like the city I've known for decades. His long-term lodgings were a *posada* and he shared the space with 'mules and wives and children'. There's the appalling story of a mother desperately trying to pimp him her obese daughter and the altogether more believable recounting of a night on the tiles with a Glaswegian and two Scouser sailors. Perhaps Laurie's low opinion of Málaga is justified given this is where his violin fell to pieces. His luck changed when, improbably, a young German he barely knew happened to have broken off with a girlfriend, who happened to play the violin, but for some reason happened to leave it with him and which he, in turn, gave to Laurie. Good story, and I don't care if it's not true.

Here's another story: Daniel and I walked the entire 60 miles to Almuñécar, badly equipped, carrying too much stuff including my own bloody violin, in suffocating temperatures in only two days…

Okay, we didn't. Bad planning, allowing only two days. Which we could spend either trying to complete a near-impossible mission or enjoy our time together.

Gerald Brenan recounts several hikes he took in the twenties, some of them covering 100 miles in two days, once when he was half-dead with 'flu' – a terrifying sickness in 1919 in Spain. I don't believe it. Lee doesn't mention the road between Málaga and Almuñécar, which makes me wonder – perhaps in self-justification – if he didn't walk it at all. He went immediately to a hotel where he stayed and worked until the outbreak of the Civil War. It seems reasonable that he knew of the offer before leaving Málaga. Even if he did walk all or some of the way he did it in early winter and, unlike us, travelled light. And we encountered another problem: the lodgings that Lee and Brenan and Cela stayed in might have been humble but at least they existed. The tourism boom, which stretches from Estepona all the way round the coast to Benidorm and Denia has changed that part of Spain's south beyond recognition. Accommodation is expensive and booked-up early. Daniel and I finally managed to book a self-catering apartment and hopped on a series of buses after four or five hours walking.

Around 8PM on the evening of Monday 17 June 2019, a century after Gerald Brenan, forty-six years since first reading *As I Walked Out One Midsummer Morning*, some four months after walking down the road from Laurie Lee's house in Slad, seven weeks after coming to Spain, I arrived with my son in Almuñécar.

They were repaving the esplanade where the most recent plaque to Lee stands, so my musical tribute got lost in the drone of the cement mixers, pounding and hammering, a back-up band for the scrape of my violin. Still, I played 'Danny Boy', 'The Bonnie Earl of Murray' – your tunes, Laurie. Even 'Scots Wha Hae', which I dislike. Then, in honour of my cycling partners, 'Mairi's Wedding'. Daniel and I recited a poem Eddie Morrison had written before we left Glasgow, 'Just Like Laurie Lee': '...*hopes and fears and dreams / memories of a land he loved / ...dusty roads that wind forever / The blistering heat that gies ye fever / The place that seeps intae yir veins...*' And for Brendan and Brian and Ana, I played 'O Andar Miudiño.'

The hotel Lee worked and played violin in was three decades too early, before the dawn of Spanish tourism, and it has since been demolished. These days it would flourish, Almuñécar now a thriving resort. Beach bars playing hip-hop, serving cocktails, the sand not the best along that coast but still attracting – Pedro Zaragoza would be proud – bikini- and Speedo-clad sunworshippers, drinking from first light into the wee small hours.

Very few people had heard of Laurie Lee. People pass the twin plaques to him daily but they go unseen, despite being mounted on an odd chimney-shaped structure in the middle of the esplanade. Lee saw it being erected in the 1980s and commented, happily, on its phallic shape. The older of the two inscriptions reads:

From the people of Almuñécar in recognition of the great writer Laurie Lee who lived in our town in 1935–36 and 1951–52, immortalising it under the pseudonym "Castillo" in his books *As I Walked Out One Midsummer Morning* and *A Rose For Winter*.

Above it, a later plaque reads, in Spanish:

Centenary of the Birth of Laurie Lee (24 June 1914–26 June 2014). "Just before the Civil War I lived in a little Andalusian fishing town... I disguised, at first, the name of the place for political reasons and referred to it as Castillo. Happily there's no need for such reticence now and I can give the town its true name: Almuñécar."

Until the 1990s all the editions of *As I Walked Out One Midsummer Morning* call Almuñécar 'Castillo' – Castletown. Lee hid the real name in an attempt to protect Republican sympathisers there. I'm not sure how effective that was... He describes in detail a coastal fishing town 50 miles from Málaga, with two hotels on the beach (unusual at the time), one of which had a Swiss owner. He paints a picture of the old castle on the hill (unlike the hotels, it is still there) and describes the attacks on nearby Nerja, which he calls 'Altofaro'. Had any of Franco's men wanted to get at the Republican activists Lee mentions, notably his friends Manolo and 'El Gato', I doubt changing names would have confused them much.

Laurie was forced to leave Spain at a dramatic time. On my first attempt I just ran out of money and confidence. On the day of his rescue a British warship was sailing up and down the coast to take home any British citizens. Most likely, Lee was not one of the more important names they had on their lists, but he got more respect from his ship's captain than I did from my British consul.

The Civil War lasted three years and Franco's regime dragged on for another thirty-six. Had I completed my intended journey I would have been bang on time to see the end of a terrible process that began the week Laurie left – the end of Franco and the beginning of the transition. I fear now, with the weakening of Europe, the rise of far-right parties like Vox, that this present journey marks a backsliding into days of division and hostility.

As I play my tribute to Laurie one lady stops and listens. She stays for the entire repertoire – about fifteen minutes long. We doubted she could have heard much of the performance through the din of the roadworks. But when I finish playing she comes up and looks for somewhere to drop some coins. I explain to her that I'm not playing for money. She doesn't say a word but forces the coins into Daniel's hand and walks away. Six euros.

Full Cycle

And my seventeen-year-old self,
was he there, waiting?
Where have you been, old man,
what happened to you, along The Way?
Oh this and that. Lost some, found some, y'know.
And what about you, kid? How'd it go?
Same. Won a few, lost a few.
How's Paul? We both ask. And Maggie and Mark and Brian
and the rest?
Answers lost in the continuous drilling,
Like machine gun fire.
You're looking tired, we both say together.
Perhaps we see something of the other in
the young man holding the mic.
What's he doing?
Oh it's for, well, this… thing.
And we nod to one another, Okay.
One a ghost on a road he never travelled,
the other, a shadow moving uncertain
somewhere further down that same road.
Buen camino.
Buen camino, *old man.*

Bringing it all Back Home

And after the commanded journey, what?
Nothing magnificent, nothing unknown.
A gazing out from far away, alone.
…Just old truth dawning: there is no next-time-round.

Seamus Heaney, 'Squarings'

Y después de este viaje
obligado, ¿qué? Nada magnífico,
nada desconocido. Este mirar
hacia afuera, desde lejos, a solas.
…sólo la verdad antigua que vuelve:
no hay próxima vez.

(Translated by Brian Hughes)

The swallows and swifts are gathering, to return to their other homes. The storks of Castile already on their way further south. Poppies beginning their long sleep, dreaming red and yellow. And I'm getting ready to go home.

The Last Busk. Doubt it'll reach the iconic status of the Last Waltz. I played the square in Relleu. A few friends came along to support. The ladies who play cards every evening smiled and laughed, clapped and tapped their feet. Then got back to their card game. Folks in the bar stepped out to see what was going on. Passers-by stopped for a moment, smiled, nodded encouragement. If there was any of Lorca's Duende it wasn't in my playing, but in the Spanish evening. Marian blue, wine red as Lent, soft draughts of jasmine from the hills. The endless chatter, slamming down of cards, clinking of glasses. In every village, every Spanish *plaza*, there's a scene like this, right now. On the chapel wall here there is a plaque, above me as I play. It reads: '*El pueblo de Relleu quiere recordar…*' (The people of Relleu wish to remember all those killed in the Civil War, on both sides, in the hope that future generations, without forgetting our history, will build together a tolerant, just and democratic Spain).

At the end of the evening I leave my violin with Christopher and Marisa at the Almàssera Vella. The second fiddle of mine now in Spain.

Moira's coming over. For a few days we'll relax, share coffees and wine with our new friends in Relleu, stare mesmerised at Puig Campana, Alicante's highest mountain, a staunch hunk of rock that seems somehow Scottish to me. The heatwave is reaching fever-pitch: 'sunlight', as poet Alan Riach has it, 'like teeth'. I feel a longing for west-coast weather – though I know fine I'll be complaining about it soon enough. Thyme-scents blowing in from the Hebrides. Waking to mornings of forty shades of silver, dozing off again in northern light. Right now it's time for decompression, getting myself back in Caledonian mode after these months of cycling, writing, being on my own for long stretches. Prepare to re-engage. I'm happy to be going back but I find myself worried about the big bad world. It feels we are increasingly at the mercy of an emotionally illiterate political class, narcissists lacking human empathy. In turn I'm finding it difficult to empathise with the people who put them in power. As if terror of the complexities and challenges of the world around them provokes a pathological need for some abusive father-figure. I'm already missing the simplicity of cycling, the uncomplicated purity of pushing one pedal after another...

It was Spain and Spanish that brought Moira and me together and we've contemplated living here ever since. It's never happened. Partly chance, but more because the pull of Scotland – and Glasgow in particular – proved stronger even than the attractions of Spain. The country and city I remember from my teens, which I described at the start of this book, now feels to me alien, a place out of a fiction. Spain showed me how to love Scotland. Back through from Lorca, Machado, Cervantes to Alasdair Gray, Ali Smith, Jackie Kay. From there, those of us who wanted to escape when we were young found Hogg, Spark, Grassic Gibbon. Through Galician pipes and Martyn Bennet, *cante jondo* and Maeve Mckinnon, we came to feel Burns and piping and Shetland fiddle music. Cycling and walking in the Campsies, venturing out to the Lomond hills and the Trossachs, ever north to the bens and lochs of the Highlands, Scotland stretches your sense of identity. My inner Gael is less inner than it once was. All these places, songs and histories, are part of all of us who choose to live in Scotland. An idea as much as a place: Celtic, Latin, Asian and Norse; flamenco notes in Tinker ballads; Chilean resistance in East Kilbride; the Tex-Mex of those childhood TV shows. I realise that, by sheer chance, the day I leave Spain is both the Día de Galicia – National Galicia Day – and the feast day of St Jaume, Santiago himself.

When St James, in one of the many tellings of the tale, left the Holy Land to convert the pagans of Spain, his boat landed somewhere along the Alicante shore. He made his way up the Marina Baja hills into the Iberian heartlands, rising up out of the sea 700 years later in his armour of seashells to do battle with Moors. In Relleu there is a little shrine built, at Padre Juan's command, around a footprint of, it's believed, Santiago himself. All roads, it seems, lead back to Galicia.

Or perhaps that's just me trying to find a shape to all these travels and encounters. Some geographical and narrative thread. As we get older it feels important to look back, to detect some kind of coherence, perhaps even meaning in our lives. How we got to here from there. I've seen memoir writing described as 'inventing the truth'. The further we get from events that feel key to us the more likely we'll get the details wrong. As Mark Twain has it: 'When I was younger I could remember anything, whether it happened or not; but I am getting old, and soon I shall remember only the latter'. Maybe I've dreamt half of this book, or cherry-picked episodes because they seem to make sense now. How lived experience, what it felt like to journey through life, rather than an audit of dates and places, allows us to invent ourselves, truthfully.

Liam and Eddie are already planning the next cycle trip – if Brendan slipped me the original gateway drug, Liam and Eddie are evil enablers, stoking my addiction. Kate O'Brien calls Spain the 'femme fatale' of countries. I know what she means. A love for Spain and the Spanish that feels slightly, and deliciously, illicit. But in a few days I'll be almost 2,000 miles north, back in my own bed, 'my head roaring with Spain' – Laurie Lee.

AFTERWORD

One Year On

Everything Passes, Everything Remains

And there's a hand, my trusty fiere,
And gie's a hand o' thine.

Robert Burns

Or, as we sang it:
Dáme la mano, compañero,
here's a hand of mine.

What a difference a plague makes.

One year ago today we were cycling out of Vigo, on our way through open roads to meet people in fiestas, village squares, restaurants. *Abrazos* (hugs) and *besos* (kisses), the *paseo* in the evening, walking from bar to bar, meeting friends and making new ones. The freedom of the road tomorrow.

As I finish this book Spain is the country most afflicted by COVID-19 in all of Europe. A land where even the wealthy tend to live in flats – because life is on the street. Being locked in our houses is difficult for all, but perhaps particularly so in a Spanish context. Many of my friends long for their villages, but cannot get there. So the rural interior gets ever emptier and sadder.

When the music stopped in the corona musical chairs Ana Zabalegui was at a meeting in Logroño. She's been stuck in a hotel there ever since, unable to move around, knowing few people. Unlike María and Ángel who left Zamora in time to hole up in their village home, Ana is miles from her beloved Monreal. 'Yes, we're confined. But we understand why. Our politicians are the only ones fighting amongst themselves,' Ana says. 'We are drenched in doubt, and fearful for our elderly.' Esteban Galán Cubillo, in elegant, urbane Valencia, paints a darker picture: 'It's terrifying. Police patrolling empty streets. Instead of *abrazos* and *besos* a macabre dance of face masks and fearful eyes. And silence, everywhere. *Tragedia, orgullo, y solidaridad.*' Grief, dignity, solidarity.

Robin and Pilar in Segovia despair at the Vox party, whose leader is claiming that 'lockdown is the greatest assault on liberty (to which we always want to add "since the days of Franco" who they lovingly call "El Abuelo" – Grandad)'.

Ángel and Marta, who hosted that boozy rambunctious lunch in Valladolid, have had the same thought: under the guise of health protection they fear a kind of growing state censorship not seen since the days of the regime. Their daughter, also Marta, like Daniel has contracted the virus, both being doctors on the frontline. Both have witnessed too much death and grief at too early an age.

Dania is quarantined with friends in a Barcelona flat. 'Our sixth week since the state of emergency was declared and reactions to confinement have been diverse, from "*policías de balcón*" (people who spend their days singling out neighbours they see on the street and cheering at displays of police brutality) to "*redes de cuidados*" (organised support networks making sure everyone has access to food and other basic goods). This disaster is shedding light on problems that have been festering for a long time. Austerity measures since 2007 have debilitated public services in a way that is now proving lethal.'

Christopher North admits that the prospect of being confined in Relleu, surrounded by almond and olive groves, was almost welcome. 'Free time and few obligations… Every evening at 8PM the village bursts into life: neighbours on balconies with saucepans and spoons, kids shouting, voices singing. Yes, it's to thank the health workers, but it's also a little demonstration: "We're alive! We're still here!"' Christopher joins in with a seventeenth-century brass bell. 'Probably the first time it's been rung for about two hundred years. In the village the police are a benign presence, exceptionally helpful with the elderly. But in the cities… the Guardia deliver massive fines for lockdown breakers. 150 euros for a first offence, 600 euros for a second.'

I'm alarmed to hear that Belén, part-time housekeeper at Almàssera Vella, was rushed into hospital yesterday. Belén is a nurse and works a couple of days a week in the hospital. Thankfully, she is recovering, and the cause was not COVID-19. So Relleu remains virus-free.

Ana Eiroa Hughes in Alicante *has* tested positive. She's been quite ill but thinks she's now finally on the mend. 'Not seeing my children and grandchildren gets harder by the minute. Everything was organised for Sean's wedding, and who knows when it will take place now.' Covid-19 is making it clear, across the globe, that those strict father figures are failing. Female leaders, instead of blaming and scapegoating – insisting we 'man up' – are deploying, more successfully, a calmer, cautious, nurturing approach. Asking communities and nations, the family in whatever form, to work together and see the pandemic, and other challenges, not in terms of 'fault' or 'war', but problems that, together, we can face and work towards solving. Teresa of Avila: 'If this is how you treat your friends, no wonder you have so many enemies.' Rosalía de Castro: *'Para el alma desolada y huérfana no hay estación risueña ni propicia.'* (For the empty and orphaned soul, there is nothing happy or healthy).

Here in Glasgow, there are daffodils instead of poppies. Childlike, blythe, today they're beginning to fade, wilting like curtseys to the fresh, new cherry blossoms. Vivacious pink and cream bubbles sparkling and popping, bursts of fleeting life. From my window the Campsie Fells are happy left alone. On the odd cycle in that direction I've seen more hawks, ferrets, tree-creepers... Hard not to think nature is saying, 'Time's up humans, we'll take it from here.'

We fear for those everywhere who already suffer from depression, for women in lockdown with abusive men, for young people who were already finding employment nearly impossible to find.

Our own daughter Emma's academic career suddenly and brutally halted. Here, as in Spain, what will matter is what comes out of the pandemic. I said in an early chapter of this book that Pedro Sánchez's Socialist government was hardly radical. But the situation has moved him to implement a universal basic income. Only Finland has experimented with such a logical, ethical, but still deemed revolutionary idea. Perhaps Spain will extend it beyond this crisis. Perhaps we'll all recognise the fundamental importance of our health care systems and social safety nets, and invest in them and their workers. All those I'm in touch with in Spain, of very different political stripes and experiences, share a certain apprehensive optimism that we might all of us, globally, come out of this better people, better societies.

Meanwhile, I dream of those long-ago nights on beaches, singing songs under the moon. Of walking up O Cebreiro, freewheelin' down the other side. I'm in touch with Liam and Eddie, over this book and a video Liam is making of our trip. Laughing at our sexagenarian antics, rhapsodising over the wonders we've seen. We long for life to return to village squares, cards and glasses slammed down, voices raised in song and conversation, *abrazos* and *besos*... It's becoming clear that this pandemic isn't going to be a short sprint, more likely a sportive, maybe a long and gruelling grand tour. We can still get on our bikes, perhaps soon even on properly laid-out cycle lanes in cities. It might be a while before the three of us will be back in the Galician hills or the plains of Extremadura, eating *lentejas* in remote villages, belting out *Where's your mamma gone? Far, far awayeeee!* for no sensible reason nor to anyone in particular. But they've been added to our memory repositories, and we can summon them up when we need to. Everything passes – but everything, in important ways, does remain.

Note on the Text

All translations, unless otherwise stated, are my own.

Throughout, I have used linguistic variants for, for example, place names – from Spanish, Catalan, Galician, Scots – as a celebration of language, culture and expression.

This book is a key element of a wider academic project, including work towards a doctorate, at Glasgow Caledonian University.

My thesis explores, from an autoethnographic perspective, literary memoirs and writers' use of memory and lived experience in their work. I am interested in the boundaries between autobiography, memoir and anti-memoir, fiction and life writing. I use qualitative research methods based on texts mentioned in this book and self-reflection to explore how writers use (co-) constructed memories to interpret and explain cultural, political, and social meaning. My aim is to draw on existing scholarship to understand how time and travel and memory change through life and the ageing process and how writers in particular use and mould past experience to explain themselves and the world to their readers.

In case any of my readers are interested in exploring some of the writers I've talked about in the book, I've included a Further Reading section, overleaf, listing some titles from my thesis bibliography.

Further Reading

BAKEWELL. SARAH. *How to Live: A Life of Montaigne in One Question and Twenty Attempts at an Answer*. 2011, Vintage, London.

BOCHNER, ARTHUR P. & ELLIS, CAROLYN. *Evocative Autoethnography: Writing Lives and Telling Stories*. 2016, Routledge, New York.

BROWN, ALAN. *Overlander*. 2019, Saraband, Manchester.

BURNS, ROBERT. *Complete Poems and Songs*. 2011, Waverley, Glasgow.

BRENAN, GERALD. *South From Granada*. 1957, Hamish Hamilton, London.

BRENAN, GERALD. *The Spanish Labyrinth*. 2014, Cambridge Press, Cambridge.

BURNET, GRAEME MACRAE. *His Bloody Project*. 2015, Saraband, Manchester.

CASTRO, ROSALÍA DE. *Obra Poética Colección*. 1975, Austral, Madrid.

CASTRO, ROSALÍA DE. *Selected Poems*, tr. Michael Smith. 2007, Shearsman Books, Swindon.

CELA, CAMILO JOSÉ. *Viaje a la Alcarria*. 1948, Austral, Madrid.

CELA, CAMILO JOSÉ. *Viaje Del Miño al Bidasoa*. 1952, Austral, Madrid.

CELA, CAMILO JOSÉ. *Viaje al Pirineo de Lérida*. 1965, Austral, Madrid.

CRACKNELL, LINDA. *Doubling Back*. 2015, Freight Books, Glasgow.

CERVANTES, MIGUEL DE. *Don Quixote*, tr. Edith Grossman. 2005, Vintage, London.

DOLAN, CHRIS. *An Anarchist's Story: The Life of Ethel Macdonald*. 2009, Birlinn, Edinburgh.

DOLAN, CHRIS. *Redlegs*. 2012, Vagabond Press, Glasgow.

GALLOWAY, JANICE. *This Is Not About Me*. 2009, Granta, London.

GIFFORD, TERRY & NORTH, CHRISTOPHER. *Al Otro Lado del Aguilar*. 2011, Overstep Books, Devon.

GRAHAM, GABRIELA CUNNINGHAME. *Santa Teresa: Her Life and Times*. 1895, A&C Black, Edinburgh.

GRAHAM, ROBERT BONTINE CUNNINGHAME. *Aurora La Cujiñi A realistic Sketch in Seville*. 2015, Leopold Classic Library, Australia.

GRAY, DANIEL. *Homage to Caledonia: Scotland and the Spanish Civil

Further Reading

War. 2009, Luath Press, Edinburgh.

GREIG, ANDREW. *The Loch Of The Green Corrie.* 2010, Quercus, London.

HANKE, L. *The Spanish struggle for justice in the conquest of America.* 1949, Southern Methodist University Press, Texas.

HEANEY, SEAMUS. *New Selected Poems 1988 – 2013.* 2014, Faber & Faber, London.

HEMINGWAY, ERNEST. *For Whom The Bell Tolls.* 1994, Arrow, New York.

HOLLOWAY, RICHARD. *Stories We Tell Ourselves.* 2020, Canongate, Edinburgh.

HUGHES, B. *'Introducción' A Seamus Heaney: Antología Poética.* 1993, Diputación Provincial, Alicante.

KAY, JACKIE. *Red Dust Road.* 2017, Picador, London.

KENNEDY, A. L. *On Bullfighting.* 2000, Yellow Jersey, London.

KLEIN, DANIEL. *Travels With Epicurus.* 2014, Oneworld Publications. London.

LARKIN, PHILIP. *Collected Poems.* 2003, Faber & Faber, London.

LEE, LAURIE. *A Rose For Winter.* 1955, Seeker and Warburg, London.

LEE, LAURIE. *Cider With Rosie.* 1959, Hogarth Press, London.

LEE, LAURIE. *As I Walked Out One Midsummer Morning.* 1969, Andre Deutsch Ltd, London.

LEE, LAURIE. *I Can't Stay Long.* 1975, André Deutsch Ltd, London.

LORCA, FEDERICO GARCÍA. *Selected Poems.* 2001, Penguin Random House, London.

MACCORMACK, DAVID. 'Evocative Autoethnography: writing lives and telling stories', *British Journal of Guidance and Counselling*, 2018, Vol 46, No. 2.

MACGILL-EAIN, SOMHAIRLE / MACLEAN, SORLEY. *O Choille gu Bearradh [From Wood to Ridge].* 1990, Carcanet, Manchester.

MACHADO, ANTONIO. *Campos de Castilla.* 1974, Ediciones Cátedra, Madrid.

MACHADO, ANTIONO. *Lands of Castile and Other Poems,* tr. Salvador Ortiz-Carboneres & Paul Burns. 2001, Oxford University Press, Oxford.

MACLAVERTY, BERNARD. *Midwinter Break.* 2017, Jonathan Cape, London.

MOAT, HELEN. *A Time of Birds*. 2020, Saraband, Manchester.

MORENO, FIDEL. *¿Qué me estás cantando?: Memoria de un siglo de canciones*. 2018, Debate, Madrid.

MUNRO, LACHIE. *An Eagle in A Hen-house: Selected Political Speeches and Writings of R. B. Cunninghame Graham*. 2017, Deveron Press, Aberdeen.

MURRAY, DONALD S. *As the Women Lay Dreaming*. 2018, Saraband, Manchester.

NORTH, CHRISTOPHER. *The Night Surveyor*. 2018, Oversteps Books, Devon.

O'BRIEN, KATE. *Farewell Spain*. 1937, House of Stratus, London.

PATERSON, DON. *The Eyes*. 1999, Faber & Faber, London.

PELIAS, RONALD J. *Writing Performance, Identity, and Everyday Life*. 2018, Routledge, Abingdon.

PRESTON, PAUL. *The Spanish Holocaust: Inquisition and Extermination in Twentieth Century Spain*. 2013, HarperCollins, London.

SIMONS, DAVID J. *An Exquisite Sense of What is Beautiful*. 2013, Saraband, Manchester.

STARKIE, WALTER. *Spanish Raggle-Taggle: Adventures with a Fiddle in North Spain*. 1961, Penguin Random House, London.

TAYLOR, ANNE. *The People's Laird: A Life of Robert Bontine Cunninghame Graham*. 2005, The Tobias Press.

VIDAL, GORE. *Palimpsest: A Memoir*. 1995, Random House, New York.

WILLIAMS, JOHN & STONES, ALISON. *The Codex Calixtinus and the Shrine of Saint James*. 1992, Narr, London.

And a couple of blogs you might be interested in…

¡Adelante! Onwards! Travels through Spain, Song and Memory
Our own blog along the road, from Slad to Almuñécar: adelante.travel.blog

Liam Kane on Vimeo
Videos and photographs of the Vigo to Valencia cycle: Sexygenarians On Tour! Plus some of our previous Spanish outings: vimeo.com/showcase/7144896

Further Reading

Don Roberto And Me
Jamie Jauncey's blog about Scotland and the Cunninghame Grahams (Jamie being one): donrobertoandme.com

ChristieBooks
Stuart Christie's site is something of a treasure trove of radical writing and ideas: christiebooks.co.uk

'Spain: Still Cause' by Christine Jones
A moving and informative film about the struggle for justice and recognition in post-Franco Spain: youtu.be/vmXyMkB81lc

Facebook pages that may be of interest include:
Scotland and the Spanish Civil War
The Cunninghame Graham Society
Camino de Santiago

Acknowledgements

First and foremost, my family. For letting me chase a hare-brained scheme and then having to listen to me talking endlessly about it. My siblings Gerry, Charles, Liz and Ann, and my in-laws, all of whom will no doubt remember things very differently. Paul and Maggie. Tom McAweaney – thanks for all the music, Tom. (Mark Dolan, Dave Whyte, Mick Morton, and David Higginson for the same reason.)

Everybody mentioned in this book: thank you all – especially Brendan Hughes and Ana Eiroa, Eddie Morrison. Liam Kane has been a vital support, from the inception of the idea through to the completion of this book. Thanks to those of you who helped make the journey possible – Ben McConville, Ann Marie di Mambro and all at Glasgow Caledonian University. Julian Calvert for his help with the blog. Friends and colleagues who helped with technical issues, in particular Mark Rikards and Peter Murray who taught us how to record on the road. Maeve Mackinnon, such talent and generosity – thanks. Fergal Doherty for his support from afar. Thanks to Nick Low, Fiona White, Janice Forsyth and all at Demus Productions and The Big Light. Mark and Maureen Anderson for their help and kindness in the Cotswolds; Christopher North for his in Relleu – and J David Simons for putting us in touch. Ana Eiroa again, for putting me up and putting up with me. To all the people we met along the road for their *amabilidad y franqueza*. And to those who made this book happen – friends and colleagues who advised me on the text, including Moira, Daniel, Emma, Mike Dolan, Eddie, Liam, Brendan, Robin Cunninghame Graham, Dania, Ana Zabalegui, Paul Cuddihy, Mike Gonzalez.

Aisling Holling for her painstaking work and for being so positive and easy to work with. Finally, and the opposite of least, Sara Hunt for her friendship, ideas, advice, and faith in me, the project and the book – I hope it's all been worth it!

LIAM KANE